Preparing
for Christian
Ministry

A
BRIDGEPOINT
BOOK

BridgePoint,
an imprint of
Baker Books,
is your connection
for the best in
serious reading
that integrates
the passion of
the heart with
the scholarship
of the mind.

Preparing for Christian Ministry

An Evangelical Approach

Edited by
David P. Gushee
and Walter C. Jackson

A BridgePoint Book

 BakerBooks

A Division of Baker Book House Co
Grand Rapids, Michigan 49516

© 1996, 1998 by David P. Gushee and Walter C. Jackson

Published by BridgePoint Books
an imprint of Baker Books
a division of Baker Book House Company
P.O. Box 6287, Grand Rapids, MI 49516-6287

Fifth printing, July 2004

Printed in the United States of America

Library of Congress Cataloging-in-Publication Data

Preparing for Christian ministry: an evangelical approach/edited by David P. Gushee, Walter C. Jackson.
   p.   cm.
"A BridgePoint book."
Includes bibliographical references.
ISBN 0-8010-9034-2
   1. Clergy—Office. 2. Pastoral theology. I. Gushee, David P., 1962– II. Jackson, Walter C., 1933– .
BV660.2.P65   1996
253—dc20   96-8799

For information about academic books, resources for Christian leaders, and all new releases available from Baker Book House, visit our web site:
http://www.bakerbooks.com

DEDICATION

THIS VOLUME IS DEDICATED TO THE FACULTY OF
THE SOUTHERN BAPTIST THEOLOGICAL SEMINARY
1859–1996;
GODLY SCHOLARS, COURAGEOUS COLLEAGUES,
DEDICATED EDUCATORS OF THE SPIRIT,
AND MENTORS OF GENERATIONS OF
MINISTERS
OF
JESUS CHRIST

CONTENTS

SECTION III Professional Formation and Tasks of Ministry

SECTION IV Global Formation and Contemporary Issues
              in Ministry

PREFACE

For many years a course entitled "Formation for Christian Ministry" has been required of all first-year students at Southern Baptist Theological Seminary in Louisville, Kentucky. The Formation course carries multiple purposes: to orient students to seminary life; to encourage students to reflect on the nature of their spiritual pilgrimage, gifts, and calling to ministry; to introduce students to the various functions and tasks of ministry; and to sketch for students some of the cutting-edge issues they will face as they begin their ministries. As well, an underlying but critical purpose of the course is to provide a meaningful small-group experience for new students in order to help them avoid sliding into anonymity and loneliness in a large institution such as Southern.

Throughout much of the history of the Formation course at the seminary, the faculty (through the faculty journal, the *Review & Expositor*) published a textbook called *Formation for Christian Ministry* for use in that class. The most recent edition of this text appeared in 1989. Seeing that no plans existed to revise that book, in the summer of 1995 several of us on the faculty began to discuss the need for a new textbook to service the Formation classes.

Two of us agreed to serve as editors of this new Formation volume. We recruited current and former Southern Baptist Theological Seminary faculty to write it.

While it is still our hope that the faculty of Southern Seminary will use this book for their Formation courses, during the course of the preparation of this text it became clear to us as editors that we ought to think more broadly about the possibilities we had before us. As we surveyed the evangelical market, we found a paucity of books that offered a broad introduction to Christian ministry. While works on specific tasks or functions of ministry can be found in abundance, most are so narrowly focused as to be inadequate as a general introduction to Christian ministry. We decided to try to help fill this gap through this book.

The editors and authors of this volume happily identify themselves as Christians, Southern Baptists, and evangelicals (in that order, for most of us). These marks of our identity are seen throughout this book. As we have prayerfully created this volume we have sought to produce a work of a particular "spirit" and tone. We hope that each chapter combines biblical theology and morality with biblical piety and compassion. We intend a text grounded in biblical authority and saturated in a biblical vision of God, the church, and ministry. We likewise intend a text that reflects and nurtures within its readers such fruit of the Holy Spirit as love, kindness, and humility (Gal. 5:22-23). We hope and pray that every page of this book communicates this vision and bears this gracious spirit.

The layout and organization of the book reflect the purposes that have long characterized the Formation curriculum at Southern Seminary. Part I, "Transitions into Community" (chaps. 1–3), contains an opening chapter by Mark Seifrid on the nature of Christian community, with a special focus on how such community can be experienced in the theological seminary. The two other chapters are quite practical in their orientation. James and Melanie Greer Nogalski address the reality of doubt and crisis during the seminary years and how to face these issues with integrity (chap. 2); Marsha Ellis Smith offers an overview of "tips and traps" for new seminary students (chap. 3).

Part II, "Personal Formation and Calling for Ministry" (chaps. 4–10), concentrates on the minister's spiritual gifts, calling, personhood, and ongoing formation for ministry. New Testament professor John Polhill opens this section by offering a thorough overview of the concept of "call" in the Scriptures (chap. 4). David Dockery and David Gushee then discuss the issue of spirituality and the minister's critical need for constant spiritual growth (chap. 5). Gerald Borchert offers an innovative approach to the issue of spiritual giftedness (chap. 6); Leigh Conver, professor of psychology of religion and pastoral care, follows up with a discussion of human personhood and personality as these affect the minister (chap. 7). A special feature of this chapter is his discussion of the use of various personality typologies and tests for ministerial self-understanding. Church historian Timothy Weber next offers a biblical, theological, and historical introduction to the church and its ministry, that God-ordained institution which the called minister of God is to serve (chap. 8). Doris Borchert offers a practical discussion of the wide variety of vocational options available to the contemporary minister (chap. 9); awareness of these diverse options and openness to previously unknown opportunities for service is an important part of formation for ministry. The section concludes with a chapter by David Gushee that focuses on the moral formation of the minister and the particular danger of sexual misconduct, with practical guidance concerning how to prevent such a calamity (chap. 10).

The third section of the book, "Professional Formation and Tasks of Ministry," attempts to introduce new ministers to the wide range of functions or tasks that ministry involves. The section is framed by two chapters from Walter Jackson, concerning leadership (chap. 11) and the exercise of authority in ministry (chap. 18). Chapter 12, "Worship Leadership," brings together the perspectives of scholars/practitioners of preaching (Craig Loscalzo) and of church music (Lloyd Mims) to consider the theology and practice of worship. David Stancil follows up addressing the ministry of shepherding (chap. 13), while John Hendrix addresses the task of teaching as it arises in the local church (chap. 14). The critical tasks of social and community ministry are addressed by Janet Furness Spressart and John Dever (chap. 15); Thom Rainer follows with a discussion of the evangelistic ministry of the church, with special attention to church planting (chap. 16). Dennis Williams then adds a discussion of the important and often difficult and delicate matter of relations among members of the church staff (chap. 17).

The final section of the book is entitled "Global Formation and Contemporary Issues in Ministry." David F. D'Amico opens this section with a discussion of the reality of increasing ethnic diversity in the United States (and around the world) and how ministers might work effectively and faithfully amidst that diversity (chap. 19). Robert Don Hughes focuses his attention on the vastly different local contexts in which ministry occurs and on the need to "contextualize" one's ministry, within appropriate biblical boundaries (chap. 20). T. Vaughn Walker and Robert Smith, Jr. address the particular ministry context of the African American church, with special attention to the unique needs and contributions of African American seminarians (chap. 21). Finally, David Gushee offers a survey of some of the most important contemporary moral issues today's seminarians will face as they go about their ministries (chap. 22). A special feature of this chapter is a discussion of the role of women in ministry.

We assume that the primary audience for this book will be new seminarians studying in Southern Baptist and evangelical seminaries. Many seminaries offer first-year courses designed to introduce new students to ministry and to seminary life. We certainly hope and believe that this book can serve as a useful text in those courses. While our Southern Baptist context is clear throughout, we have sought to write and edit in a way that welcomes and includes non-Southern Baptist evangelicals as well.

As well, we are hoping that *Preparing for Christian Ministry* will be selected for use at the college level. Many Bible colleges and Christian universities offer courses in Christian ministry and are involved in preparing students either to go directly into ministry or on to seminary. This book is written in such a way as to be appropriate for college students who are considering ministry and for ministry studies courses at the college level.

We also nurture the hope that this book will find its way onto the shelves of Christian bookstores unrelated to colleges and seminaries. We envision the man or woman in midlife who suddenly (or gradually!) senses a call to ministry. Frequently this sense of call is bewildering and even frightening. It involves a fundamental redirection of life. Is God really calling *me* into ministry? We hope that ours will be a book that God can use to help such folks determine God's direction for their lives.

* * *

The editors wish to offer grateful thanks to the many people who made this book possible. First, we are extremely grateful to those who have contributed chapters. These men and women are all God-called ministers of the gospel of Jesus Christ. Most serve full-time in the preparation of ministers to serve the churches. They write out of both personal experience in ministry and extensive academic research and preparation. While at the beginning of this project all were on the faculty of Southern Baptist Theological Seminary, by now several serve in other capacities. Their diverse places of service, we believe, have enriched this work.

We are grateful to the editorial board of the *Review & Expositor* for allowing us to adapt and use three chapters from the last edition of their book, *Formation for Christian Ministry* (chaps. 9, 11, 18). Thanks for your gracious cooperation as we have "flown the coop" and gone out on our own with this project.

We are also thankful to David Dockery, formerly Vice President for Academic Administration at Southern Seminary, and now President of Union University in Jackson, Tennessee (and a contributor to this volume). Though this work is not an "official" product of Southern Baptist Theological Seminary, Dockery offered the editors considerable support and help during our work. We also are glad to acknowledge the hours of word processing and editing help provided by the very fine secretarial staff that serves in ministry alongside the faculty and administration at Southern. Thanks for a job well done!

Finally, we are grateful to Robert Hosack and the other members of the team at BridgePoint/Victor Books for the care, attention, and skill with which they have handled this book. This is a publishing house that clearly sees its work as a ministry, and for this we are grateful to God.

We send this book into the world with the prayer that God will bless all who read it with a deepened passion for Jesus Christ and for the ministry of the Gospel.

David P. Gushee and Walter C. Jackson, editors

TRANSITIONS
INTO
COMMUNITY

1

THE NATURE OF CHRISTIAN COMMUNITY AND THE THEOLOGICAL SEMINARY

MARK A. SEIFRID

Already in the middle of the nineteenth century the social philosopher Alexis de Tocqueville described Americans as especially disposed to "individualism," which he characterized as a "habit of the heart," to withdraw to "a little society formed to (one's) own taste." In an important study which bears de Tocqueville's phrase in its title, Robert Bellah and others have described how this mind-set has largely captured American society.[1] If we are honest with ourselves, it is not hard to see various ways in which this inclination has affected our participation in Christian community. In the first place, it has long been true that most of us worship with those who are like us in social and economic status. Many of us also readily change our church membership, breaking ties with other believers rather easily. Our choice of a local church has become very often a matter of personal taste in style of worship and availability of programs rather than a matter of conviction. A surprisingly large number of professing Christians regard beliefs as wholly private, to be devel-

Mark A. Seifrid is Associate Professor of New Testament Interpretation at the Southern Baptist Theological Seminary in Louisville, Kentucky.

oped individually and often apart from the church or tradition of which they are members.[2] And if our beliefs are a private matter, so is our personal conduct. When is the last time we accepted correction from another Christian? When is the last time we had enough concern and courage to give it?

THE COMMUNION OF THE SAINTS

Despite such glaring weaknesses widespread in American church life, most evangelicals have tasted something of true Christian fellowship and long for a deeper experience of it. Yet even such longing might contain a danger in and of itself. Our desire for fellowship just might distract us from thinking carefully and biblically about the distinctive character of Christian community. It is easy to accept a lesser—and therefore destructive—substitute for the community to which God has called us in Christ. The Scriptures instruct us that true community is present on earth wherever the gospel is proclaimed, believed, and obeyed. God in his redemptive work in Christ has already created "the communion of the saints." To believe in Christ is to share in Christ, and to share in Christ is to be a member of the new humanity which is a present *reality* in him (Gal. 3:28; Eph. 2:21-22; Col. 3:9-11). Christian community is, above all else, Christ indwelling his people. It is crucial for us to recognize then, that it is *Christ alone* who builds his church (Matt. 16:18). Christ's cross, not our endeavor, sets us apart, sanctifies us in the truth, and makes us one with one another (John 17:17-23). It is in receiving the mercy of God that we are made the people of God (1 Peter 2:9-11; Rom. 9:22-26). Through Christ, God builds us together with other believers into a spiritual house and a holy priesthood (1 Peter 2:4-7). We do not generate community with one another by our efforts, by our meetings, or by our practices. We gratefully receive the community which God has given us in Christ. To reject that community would be nothing other than disobedience to the gospel.

This does not imply, of course, that we and all Christians fully know and participate in the community which God has created for us in Christ. In the first place, there are obvious degrees of spiritual health and maturity among churches (and other associations of believers) just as there are among individual Christians.

More fundamentally, we must recognize that the concrete experience of fellowship in this life *always* falls short of the fullness to be consummated at the eschaton. It is a sign of danger when we become satisfied or smug about the quality of our fellowship. We have then lost sight of our calling, in both its demands upon us and the deep riches which it yet offers us. We are all to grow together into nothing less than the "full stature of Christ" (Eph. 4:13, NRSVB), with all the unity, knowledge, and character which that implies. Even as a "community of saints" we presently remain a "community of sinners." Our spiritual health depends on our constant recognition of this vital truth, to which we will return more than once in what follows.

In regard to this inherent paradox of the present Christian experience of community, it is instructive to consider Paul's response to the failure of the Corinthian congregation (1 Cor. 1:10-12). For Paul, the Corinthian factions represented a denial of Christ and his work: "What!" Paul responds to the report of the situation in Corinth, "Has *Christ* been divided?" (1 Cor. 1:13, NASB) The Corinthians had been called together, "with all who in every place call on the name of our Lord Jesus Christ" (1 Cor. 1:2, NASB). They were already the very temple of God (1 Cor. 3:16). They had been baptized by one Spirit into one body (1 Cor. 12:12-13). Seen from the perspective of the cross and resurrection, the community of the Corinthian Christians was complete. For this reason, their behavior brought shame on Christ himself, and in their self-centered violation of the Lord's Supper they incurred divine judgment (1 Cor. 11:27-32). The implications for our context are obvious. Despite our weaknesses, Christ himself dwells with and among us. He is our true community, although we grasp and realize this reality only partially here and now. We receive this fellowship as a gift from God, and lay hold of it ever more firmly and fully as we progress in faith and obedience to Christ. We must, in fact, continue to grow into community, however significant our present experience might be; otherwise we deny the gospel itself. If we abuse and disregard what God has done for us in Christ, we stand in danger of the same divine discipline which came upon the Corinthians.

Dietrich Bonhoeffer, in his helpful book on Christian fellowship, *Life Together*, draws out two implications of this truth which are worth considering. He observes that since true community is a God-given reality into which we enter, rather than a product of our own piety, we must set aside our own ideals of community. Our fellowship must not be guided by what we dream of or expect from others, but by that which God requires of us. Elsewhere, Bonhoeffer rightly applies to the formation of community the biblical irony that "the one who loses his life, keeps it."[3] The Christian finds community not through seeking community, which may ultimately represent self-interest, but through the exercise of love for the other. We, therefore, must not allow the disappointments of any particular Christian community to make us bitter or judgmental, but pray that God might allow us all to taste more of the fellowship which the earliest church knew (Acts 2:46). Imperfection and failure were not absent from the earliest church (Acts 6:1; 15:37-41) and will remain among us until the kingdom is consummated. The New Testament writers maintained this realistic view of Christian fellowship. "Above all else," Peter urges, "keep fervent in your love for one another, because love covers a multitude of sins" (1 Peter 4:8, NASB). Echoing the words of Jesus, James warns that we are not to speak evil about one another or judge one another. That is not our task. There is only one Lawgiver and Judge (James 4:11-12; cf. Matt. 7:1-5). Rather than having an eye for one another's faults, we must have an eye for the beauty of Christ as he manifests himself in the love, faith, and obedience of others. Bonhoeffer likewise urges that we must begin with thankfulness for the fellowship which God gives us here and now, with all its faults.

> If we do not give thanks daily for the Christian fellowship in which we have been placed, even where there is no great experience, no discoverable riches, but much weakness, small faith and difficulty; if on the contrary, we only keep complaining to God that everything is so paltry and petty, so far from what we expected, then we hinder God from letting our fellowship grow according to the measure and riches which are there for us all in Jesus Christ.[4]

Secondly, Bonhoeffer points to a crucial distinction between human love and Christian community. The vitality of our Christian life together *depends on* our "ability to distinguish between a human ideal and God's reality, between spiritual and human community."[5] Despite the considerable power of human love, sin is always operative within it, threatening the domination of others.[6] Fallen human love has an inherently selfish aspect—"dark ambitions."[7] Behind perverted natural "love" lies ultimately the desire for pleasure rather than for service, the subjection of other human beings to our will, rather than their freedom in and for Christ. Such false love seeks to bind persons to us and to our purposes, rather than directing them to Christ. In contrast, Christian fellowship is always indirect, mediated by Christ and his will for the other person, not ours. We therefore must view other persons, not for what they are in and of themselves, but for what Christ wills them to be. We must neither exploit them for their gifts, nor despise them for their weaknesses, but in both instances seek the furtherance of Christ's purposes for them.

We might add the observation that mere human intentions generally are not immediately apparent. We often hide our true motives from ourselves beneath a Christian veneer. In all but the most extreme instances, we and our churches do not display the sickness that, say, a sect like the Branch Davidians at Waco did. But it remains true that the degree of our health depends upon our awareness that true community takes place in and through Jesus Christ alone. Bonhoeffer expresses this thought beautifully:

> Our community with one another consists solely in what Christ has done to both of us. This is true not merely at the beginning, as though in the course of time something else were to be added to our community; it remains so for all the future and to all eternity. I have community with others and I shall continue to have it only through Jesus Christ. The more genuine and the deeper our community becomes, the more will everything else between us recede, the more clearly and purely will Jesus Christ and his work become the one and only thing that is vital between us.[8]

CHRISTIAN COMMUNITY IN PRACTICE

The centrality of Christ and his work to our experience of community carries several important implications. In the first place, it means that true community exists only in conjunction with worship. It is this atmosphere of worship which characterized the fellowship of the earliest church (Acts 2:46-47; 4:24-31) and runs like a thread through the New Testament. Paul prays that the Roman church might live in harmony so that they might "together . . . with one voice glorify the God and Father of our Lord Jesus Christ" (Rom. 15:6, NRSVB). Peter tells us that we have been made to be God's own people, "so that you may proclaim the excellencies of him who called you out of darkness into his marvelous light" (1 Peter 2:9, NASB). The heavenly communion of the saints appears in the book of Revelation as those who sing in praise to God and Christ (5:9-14; 7:9-10; 11:16-19). Our assembling together here and now is an anticipation of our final and eternal gathering around the throne of God to render to him the glory which is his alone. It is first and foremost the worship of God which draws us together in visible fellowship. Therefore, the gathering of the church where the Word of God is proclaimed, and where we remember what Christ has done for us in the celebration of the Lord's Supper, is the indispensable and central aspect of true Christian community.

That means, for example, that small groups, if they are to further Christian community, must do something more than create friendships among members. It also means that there are limits and guidelines to adapting our worship services to be "user-friendly." We gather as a church to do what the world refuses to do, to worship the one true God in the name of Christ. In this sense, our services of worship must necessarily be a scandal to the world, even as they give invitation: "Come, let us worship and bow down; let us kneel before the Lord our Maker" (Ps. 95:6).

Moreover, the centrality of Christ to community means that Christian fellowship is founded upon and sustained by our common confession of the truth. Often Christians suppose that love and doctrine are inherently opposed to one another, and that the path to fellowship lies in setting aside questions of belief. As we have seen already, nothing could be more misleading. We all know of unhappy and unfruitful disputes over matters of indifference. And even worse, we know of those who have seemingly contended for the gospel in a very unchristlike manner. But these transgressions should not blind us to the essential character of

Christian community. It is precisely by speaking the truth (in love!) that we grow into Christ our head, that is, into true community (Eph. 4:11). The quality of our fellowship depends upon our discerning and embracing the truth of Christ in our present circumstances, in all which that entails for us. This growth into the truth, in turn, requires our readiness to be corrected by others theologically, and our willingness to lovingly do the same for them when the truth demands it. The perfection in which we all shall know fully just as we have been known has not yet arrived (1 Cor. 13:12). Until then, we must continue to admonish and be admonished. It is this mutual correction which Paul regards as the mark of a mature Christian community (Rom. 15:14).

If this image seems harsh and undesirable, we should consider the biblical perspective on the alternative. According to the apostolic witness in 1 John, community is possible only through the gospel, which establishes our fellowship with the Father and the Son and *thereby* our fellowship with one another (1:3). It is such communion which rejoices in the inclusion of others, and seeks to embrace even the whole world (1:4; 2:2). Outside, in the "world," only self-centered desires and boasting are present, no matter how deceptively they might clothe themselves in the trappings of love (2:15-16). Mere "human love," which has no regard for the truth, cannot tolerate real difference since it seeks unity in itself, by binding others to itself. If it cannot make the other conform, it will withdraw to its own circle (2:19; cf. Gal. 4:18).[9] Those in the darkness hate the "other," the one who practices righteousness, just as Cain murdered Abel (3:11-14). Only by believing the gospel, which proclaims Christ's laying down of his life on our behalf, do we know what love is (3:16). And this love is transforming love, which sets us on the path of obedience (2:3-4; 3:6-8; 5:2-5). The community of love, therefore, is sustained by its fidelity to the gospel in word and deed. The church in its exercise of discipline always seeks restoration, always invites, but it always does so by inviting to the truth of the gospel, the holy love which constitutes the life of the community itself (5:14-17).

Yet a third point is to be drawn from the centrality of Christ to community: fellowship, because it is located in Christ, does not depend upon secondary and outward matters of gender, role, or social status. It is the very beauty of such community that such boundaries are transcended. When Paul speaks of "neither Jew nor Greek, slave nor free, male nor female" in Christ (Gal. 3:28), he does not at all mean that these distinctions have been obliterated (cf. 1 Cor. 7:8-24), but that they have been overcome, *despite* their continuance in the present age. In the earliest church, slave and master shared the same Communion table, a fellowship that was bound to have its impact on their daily lives. There is much more to be said about this matter, but here we want only to observe that when Christians from different social classes or cultures join together for fellowship, labor, and worship (as they did in the earliest churches), there is a greater possibility for *true* fellowship, no matter how large the difficulties in coming together might be. When the obstacles have been overcome, the self-interest which might otherwise bind human beings together is more or less absent. We are directed to Christ more simply and purely as the basis of our unity. Who hasn't sensed something of this when worshiping with Christians from other parts of the world, or other cultures, or other races?

Another aspect of this thought deserves attention. Since true community is found in Christ, and not in any quality in us, the growth of true Christian fellowship *furthers* rather than diminishes *our individual gifts and callings*. This diversity in unity is a mark of the Spirit of God, who is the power and source of our love for one another, and who coordinates our mutual service (1 Cor. 12:12-13; Eph. 2:21-22). Of course, this form of community is contrary to our natural tendencies. We are inclined to self-love and to the exploitation of the gifts of others for our own ends. Moreover, group expectations tend to reinforce sameness. We tend to associate with those who think, live, and act as we do. In other words, we are not shielded from individualism, particularly not as de Tocqueville defined it, simply because we are part of a group or even of a church. Like the tongues-speakers in Corinth, all of us are tempted to measure others by *our* gifts and to reduce our fellowship to those who fit our ideals. God, in contrast, delights in the individual differences which he has created: the body of Christ is not one member, but many (1 Cor. 12:14).

We are not thereby released to unbridled individualism, of course. In a beautiful way, true Christian community and individuality strengthen one another. Precisely in seeking to serve we find ourselves. Congregational surveys which ask church members (or seminarians) to identify their gifts would be more useful if they included the discovery of gifts through service. We are closer to the biblical model when we say, "Here are some tasks which need attention in our church. Perhaps there are others which you see. Scripture teaches that each one of us has been given a gift for the benefit of the body. Christ calls you to consider prayerfully what task or tasks you will take up. Only through the joy of service can you discover your gift." Conversely, the church exists to strengthen each of us individually in our obedience to Christ. We should not forget that we remain "sinners" who need the exhortation, encouragement, and comfort which God extends to us through the communion of the saints. Not only our desire to share in corporate worship, but also our own weaknesses call us to gather together regularly with other believers. "Let us not give up meeting together as some are in the habit of doing," the author of Hebrews urges, "but let us encourage one another—and all the more so, as you see the Day approaching" (Heb. 10:25).

The church thrives and grows, then, not by binding individuals ever more tightly to its earthly form, as if they existed only in order to come to our meetings and carry out our programs. We must not confuse the present, visible manifestation of the church with our eternal rest. Rather, the community thrives by binding each one more closely to Christ and to his will for her or him. We gather to worship and serve Christ, who sends us each forth to different deeds of discipleship and witness in the world, and who will continue to do so until he comes again. In tasks such as these the life of the community is strengthened. Since it is Christ alone who is the basis of our fellowship, our participation in gathered community will depend on how firmly each of us is intent on Christ's purposes and not our own (Phil. 2:2-4).

We have returned to the essential paradox which we touched upon earlier. Believers in Christ necessarily come together in visible fellowship. We set apart times and places in which to gather. Yet it is not the visible gathering which produces or ensures community. Rather, the gospel bears true community as its fruit. We must beware of the illusion of community. When large numbers of people gather to enjoy a performance or a concert, it can appear that community exists in their common enjoyment. But this is not true community: the event has no power or authority to bind persons together in love permanently or effectively. All of us know that even in the midst of festive gatherings it is quite possible to be, and to sense, that we are entirely alone. The outward unity may hide the deepest disunity and even animosity. This should again caution us against attempts to generate community by our own techniques or activities!

On the other hand, the Christian may be entirely alone, isolated from others due to sickness, labor, persecution, or even simply geographical distance, and yet he or she is not at all alone. In fact, in its trials on this earth the church displays precisely this outward loneliness, but simultaneously the deepest inner unity through its participation in Christ.[10] Wherever Christ is there is the communion of the saints. The Apostle Paul understood that he was present with his congregations, even when he was absent from them (1 Cor. 5:3; Col. 2:5). In fact, the quality of our joining together depends in considerable measure on our recognizing the bond of fellowship which unites us when we are apart. One essential expression of this unity is our prayer for one another in Christ, prayer which must extend beyond the limits of our own church and denomination. "I want you to know, how much I am struggling for you," writes Paul to the church in Colossae, a church which he had not visited (Col. 2:1, NRSVB). And that "struggle" is nothing other than his prayer on their behalf (cf. Col. 1:9-10; 4:12). Jesus' instruction to his disciples on prayer implies that even in our private devotions we are to remain conscious that we pray as part of the community of the saints. "Pray then in this way, '*Our* Father, in heaven. . .'" (Matt. 6:9, cf. 6:6). As Jan Lochmann observes, the Lord's Prayer "is not an *I* prayer but a *We* prayer."[11] In short, Christian community and individuality are not mutually exclusive, but interdependent. And this is so because sharing in Christ—and this alone, not our coming together—makes us one.

Christian community flourishes not only by strengthening individual discipleship, but also by looking outward to the redemptive intent of God in this fallen world. The incomplete character of our experience of Christian community is due not only to our remaining sinfulness, but also to the unfinished state of God's work on earth. According to Paul, we cannot know and share with one another the full dimensions of Christ's love apart from the community of "all the saints" (Eph. 3:18). Only in seeing Christ's love concretely displayed in the redemption of his people from all the families of the earth will we come to our fullest grasp of the greatness of that love: Paul's prayer in Ephesians 3 pushes forward to the eschaton. The quality of our fellowship here and now depends on our giving ourselves to the completion of this saving purpose of God, with all its implications for our prayer, witness, and engagement in missions. We necessarily participate in particular churches, and particular prayer, Bible study, and fellowship groups. Yet true community is maintained in these contexts by turning our attention to God's larger purpose of establishing the full "communion of the saints."

This truth is especially applicable to small groups. Although they very often are a means to community, they may, in reality, become quite individualistic in character and must be rightly led if they are to further Christian community.[12] We will examine at least four conditions which are necessary for this to take place.

First, there must be an open commitment to the authority of the Scripture and to its binding *truth*. This is particularly important for Bible study groups, where there must be mutual correction in the light of the meaning of the text and not just a sharing of viewpoints.

Second, group members ought to agree to practice accountability to one another so as to live in accordance with the Scripture. We must find ways to encourage and admonish one another rightly and positively (Col. 3:16). Likewise, in a way which respects the privacy of others, we ought to fulfill James' injunction to "confess your sins to each other and pray for each other, so that you might be healed" (James 5:16).

Third, prayer in a small group must intentionally extend beyond the needs of its members, if it is to be an expression of Christian community. (This applies to church prayer meetings as well!) It is very helpful to follow the pattern of the Lord's Prayer or the prayers of Paul in order rightly to focus our worship, thanksgiving, and petitions.

Finally, the group must function as part of the larger church body. This might mean that it will disband after it has served a specific purpose. Or it may mean that it deliberately remains open to new members, or the formation of new groups if it should become too large.

In many cases small groups, if they are functioning properly, may fill a void that exists in modern American church life. The earliest house-churches encouraged considerable congregational participation in worship, for which participants were held *accountable* (e.g., 1 Cor. 14:26-33). Personal exhortation can only take place in a group of limited size. In this way, by furthering individual responsibility, small groups may be a vehicle for growth into community.

Last, but certainly not least, we should remember that in Christian fellowship the sharing of spiritual realities and the sharing of material goods cannot be separated. Indeed, the word *koinōnia* has both senses within its range of meaning, and sometimes is used with a certain ambiguity. When Paul thanks God for the Philippians' participation (*koinōnia*) in the gospel (Phil. 1:5), it is not entirely clear whether he has in mind the faith of the Philippians or the monetary gift which they had sent to him. In this context, for Paul, there is no strong distinction between the two: the latter is the necessary expression of the former. Likewise, the other New Testament writers regard the tangible expression of love as essential to Christian community (James 2:14-17; 1 John 3:16-17).

CHRISTIAN COMMUNITY IN THE SEMINARY SETTING

The life of the theological seminary presents its own possibilities for Christian fellowship, as well as perils related to it. In thinking about the seminary, it is first of all important to understand its relation to the churches which it serves. Institutions such as the seminary derive their existence from partial and temporally limited goals. That includes even the missionary task of the churches, which will come to an end when Christ appears to consummate the kingdom. In contrast, the earthly church both locally and universally is the present expression, however weak and feeble, of the community of love, which will continue into eternity. Other forms of Christian fellowship, as indispensable as they are, must not become substitutes for the life of the church. Basil Manly, Jr. included this very thought in his hymn written for the Southern Baptist Theological Seminary, "Soldiers of Christ in Truth Arrayed":

> We meet to part, but part to meet
> When earthly labors are complete
> To join in yet more blest employ
> In an eternal world of joy.

We seek Christian community in the theological seminary then, not as an end in itself but precisely because the seminary is a goal-directed extension of the churches, which represent Christ's community of love in its earthly form. The depth of our experience of community in the life of the seminary will depend on our carrying out the responsibilities we have been given in service to Christ. Christian community is to be found not merely in the chapel, or in small groups, or conversation with others, but in the very task of study which brings us here. The moment we think that community is to be found solely outside the classroom, we have enervated our fellowship. We join together precisely in our common duty. Of course that means that our learning and teaching are to be carried out in an attitude of service and worship. The atmosphere of the chapel is to penetrate the classroom. B.B. Warfield, whose essay on the "Religious Life of Theological Students" is still worth reading, asks the appropriate question: "Why should you turn from God when you turn to your books, or feel that you must turn from your books in order to turn to God?"[13] A consciousness that we have been brought together by a much larger task may help to protect us from the temptation of comparing ourselves with one another. No place of Christian service shields us from that temptation, but our regular contact with one another, and the inescapable reality of grades, make us especially vulnerable here to envy and pride as well as to other forms of academic sin. It is necessary to keep in view Christ's call upon each of us, and to encourage one another to excellence in service of the gospel.

In order for the chapel to penetrate the classroom, the classroom must not be severed from the chapel. Our participation in chapel constitutes our confession that our labor over books is labor for Christ, in which we seek to bring every thought captive to Christ (2 Cor. 10:5). The end of all our theology must be doxology, and doxology, of necessity, calls us to gather together, since we worship as the community of the redeemed. We gather together then, not merely to hear the speakers we prefer. Nor do we gather together only when the service promises to encourage us. Even when the music does not move us, even when we wish for better preaching, we gather together, because we gather together for worship. And in doing so, we must both give thanks for the experience of fellowship God allows us and pray fervently that it might yet be deepened: that our preaching might be truer and more penetrating, that our prayer as a community might more fully grasp the will of God for us, that our singing together might more fully reflect our future song before the throne.

No doubt we will want to supplement the worship in chapel with fellowship in smaller groups which gather for prayer, Bible study, and the like. As we have noted already, this form of fellowship allows for dimensions of community which the Scriptures urge upon us and which are lacking in a larger assembly. In regard to such groups, we mustn't overlook the wonderful opportunity that the seminary offers us to reach across racial barriers and to forge relationships with believers from other nations. It is in these very relationships that true Christian community is most evident, and most precious. Shouldn't we take advantage of our life together in this way?

N O T E S

1. Robert N. Bellah, et al., *Habits of the Heart: Individualism and Commitment in American Life* (New York: Harper and Row, 1985). See especially the chapter on "Religion," 219–49.

2. Ibid., 228.

3. Dietrich Bonhoeffer, *Sanctorum Communio: Eine dogmatische Untersuchung zur Soziologie der Kirche* (Munich: C. Kaiser, 1986), 115.

4. Dietrich Bonhoeffer, *Life Together*, trans. and introduced by John W. Doberstein (New York: Harper and Brothers, 1954), 29.

5. Ibid., 34.

6. It is worth noting that even marriage and family life may manifest this disorder of our fallen state. Yet, as Bonhoeffer points out, the danger here is

diminished somewhat by the limited purpose of marriage.

7. With the expression "human" (Ger., *seelisch*), Bonhoeffer refers to the Greek word *psychikos*.

8. Bonhoeffer, *Life Together*, 25–26.

9. Ibid., 31–39.

10. Ibid., 95.

11. Jan M. Lochman, *The Lord's Prayer*, trans. Geoffrey Bromiley (Grand Rapids: Eerdmans, 1990), 24.

12. See Robert Wuthnow, ed., *"I Come Away Stronger": How Small Groups Are Shaping American Religion* (Grand Rapids: Eerdmans, 1994).

13. Benjamin Breckenridge Warfield, "The Religious Life of Theological Students," in *The Princeton Theology: 1812-1921*, ed. Mark A. Noll (Grand Rapids: Baker, 1983), 263.

FOR FURTHER READING

Bellah, Robert N., et al. *Habits of the Heart: Individualism and Commitment in American Life*. New York: Harper and Row, 1985.

Bonhoeffer, Dietrich. *Life Together*. Translated and introduced by John W. Doberstein. New York: Harper and Brothers, 1954.

Carson, D.A. *The Church in the Bible and the World*. Grand Rapids: Baker, 1987.

Grudem, Wayne A. *Systematic Theology: An Introduction to Biblical Doctrine*. Grand Rapids: Zondervan, 1994.

Guthrie, Donald. "The Church." In *New Testament Theology*. Downers Grove, Ill.: InterVarsity, 1981.

Snyder, Howard A. *The Community of the King*. Downers Grove, Ill.: InterVarsity, 1977.

Warfield, Benjamin Breckenridge. "The Religious Life of Theological Students." In *Selected Shorter Writings of Benjamin B. Warfield*, edited by John E. Meeter, 411–25. Phillipsburg, N.J.: Presbyterian and Reformed, 1970.

Wuthnow, Robert, ed. *"I Come Away Stronger": How Small Groups Are Shaping American Religion*. Grand Rapids: Eerdmans, 1994.

2

FACING DOUBT AND CRISIS WITH INTEGRITY IN A SEMINARY SETTING

MELANIE GREER NOGALSKI
AND
JAMES D. NOGALSKI

Beginning a new school experience always brings out varied emotions for a student, whether it's the first semester of high school or the first term of seminary. Picture this scene as an example: a first semester seminary student makes an appointment to see a professor, ostensibly to clarify questions about the Bible. As the conference proceeds, the student begins sharing personal concerns. "I came to seminary, knowing that God called me into ministry," he begins. "But, I had no idea that there would be this much stress. I can only find a part-time job at night. I have to study every free moment, whether that is convenient or not. And there is so much to study and read: Old Testament, New Testament, Church History, Greek, Educational Theory. The list just keeps growing. I am confused about some of the things I am reading. When I surrendered to my call, I felt so good and so confident that this was the right decision. But now I am not so sure.

Melanie Greer Nogalski is Director of Academic Counseling and Academic Archives, James D. Nogalski is Assistant Professor of Old Testament Interpretation, both at the Southern Baptist Theological Seminary in Louisville, Kentucky.

Is it possible that I misunderstood my call?"

This student's experience is common among every entering group of seminarians, although the details and the questions may vary slightly. Even seasoned ministers who have engaged in vocational ministry prior to embarking on the path of theological education may experience questions when refining their call. Questions may arise as you seek vocational direction for your particular place in ministry. These questions create a genuine moment of crisis involving identity concerns, spirituality, or vocational certainty. What do you do if you find yourself in such a crisis?

These issues may impel you to reexamine your call to ministry. The intensity of this questioning will vary among students because the struggle is very personal. However, it may also involve family and friends, as well as how you view the call to serve the church. Take a moment to remember how you first experienced your call.

How did your call to ministry differ from the call of every Christian to serve Christ? What specific task did you feel best suited your gifts and God's leadership at that point? How do you see your vocational direction serving the church and bringing others into a saving relationship with Jesus Christ?

CALL EXPERIENCE AND FAITH RESPONSES

The Bible provides many examples of persons who have been singled out for a particular task. We often presume that every person called by God responded elatedly to the opportunity. But the Bible records a wide variety of initial responses to God's call. In Exodus 3, Moses essentially tells God, "You can't mean me," which contrasts markedly to Isaiah's dramatic response, "Here am I, send me" (Isa. 6:8). Jonah's flight of anger (Jonah 1:3; cf. 4:1-3) implies that he basically responded to God: "I don't want it to be me." Compare Jonah's response with the Galilean fishermen who left everything they owned to follow an unknown teacher from Nazareth. And Paul, the great apostle, took considerable time before proceeding with the task to which he was called (see Gal. 1).

How do these responses help you? You may be able to identify with some of these biblical examples. You may be facing a future in ministry with great eagerness, or with some trepidation. You may be coming to seminary fresh from a dramatic call experience, or your experience may involve an unfolding, gradual understanding of God's direction for your life, which you have been able to articulate only recently. You may be beginning seminary early in adulthood, with a clear vision of a ministry that will guide your entire future, or you may experience a call into vocational ministry after having invested years in another career. Perhaps the move to seminary and the change of careers has required great financial and familial sacrifice.

The range of emotions you experience includes excitement, relief, and expectation on the one hand and anxiety, dread, and fear on the other. In the collision of expectations with the day-to-day grind of work and study, some questions about the nature of call and purpose in ministry are perhaps inevitable. What are some of your questions in beginning the educational journey? Can you identify some of the emotions you have felt?

ISSUES OF FAITH AND DOUBT

It may seem ironic at first that seminary is a place where most persons called to ministry encounter various levels of doubt about their calling or their ability to fulfill it. However, experience indicates that students do struggle so it may be helpful to highlight some of the areas around which doubt develops. These include confidence, spiritual gifts, vocational choices, ministry tasks, belief systems, and external crises.

You may feel intimidated by the personhood/maturity/talents you perceive in your peers (Moses initially responded that Aaron was more qualified!). Or, you may be cognizant for the first time that numerous vocational choices exist within ministry. As you develop an awareness of ministry options, suddenly your vocational menu may be expanded far beyond what was available before coming to seminary. As a result, you may find excitement in the many places available for the practice of ministry. Even now you may be attempting to focus upon one particular kind of ministry from a range of interesting and intriguing areas in which you feel God has gifted you. You may be moving from multiple possibilities to a singular direction. Or, on the other hand, you may already be certain of your vocational direction early in your educational career. If so, you may find it easier to be singularly focused, but you will need to be sensitive to other students who are still defining and clarifying their specific calls.

How do you clarify the particular direction your ministry will take? This process will involve much prayer, soul searching, and listening. Listening to the stories of others will help immensely, but listening for the many ways God will communicate to you will provide the most definitive route.

Listening and learning from peers may spark new doubts or doctrinal questions. You now share your life with others who come from different states, backgrounds, and church experiences. Prior to seminary, your opportunity to share with other Christians from diverse backgrounds may have been limited. But now you are engaged in dialogue with others whose spiritual experience or doctrinal perspective may be different than yours.

You may have thought that seminary would clarify some of your doctrinal questions. Now, however, while you find much that coincides with what you had learned in the past, you find there are other perspectives to consider. Perhaps you find yourself trying to convince others to believe exactly as you, or you find others insisting you use *their* words to describe *your* beliefs.

You might find this interaction emotionally and spiritually exhausting, and you may wonder why Christians can't agree on all of the fine points of interpretation. For the moments of discomfort you experience, there will be many more moments when you *do* connect with another student and realize that uniformity on all issues is not a prerequisite for sharing the path with another traveler. You may discover that a "heart for ministry" beats strongly in persons of differing theological convictions. In the years to come, you may look back on your seminary experience and realize that it presented a unique opportunity to share, to learn, and to be challenged.

In addition to assessing spiritual gifts and refining vocational goals, the task of ministry is another area which sparks questions. The task of ministry may seem overwhelming as one moves toward the corporate responsibilities of guiding the spiritual welfare of others. Seminary classes typically focus on individual skill development or the development of programs which will assist in leadership, motivation, and discipling of others. Yet you may wonder, "How can I do these things? Will people respond to me? What if I fail? How do I deal with discouragement?"

Internal crises arise from the challenges mentioned above. Sometimes, however, these internal issues are compounded by external crises such as marital difficulties, family medical problems, financial debts, and vocational uncertainty or job termination. Perhaps you are experiencing one of these crises or have come in contact with another student who is undergoing such trauma. One might wonder why those called to God's service suffer in such a fashion. Or, you might ask how you can make it through seminary with such huge obstacles in the way. Finally, you may consider if it is God's will for you to be in seminary at all.

To be sure, not all of these crises will be encountered during your seminary experience. However, students who experience crises, and who are already overloaded with financial and emotional burdens, may not have enough time to sort through the necessary questions to find resolution. Life can become one big blur, with "just finish the semester" as the prevailing attitude. Given all of the areas which can cause doubt, what can be done to cope productively if you find yourself wrestling with these or other issues?

FACING DOUBT WITH INTEGRITY

Above all, it is important to face these issues honestly. The issues of doubt that you encounter regarding your own faith and your understanding of ministry can affect career direction, effectiveness, and satisfaction. The manner in which one handles the questions that arise early in a career can set a pattern for the future. Thus, facing these questions with integrity from the beginning will provide a stable foundation from which to build an enduring, mature ministry.

Facing doubt with integrity affects the development of Christian intellect, faith, and character. Various attitudes about doubt among seminary students may be characterized. Some will deny they experience doubt, often because they understand doubt as a threat to God's sovereignty or even to their own salvation. Others attempt to wrestle with doubt, without succumbing to defeatism (like Jacob at the Jabbok). A few let doubt overwhelm them and thwart their calling, at least temporarily (as when Peter denied Christ). Still others embrace doubt until they create a barrier which hinders faith development. For these persons doubt may be raised to an art form, and they may revel in questions but never again experience the confidence and certainty of faith. Consider where you might classify yourself among these attitudes.

To be sure, constant *preoccupation* with doubt prevents one from drawing upon the strength of his or her spiritual resources, but systematically avoiding the nagging questions which arise also hinders spiritual development. Most persons preparing for ministry will learn to confront questions honestly and will realize that some issues cannot be answered immediately or definitively. In many ways, students learn to function constructively and productively as ministers within the paradox: we possess the answers of faith, but we don't have the answers to all of life's mysteries.

Facing doubt about vocational questions honestly sometimes involves narrowing the parameters in the aftermath of a general call to ministry. Such honing requires wrestling with the implications of accepting your call. This task strengthens and affirms God's calling in your life. For some, however, moving toward the ownership of a call leads to the discovery that it is not what one first thought. For example, some young adults may presume a logical progression from youth group leader to professional minister, only later to recognize it was not God's call into vocational ministry. Other persons come to seminary after experiencing career turmoil, following layoffs or professional stagnation. For many, the call to ministry in a second career leads to great rewards, but others find that seminary is only a transition to yet another arena of service. They too may realize that vocational ministry beyond seminary is not the best use of their gifts.

Even seasoned ministers revisit career goals periodically. At this point of vocational refocusing, it is possible that some will leave professional ministry. Since vocational questioning potentially implies that a person may choose a profession other than ministry, some try to avoid this area of questioning as dangerous.

However, avoidance of genuine questions only postpones the moment of crisis and detracts from the need to reaffirm one's commitment to ministry during unproductive or discouraging periods. Ministers who incorporate vocational doubts and questions into their spiritual pilgrimages learn to become comfortable with their calling to ministry even when they experience difficulties in their personal or professional lives. They integrate decisions, spiritual maturity, opportunities, and skills into productive ministry. For the seminary student beginning this path, it is very important to ask, "How do I face doubt with integrity?"

TAKING CHARGE OF DOUBT

Spiritual Resources

The most important resource in questions of doubt is your own spiritual mettle. Personal faith in Christ is the anchor which cannot be forgotten or supplanted. Internal struggles are very real and you cannot expect to be exempt from them. People turn to ministers for spiritual guidance. Insights gained by passing through your own struggles will be pivotal to your ministry as a fellow struggler through whom God can speak. Your own trials will deepen faith. The search for a deeper understanding of God and his purpose for your life will provide a depth and security which others will recognize and which will make you more effective in ministering to them.

Another aspect related to your spiritual health involves significant relationships and priorities. They need continual attention. Relationships cannot be put on hold until after a person finishes seminary. Time spent with spouse (and family) is a fundamental responsibility for married students and yet one which can too easily be ignored. "Catch-up time" rarely occurs and only communicates that everything else is more important than one's marriage or family. Spouses undergo enormous strains, and students should engage their spouses in mutual spiritual and personal development. Patterns developed in seminary will likely be repeated later in a place of ministry. Creating positive patterns of good communication, shared decision-making skills, common vision of purpose, and reciprocal affirmation of personhood constitute the basis for strong, healthy relationships. Initiating these fundamentals in seminary will prepare students and spouses to endure the demands which ministry places upon families.

Community Support

Another vital resource is the role of community support. Community support will be found in the seminary and the church. Seminary is an obvious place to seek help, since other students encounter the same problems. No one can empathize with you like another student experiencing the same questions. You must learn to avoid the danger, however, of using conversations with other students only as a time to lament the pressure under which seminarians operate. The real benefit in peer relationships lies in their constructive potential to strengthen the participants. Ministers develop lifelong friendships in seminary and learn patterns for the development of future relationships with other ministers which are significant for support later in ministry settings.

Everyone needs a "safety net"—friends to whom you can turn during low periods in ministry. It is important to keep in touch with close friends after seminary and to update one another regarding personal and professional development. Meeting an old friend from the past and "debriefing," even every few years, can be very healthy and provide the periodic reflection necessary to keep ministry focused and meaningful.

Seminary does not automatically create friendships, however, so you must take the initiative to develop relationships. Strong peer relationships are as important to education as any course work. Students who commute and have little time to visit with other students must develop creative ways to establish friendships. Many form meaningful relationships by commuting with other students, talking and sharing while they travel. The quality of such relationships is more important than the quantity.

The church is a source of community support and has a vital place in your past and present. If possible, it is good to stay connected with your home church (your spiritual roots). Today's transient society can complicate this effort, but it is important to retain ties with past church experiences which can be transferred into the present. Knowing of the prayers of others who care about your well-being will generate fortitude and a sense of responsibility to the task to which you are called.

It is also vital for spiritual and professional development that one find a supporting congregation during seminary. For some students, this congregation may be a first pastorate or staff position. Others may not find remunerative ministerial positions, but there are always local churches where you can learn about ministry through leadership in church programs (such as Sunday School, supervised ministry, clinical pastoral education, etc.). During seminary days, students are best advised to stay connected with people whom they will serve after seminary.

Community support within the church also involves mentor relationships. Local pastors and other professional church workers are important resources in developing ministerial identity. Professors and other seminary personnel can also be important mentors. Such relationships must be fostered deliberately. These relationships do not always require a great deal of time, but they do necessitate a commitment to keep mentors informed about personal and professional development.

Character Development
The role of character development in taking charge of doubt is also important in ministry. Strong character requires you to use common sense as a means of minimizing external crises. You must recognize problems in the developing stage, find appropriate responses, *and* move toward correcting or negotiating through them.

Physical and mental overload is a very common problem among seminary students. You must take care of your health by getting enough sleep and exercise. A student cannot expect to work a forty hour week, take four or five courses, work in a church, and remain alert and energetic, or even sane. Given the problem of financial restraints, you should examine your lifestyle, eliminate as many nonessential obligations as possible, and reduce the academic workload to a manageable level. Even if it takes a year longer to complete your degree, it is more beneficial for all concerned (students and churches) that you gain as much as possible from seminary, and that you be as financially stable as possible when you finish.

Another aspect of character development involves personal responsibility. Integrity requires persons to assume responsibility for their own actions, relationships, and utilization of resources. This issue relates to stewardship and professional ethics. A minister cannot expect to be a model of Christian responsibility to a church when ignoring his or her own actions and behavior. The attitude of "I am in charge, therefore whatever I do is permissible" has led too many ministers into financial problems, extramarital affairs, and interpersonal conflict. Personal responsibility is not something to be taken lightly, nor should developing problems be ignored.

Taking charge of doubt requires active engagement in the problems which emerge in any kind of ministry. Merely waiting passively until things work out robs the minister of opportunities to grow spiritually, to receive or to give appropriate levels of support, and to develop character qualities necessary for a healthy life. Facing occasional periods of doubt can increase your sense of purpose, call, and commitment to ministry.

The Cyclical Nature of Doubt

After graduating from seminary, students are often surprised by the transition which takes place from student life to professional life. In seminary, the goal of completion is a major driving force for the student. Students may be caught off guard by the adjustment to a life in which they must set and meet their own deadlines and in which they must establish and implement ministry goals which *they* deem important.

Many people learn at that time the unhappy truth that the overload which occurs in their lives as students, continues into ministry settings. There is always another family to visit, another call to make, another lesson to prepare, another letter to write. Thus, the strategies one develops as a student for coping with the demands on time, emotions, family life, and faith life will be reemployed and adjusted for other settings.

Overwhelming demands may cause ministers to ask again, "Am I in the right profession?" "Does God want me in ministry when I am having problems meeting all the needs of those around me?" Disappointment may become a factor for a minister in a church where things are not "happening" fast enough.

Burnout can occur when both the minister and the church have unrealistic expectations of what can be accomplished. Aging ministers face rejection from churches who want younger people to lead the flock. Every minister can tell stories of personal crises which cause them to wonder, "Why am I here?"

One common, yet debilitating, response occurs when ministers interpret the reemergence of doubt as God's signal that the grass is greener someplace else or that it is time to seek another profession. Too many ministers and churches run away from problems rather than work through the (sometimes painful) process of resolution and reconciliation. Too often, ministers fail to realize that vocational doubts and questions are a part of normal adult development. Most professionals have similar questions and problems. Yet for ministers, the professional stakes are much higher because they involve a person's faith life, family life, vocational identity, and a divine call!

Productive responses can be incorporated into your professional arsenal of support. Ministers should take care to reduce overload by establishing boundaries for personal and family time. They may need to educate the church to honor these commitments and to see them as worthy of emulation for members of their congregations. Ministers also need to anticipate the need for "safety nets" (colleagues, friends, other professionals) and ministers from area churches (even other denominations). Ministers can profit by becoming mentors to seminarians and by sharing their own experiences with those who are engaged in learning about ministry as novice professionals. Ministers should relate caringly to young people in their church who feel a call to ministry and who may be experiencing the associated joys or doubts of such a calling. Ministers also help themselves by continuing their own education and development. Conferences, continuing education courses, local ministerial associations, or professional organizations geared toward specific ministry roles can support, energize, and renew one's spirit.

The focus of this article has moved deliberately from student experience to professional aspects of ministry. While many of the issues raised here may resonate with the life experiences of both students and professional ministers, the reality is that such questions cannot be examined publicly. Doubts and questions are very private and part of your "interior dialogue." Emotional low points can be very isolating and, if left in the realm of interior dialogue, potentially destructive to your life and ministry. Periods of doubt and crisis are not simply problems which can be isolated into a single sphere of life.

For this reason, you must foster the courage to face doubts with honesty, realism, and commitment to a positive resolution. By resolving doubt positively, you continue to mature in faith and to seek spiritual depth, thereby increasing your potential to function productively as a minister of Christ.

For Further Reading

Broholm, Richard R. "How Can You Believe You're a Minister When the Church Keeps Telling You You're Not." *American Baptist Quarterly* 3 (1984): 175–83.

Engram, Ann T. "A Mentor's Reflection." *St. Luke's Journal of Theology* 27 (1984): 279–85.

Fowler, James W. *Stages of Faith: The Psychology of Human Development and the Quest for Meaning.* San Francisco: Harper and Row, 1981.

Habermas, Ronald T. "Doubt Is Not a Four-Letter Word." *Religious Education* 84 (1989): 402–10.

Hartshorne, Marion H. "Faith Without Doubt Is Dead." *Theology Today* 13 (1956): 63–71.

Jensen, Mark. *Shattered Vocations.* Nashville: Broadman, 1990.

Malone, Nancy M. "Faith That Works." *Cross Currents* 40 (1990): 147–227.

Marty, Martin. *A Cry of Absence: Reflections for the Winter of the Heart.* San Francisco: Harper, 1983.

Nelson, Melvin R. "Psychology of Spiritual Conflict." *Journal of Psychology and Theology* 4 (1976): 34–41.

Oates, Wayne E. *Managing Your Stress*. Indianapolis: Bierce Associates, 1983.

Oates, Wayne E., ed. *The Minister's Own Mental Health*. Great Neck, N.Y.: Channel, 1955.

St. John of the Cross. *Dark Night of the Soul: A Classic in the Literature of Mysticism*. Translated by E. Allison Peers. Garden City, N.Y.: Doubleday, 1959.

Whittaker, John H. "Wise and Simple Faith: An Address to Sceptics." *Theology* 81 (1978): 323–31.

THE SEMINARY EXPERIENCE: TIPS AND TRAPS

MARSHA A. ELLIS SMITH

If you are headed to seminary, or even contemplating the possibility, then this is a chapter you don't want to miss. I will be sharing some practical advice that you will need in order to have the best of all seminary experiences. Thus, I will be writing in a "student-friendly" style; I want you to feel like I am speaking directly to your questions and concerns.

Seminary is a life-changing event. To enter it both with fear and trepidation *and* with excitement and enthusiasm is normal. Some advice, however, is helpful (make that essential!) as you move toward it. To share this help, I'll be giving you two lists: one of tips to guide and one of traps or misconceptions to avoid. Some will seem funny, some impossible, and still others confusing. However, all of them contain bits and pieces—sometimes even large chunks—that you can apply to your preparation for, or your daily living out of, the seminary experience. Some ideas will apply more than others. Many have been offered to me by current students; others came from student spouses, veteran seminary

Marsha A. Ellis Smith is Associate Vice President for Academic Administration at the Southern Baptist Theological Seminary in Louisville, Kentucky.

staff people, and my own experience—speaking as one who earned two seminary degrees. My hope is that each tip and trap will help you to get the most from your seminary years.

THE TEN BEST TIPS
FOR NEW SEMINARY STUDENTS

1. Plan for Your Seminary Career Financially, Spiritually, and Educationally.
I believe that our God shows us his penchant for order in the world around us. He also shows us in that same world that he is not opposed to spontaneity. Therefore, while God does sometimes call persons to seminary with little time for preplanning, I believe that this is the exception to the rule. Your seminary experience will be greatly enhanced if you have made time to think about your move and plan for it. This is particularly applicable if you are moving an entire family from one location to another to attend school.

Plan to survive financially. Do you have savings that can be used, job prospects in the new location, family or friends who are paying the bills for you? If you are married, are your children at an age where you or your spouse is needed at home? If so, can you "make ends meet" with one spouse at home and one attending school full-time? Would a part-time school/part-time job situation be a better plan? What about your house—can you sell it? These and similar questions should be answered forthrightly before you get to seminary. Because there will be plenty of issues to face after you arrive on campus, the more decisions you can make beforehand the better.

Closely perusing your school's catalog is also a beneficial discipline. Get familiar with the school, the faculty, and the programs which seem best suited for your particular vocational objectives. (And, oh yes, make sure to send in your application by the deadline date. This is a very important detail.)

2. Get to Campus before the First Week of Classes!
Although one can arrive at seminary and register for classes in the same week (or same day for that matter), it will wreak less

havoc on you (and your family!) if you plan to arrive one to two months prior to your first semester. Whether single or married, there are many benefits to arriving that early. Job hunting may take more time than planned and just getting settled into a new home is time-consuming, stressful, and emotionally draining. Also, there may be additional matriculation details that can't be taken care of until after arriving on campus. Items like your new address and phone number (for both work and school) are needed. Further, you might be able to get other business taken care of—like obtaining a campus post office box, setting up an account with the school, and becoming familiar with the library and other classroom and recreational facilities. At some schools these types of issues can be handled before registration, but at others registration has to take place first.

3. Study Hard.

Does this even need to be listed as a tip? Unfortunately, yes! I have heard students say that they came to seminary "to minister, not to learn." Realizing that God calls men and women to seminary for different reasons, I still believe that, above all else, he calls them first to learn. Why would one come to seminary if not to learn how to be a good minister? And so, this tip reminds us that our primary responsibility to God is to learn all that he has for us while we are in seminary.

Seminary is a time like no other in your life. I look back on my seminary experience and know that it was a blessed time, filled with God's grace in a way unlike any other time in my life. A lifetime bond is often created between people who were students or student spouses together in seminary. Years later when meeting again you will reminisce about both the good and the difficult times that have given you memories for a lifetime.

There may even be some required classes where you will have to remind yourself that your study responsibility is one you owe to God and not to a professor or even to the seminary. And then there will be those classes that you wish would never end. Warning: do not measure your *responsibility* to study by your *level of desire* to study in any specific class. Measure it instead by your responsibility to do your best in whatever situation God places you.

4. Play Hard.

In the same way that you have a responsibility to study, you also have one to play. When I was preparing for the doctoral entrance exams at seminary, I was trying to study eight hours a day with only periodic five-minute breaks. I soon discovered that I was not able to concentrate effectively and was becoming frustrated. I confessed to a professor, whom I greatly respected, my concern over not being ready for the exams because of my inability to concentrate. His sage advice was to punctuate my concentrated study periods (two-three hours) with breaks throughout the day and to not try to study eight full hours each day. I took his counsel seriously and was able to study much more effectively with the breaks.

Recently, Christian books and studies have been emphasizing our responsibility to use leisure time wisely, to the glory of God. Getting the most out of your leisure time is as important as getting the most out of your study time. Whether taking your dog for a walk, playing intramural basketball, or swimming a few laps, your body needs exercise to keep it healthy just as your mind needs intellectual stimulation to keep it sharp. And both are necessary to keep you a healthy, whole person.

5. Learn That Stress Is a Real and Active Part of Your Life at Seminary!

Stress will be a constant companion during seminary life. Stress is not a "bad" thing in itself. It can be used creatively. Some stress or tension in our lives helps to stimulate us to function effectively. But an overabundance of stress can be debilitating; it can cause one to become immobilized.

Some stress will always be present. Any kind of change—whether for the better or the worse—causes some amount of stress. Simply being a new seminary student is a stress factor. If attending seminary means a move from a different part of the country, or from another country, this only adds to the initial stress. Stress will be a part of this experience, as it is with all of life. The important thing is to learn how to live with this knowledge.

Consider these two ways of dealing with stress. First, learn to alleviate whatever stress you can. Learn to say no when you need to do so. Don't do everything you are asked to do. You do not have to speak at every church function, even if you are on the staff! You do not have to serve on every student committee at seminary. You don't even have to go to every social event to which you are invited! Second, learn how to deal creatively with the stress that you cannot get rid of. Approach a huge project one small step at a time. Don't wait until the last minute and be forced to "pull an all-nighter" to get it finished! Take breaks from your work (as mentioned in tip 4). Take time for yourself. Learn to relax in the midst of your stressful life. A short break in the middle of a heated discussion or in the middle of a heated day can save a friendship, a marriage, or a life.

6. Get to Know Your Professors.

In talking with former students about what seminary meant to them, their level of appreciation seems to hinge on their involvement with the seminary community. If they felt a sense of community with others at seminary, then their appreciation for those years is high. If they had little contact with others during that time, they tend not to have much appreciation for their seminary experience.

Whatever else you do, get to know your professors. I learned a great deal from my teachers in the classroom, but I also learned from watching them live out in "real life" what they taught in class lectures. I watched professors deal with major life issues—one's own terminal illness and death, the terminal illness and death of a spouse, a child's bad decision and the resulting difficulties, a spouse's midlife crisis and resulting divorce—and saw God's grace lift them up and give them strength for each day. I learned much about Christian spirituality in the laboratory of life walk by watching my professors' reactions to their own life experiences.

Here's a simple suggestion: take a professor to lunch. If the thought of that intimidates you, get two or three of your classmates together and make it a group outing. Stopping by a professor's office for a quick visit is another way to build relationships (but get to know their office hours and make appointments!). The benefits of developing personal relationships with those from whom you are learning are well worth the effort expended in so doing.

7a. Find Ways to Mesh Your Family Life with Your Seminary Life (Married Student Version).

If a spouse does not feel like part of the seminary experience, he or she will have difficulty committing to the years it will take to get the degree. When you are married, God's will for one of you ends up (practically speaking) being God's will for both of you. Coming to seminary is a major decision to which both partners must be committed. If there are children involved, care needs to be taken to involve them in the "family decision-making process." Thankfully, many resources are available to help make this transition a positive experience for your family.

Once on campus, take as much opportunity as time allows to build fellowship between you and your family—and other students and their families. Experience teaches that it is very difficult for a spouse who knows none of the people with whom his wife or her husband associates in the classroom and on campus. The more you can involve your spouse, the more your spouse will feel a part of your seminary experience and the less isolated he or she will be. It should really be viewed not as "my" seminary experience by you, but as "our" seminary experience by the both of you.

7b. Find Ways to Get to Know Other Seminary Students (Single Student Version).

The first rule for the "single student" is get out there and meet people! Your situation is different from the married student in that your "family" on campus is you. (Although if you are in the single-again status, you may have children with you at seminary.) You may be lamenting your singleness right now, wondering if this will be your status for the rest of your life. Or you may have worked through it and now trust God that you will get married when and if it is his will. Whatever your perspective, be aware that you need to develop a sense of community with your fellow seminary students in the here and now. There will be other single students at your seminary who will need the same fellowship that you do. Some of the best and longest of friendships are begun during seminary years.

Take the opportunity to get to know some married couples; it is a good experience to relate to the families of students you know from class—both for you and for them. We all need a variety of friends who are in various passages of life. It makes for a richly colored tapestry of friends from whom we can learn a tremendous amount.

8. Get to Know as Many People from as Many Cultures as Possible.

Seminary can be a great time to get to know Christian brothers and sisters from parts of the world that you may never get a chance to visit—people from wonderfully diverse cultural backgrounds. Getting to know these persons will enrich your life. They are the living example to you (as you will be to them!) that God can reach into any life in any culture and bring that life to himself. In fact, it is a reminder that God seems to love the variety he wove into his universe.

Take every opportunity that time allows to get to know people who are different from you—whether you are a native or international student. If you and your family are international students, take every chance to get to know students and student families here in this country. Get to know the language and customs of this country (and also encourage your family to do so) to the extent that you can function and communicate while you are here in seminary. Your life will be enhanced by your effort.

9. Try to Survive Seminary without Being the Exception to Every Rule!

This suggestion comes from staff persons more than seminary students. Every institution of higher education has rules and regulations that students are required to follow. Contrary to popular belief, rules are not made to be broken. Administrators take no delight in denying student requests. However, sometimes "no" must be said. Although exceptions are sometimes made to rules, exceptions should be the exception—not the rule! Most rules have solid reasoning behind them. Making exceptions must be due to extremely extenuating circumstances.

Play by the rules regularly. That way when you do need to be the exception you may be treated more favorably. Perhaps a practical example would help. If you do have a question regarding seminary policy—like registration, grades, or degree program—

make an effort to find the right office to answer your question. Administrators can serve more effectively when assisting an informed clientele. Don't depend on hearsay for information; go directly to the source.

10. *Know That God Brought You Here and He Will Give You Grace for the Experience.*
Last and most important—God is in control. It is he who brought you to seminary, and he will get you through it with his grace. Seminary is a great experience. But even when it gets difficult, God will give you the strength to make it, just like he has been there to help you in the past. Stand on the words of the writer of Proverbs 3:5-6: "Trust in the Lord with all your heart and lean not on your own understanding; in all your ways acknowledge him, and he will make your paths straight."

THE TEN WORST TRAPS FOR NEW SEMINARY STUDENTS

1. *God Called Me Here, So He Will Take Care of Everything.*
Beware of leaving everything in the lap of God. We are not Christian robots, simply wound up to follow his will. We are given freedom to make decisions, always in connection, however, with his guidance. He expects us to use the gifts he has given us. And one of God's greatest gifts is our ability to think through alternatives and make decisions.

For instance, it is *your* responsibility to read information sent to you from the seminary you have chosen, whether it is the application material before you enter or notices in your post office box once you have become a student. Always read the fine print, literally and figuratively, and trust the Lord to give you discernment. Be all that God made you; keep moving ahead with all the energy and brain power you can muster—always under his grace and guidance.

2. *Seminary Is Like a Big Spiritual Pep Rally.*
The seminary is a spiritual institution, but it is also an academic institution. God brings people to seminary to learn and to pre-

pare them for the ministry to which he has called them. Seminary brings its own rich share of spiritual experiences, however it is not an ongoing pep rally. There will, of course, be spiritual highs which you will experience, but we are not created by God to function that way. It would be unnatural and a little unhealthy.

Spiritual formation will take place both inside and outside the classroom setting, but your primary focus should be on coming to seminary to study. And further, be prepared to experience both spiritual highs and lows as you will even after you have begun your formal ministry.

3. Seminary Life Will Be Wonderful without Any Loneliness.

There are many adjustments necessary for those entering seminary, and that will include loneliness for some. Depending on your situation before coming to seminary, this loneliness will play itself out in various ways. If you have left a stable home environment, you might face more adjustment challenges than one who has lived a more "nomadic" lifestyle. It is not a sign of failure if you do not feel "at home" after several months at seminary. Nor is it a sign of failure to get homesick every now and then, even after being at seminary for a year or so. Those are normal and natural feelings.

There are various kinds of loneliness—yearning for a best friend, for a dating partner, for a community of caring. When any of these are missing, some time of loneliness is likely to follow. During these lonely moments remember that God loves you more than you can imagine, and he will give you strength and comfort in your dark times.

4. Anyone Whose Opinion Differs from Mine Is Wrong/Bad/Evil!

Deep within every person's life is some level of fear of those who are different than themselves. Everyone is taught that strangers tend to steal or that they may hurt you. News of rampant abuse in our culture is broadcast into our homes on television news every day. "Stranger fear" is a given commodity in our nation. The ever-present media reinforces the "stranger fear" message. We are, with quite some clear examples of reasons why, driven by this "stranger fear." This fear was quite well known to biblical-era citizens. They too feared for life, limb, and property at the hands of the stranger.

One of the major differences between the Hebrew children of

Abraham and their contemporaries was their religious teaching about hospitality. Any traveler appearing at a Hebrew doorstep was to be given three days and two nights of lodging, food, and care. Though infidels, or nonbelievers, they were to be cared for, protected, and invited to the family table. The root of Jesus' teaching about loving your enemy arises from the same mind-set. Christians are to be open and hospitable to others, to meet them face to face, and to attempt both to learn from them and to teach those whose ideas are different from their own.

Today, as in ancient times, hospitality is likely only to be extended to family or to intimate friends. In addition, friends are likely to be defined as those who look like us, live like us, believe like us, and behave like us. We feel comfortable around those who associate with the same groups, who espouse the same beliefs, and who live in the same manner as we do. The opposite is also true. The prohibition against strangers is strong.

In some places, this fear of the stranger has been extended to fear of the stranger's ideas. Surely, many of us have been taught that if another person speaks ideas different from our own, then that stranger and all about him/her is suspect.

Surprisingly enough, you will discover among your peers in the seminary people who actually believe exactly as you do. You will also discover others who hold strongly to beliefs that are somewhat or even markedly different from your own.

A great test of faith is to be able to give testimony to your own belief while being open to give others the courtesy of a listening ear when they speak of beliefs different from your own. You should not surrender your faith in such contexts, but hopefully be open to listen as you seek to understand the lives and faith commitments of others.

Seminary typically provides an ideal context for being challenged by ideas with which we disagree. Try to listen to those with new or different ideas. The mental and theological stretching is good for the mind and the soul. Frankly, if we stop listening and talking to people different from ourselves, we not only stop growing, we lose any opportunity to share our own ideas. Further, one of the worst dangers of this is that we also lose any opportunity to witness to those out in the world who do not know Christ. That should make us stop and think!

5. Bible Study for Classes Can Replace My Devotional Time Right Now.

One of the most difficult obstacles to maintaining one's spirituality in seminary is a lack of consistency in daily devotional time. The seminary student's great temptation is to allow his or her Bible reading for classes to replace a regular daily devotional time. It is far too easy to say, "I read my Bible today for Old Testament class, so I can wait until tomorrow to read devotionally." All too soon "tomorrow" becomes the next day and the next day, and soon your personal devotions begin to suffer, as does your spiritual life. Take care to reserve time to read your Bible devotionally, when you can let God speak to you through the text apart from any classroom study.

Also, don't forget your quiet time in prayer with God either. Most seminaries have courses on individual spiritual formation required in many degree programs. These are very helpful, but one course won't carry you spiritually through your seminary years. You must develop and sustain a consistent devotional life. This will help you to balance the rigors of study now as well as those of ministry later.

6. I'd Better Not Ask Any Questions; I Don't Want to Look Stupid.

If you do not have the freedom to ask questions at seminary, you don't have that freedom anywhere! This is your chance to learn from the "experts." You are preparing for Christian ministry. Don't be intimidated by what you *think* your classmates know! People come to seminary from all kinds of educational and professional backgrounds—some come straight from college (including Bible and theology majors!) while others have been in the workplace for years. All these backgrounds are thrown together into ethics, theology, and biblical studies classes. The quiet students may indeed know all of the answers and thus not need to ask questions. However, they probably are just as afraid to ask a question as you are and may need the answer as much as, if not more than, you do! If you have a question but are hesitant to ask it in the classroom, make sure to set up an office appointment with your professor to get your answer. No matter how you choose to do it, make sure to ask your questions!

7. My Studies Are More Important Than Anything Else in My Life.

The information and skills you will learn through your classes are a crucial part of the seminary experience. In fact, it is the anticipation of that learning that brings one to seminary. However, sometimes classes should not be your top priority. Your own illness or that of a spouse, child, or other family member may cause you to put your class work on the back burner. Your health (both mental and physical) and the health of those closest to you has to take priority at times. There may even be times when a family event must take priority over your seminary work. Only you—with God's guidance—will be able to determine when your priorities must be modified. Always keep in mind that your main goal at seminary is to prepare yourself to carry out God's calling in your life. Knowing that, you must adjust priorities when necessary to deal with life's emergencies and opportunities.

8. My Life Is on Hold While I Am in Seminary.

While you may view your life as being on hold during your seminary years, remember that is not the case for those with whom you are closely associated. Your friends' lives continue, family members age, children develop, and spouses' needs change and evolve. Their lives are marching on uninterrupted. If caution is not taken to be sensitive to these "significant others," there will be hurt feelings and broken relationships. I know a professor who credits his Ph.D. degree with the problems his children have experienced in their young adult lives. When they were youngsters he was not available to spend quality time with them; sadly, they have reaped the consequences of his absence in their lives.

Life goes on while you are in seminary, for both you and your loved ones. Don't lose those you love in the name of devotion to God. This does not honor God in any way. Protect the ones you love; live life.

9. I Must Not Be Doing Things Right Because I Am Not Doing As Well As _____.

This trap and number 10 are related, so I will only make a few emphatic remarks about this one. *Do not compare yourself to anyone else!* Your only responsibility is to do the best that *you* can do—

not the best that your classmates can do. We are all uniquely made in God's image; we have different gifts, strengths, and weaknesses. God will not ask you why you did not do as well as the student at the next desk; he will ask what you did with what you were given.

In our competitive culture it is hard to avoid measuring ourselves against each other, but the difficulty of the task is not ours to determine. We are only responsible for our own development—under God's guidance.

10. I Am Superman/Superwoman/Superseminarian.

This "super" identity deception causes individuals to take on more tasks than they should and inevitably leads to "burnout." For example, seminary courses are different from college classes—you may not be able to take as many hours on the graduate level as you had hoped. That's okay. Your seminary experience does not have to be a race against time! Give yourself enough time for the knowledge you are putting into your head to take up residence!

This "superhuman" syndrome has a tendency to sneak up on one. You won't realize you are trying to do too much until suddenly you are already overwhelmed. And this applies to all areas of your life—school, work, family and, yes, even church work! Watch your schedule; pray about how you use your time. Beware of the tyranny of the urgent.

We are called to be good stewards of all that we are and all that we do. Become as conscious of the value of your time as you are of your money, and just this knowledge will empower you to take better control of it. If you don't currently keep a calendar, get one to organize your busy life. Use it to jot down dates of assignments and important events (school, family, work, and church). Become as organized as you can without becoming a slave to that organization. If you can learn this lesson in seminary, you will have a much more productive ministry after graduation.

CONCLUSION

This chapter has presented a rather rapid overflight of subjects and suggestions useful to you as you begin and continue your seminary career. I hope some of the ideas here will make your "settling in" a little more easy for you.

Entering seminary, in and of itself, is an activity of faith. It is clearly a practical adventure for Christians who sense God calling them into a lifetime of vocational ministry. Like all institutions, seminaries can be intimidating to a newcomer. Unfamiliar procedures, new persons, and a challenging academic environment have always been a challenge. However, I trust you will find your seminary to be a comfortable place to live, learn, and serve. This will certainly happen for you as you begin to explore new relationships with peers, professors, and administrators in your new place of ministry.

As a final word, I recommend that you use your move into the seminary community as an opportunity to exercise the three major common denominators of ministry relations. The first is the art of *initiative*. Throughout your life, you will need to be able to move toward people and situations with appropriate amounts of energy and resourcefulness. Ministers do not characteristically sit around and wait for a specific invitation to begin ministry. They listen carefully to the promptings of the Holy Spirit, to be sure, but the hallmark of ministry is the art of moving toward the person or situation needing to be addressed. Every new person and event as you enter the seminary is an opportunity to practice appropriate initiative. I warmly recommend that you begin that practice as soon as possible.

The second art of ministry is *urgency*. This is the practice of doing as many things right away as is reasonably possible. Life is too short to postpone whatever needs to be done for another time. Procrastination is the practice of borrowing time from one of your tomorrows, like overloading your only credit card before going on a trip. The fewer things you have left over to be completed tomorrow, the more free and flexible you will be to accomplish tomorrow's challenges and pleasures tomorrow. I recommend that you deal with your classroom work, library research, and other requirements of each day with this kind of appropriate urgency.

Finally, I recommend that you practice the art of *closure*. Even when you take initiative, you may inadvertently leave out something and leave odds and ends undone. If this happened in a court of law, the case would still be open—and not closed. As frequently as you are able, complete assignments, conversations, and tasks while you have them in your mind and hand, and move on to the rest of your life. Initiative, urgency, and closure are important, but the greatest of these is closure.

I invite you to move along and to read the rest of the chapters in this book. They offer many clear and helpful suggestions along with much wisdom about ministry. I hope you enjoy your time in seminary, your first ministry studies class, and every one of your lifelong career opportunities to do ministry. I pray you find the tips helpful—helpful enough to avoid the traps which may await any of us whenever we move to a new location. God bless you as you continue your studies for ministry.

FOR FURTHER READING

George, Denise. *How to be a Seminary Student and Survive.* Nashville: Broadman, 1981.

PERSONAL
FORMATION AND
CALLING FOR
MINISTRY

4

TOWARD A BIBLICAL VIEW OF CALL

JOHN POLHILL

Each of us has our own story about our call into the ministry. Most of us are convinced that our call was legitimate and fit the biblical pattern. Yet if we pick up a concordance and check out the passages which relate to a "call" or "calling," most likely we will be surprised by what we find. The Bible actually presents a much different picture of calling than the common view among Christians today.

Take the phrase "call to full-time Christian service," for example. In at least two respects this familiar phrase is at odds with the biblical passages which speak of a call. First, it assumes that a call is reserved for a restricted group of people, whereas, in fact, the New Testament speaks of all Christians as being called. Second, it assumes a full-time, fully supported professional ministry. It is doubtful that such a professional ministry existed at all in New Testament times. Let us take a fresh look at what the Bible really says about the concept of "the call to ministry."

John Polhill is J.B. Harrison Professor of New Testament Interpretation, and Associate Dean, School of Theology, at the Southern Baptist Theological Seminary, Louisville, Kentucky.

CALLING IN THE GENERAL SENSE

The New Testament primarily speaks of a "call" or "calling" in a general sense. All Christians are "called." This "calling" is God's invitation to share in the salvation offered through Christ. It is not specifically a call to service. It is rather a call to membership in the church, the body of Christ.

The root word for calling in the Greek New Testament is *kaleo*. This verb, "to call," shares many of the same meanings as our English verb "to call." Its most common use in the New Testament is in naming something, as in "a city *called* Nazareth" (Matt. 2:23, NASB) and "you shall *call* his name John" (Luke 1:13, NKJV). Much less frequently, it has the meaning to call someone over, to summon them—as when the Sanhedrin summons the apostles in Acts 4:18, or Herod summons the magi in Matthew 2:7. Other usages have the meaning of "invite," and with this meaning we move into more of a religious sphere. It has this meaning in Jesus' parable of the king's invitation to the wedding feast of his son (Matt. 22:1-10), as well as his parable of the excuses for refusing the invitation to the great banquet (Luke 14:15-24). These parables rather transparently depict God's invitation or "calling" to share in the joy of his salvation, to take one's seat in the heavenly banquet hall.

Paul frequently uses the verb "to call" in this more restricted sense of God's invitation to share in his salvation. One is *"called into fellowship with his Son Jesus Christ"* (1 Cor. 1:9). Paul urges the Corinthians to continue in the situation in life in which they were originally called (1 Cor. 7:17-24). The reference is obviously to the time of their commitment to Christ and call into the body of Christ. In Ephesians, Paul speaks of the hope which belongs to our calling; that is, the eternal hope which accompanies belonging to God's people in Christ (Eph. 4:1, 4). Likewise, 1 Timothy 6:12 speaks of being called to eternal life. In 2 Timothy 1:9, God's calling is synonymous with his salvation, and 1 Peter 5:10 describes the Christian call as a call to "eternal glory." One readily sees that in the New Testament epistles God's calling is his invitation to eternal life in Christ.

When one examines the New Testament usage of the noun form "calling" (*klesis*) and the adjective form "called" (*kletos*) the religious meaning is the only one that appears. Both terms refer to God's calling to salvation and discipleship and not to a special call to ministry. There is one exception—when Paul speaks of his call to be an apostle. We will examine that usage in the next section and at present will restrict ourselves to the more common uses of "calling" and "called," which refer almost exclusively to God's calling Christians to salvation. One's "calling" (*klesis*) is when they first come to faith in Christ (1 Cor. 1:26; 7:20). Calling is thus closely connected with the hope of eternal life in Christ (Eph. 1:18; 4:4). It is the higher, heavenly calling of God to faithful discipleship (Phil. 3:14; 2 Thes. 1:11). The one who is "called" (*kletos*) is "sanctified," "set apart" in Christ Jesus (Rom. 1:7; 1 Cor. 1:2; Jude 1). God's salvation, his calling, is inclusive. It embraces all peoples without distinction, Jews and Gentiles alike (Rom. 1:16; 1 Cor. 1:24).

"Calling" and "election" express the same reality, and so it is no surprise to find the two terms together in several places. In 2 Peter 1:10 they occur together and are virtually synonymous. First Peter 2:9 places God's "called" together with other designations of his people—"a chosen people, a royal priesthood, a holy nation, a people belonging to God." In Revelation 17:14, those who belong to the Lamb are described in three basically synonymous terms—"called, chosen, and faithful." In short, "called" is equivalent to "chosen" and "elect." God's call is always prior to our response. Salvation is God's prerogative. He chooses, he calls, he sends out the invitation. We respond to his call. One somewhat enigmatic statement, found in Matthew 22:14, may seem on the surface to contradict this claim: "Many are called, but few are chosen" (NASB). Here, Jesus' parable is actually making a different point. "Called" in this text is being used in its more general sense, as "invited," not in the more common New Testament sense, as a reference to those who have already responded positively to God's invitation and thus belong to the elect.

It should be noted that the regular New Testament term for church is *ekklesia*, another noun which derives from the verb "to call." It means, "those who are called out." The church, the body of Christ, consists of those who are called out, set apart as God's own people. This fits the pattern as we have seen it. The Christian calling in its characteristic New Testament sense is the call into the church, God's people, the body of Christ.

Does this mean that "calling" has nothing to do with service or ministry? Quite the contrary, it implies that the concept of Christian calling or vocation applies to all Christians, not to a limited group. Many of the passages which speak of calling emphasize service, steadfastness, discipleship, walking worthily of one's calling, pressing forward toward the goal. All Christians are called to serve. The minister's task is to lead others to affirm their calling and discover their own place of ministry.

CALLING IN THE RESTRICTIVE SENSE

In the early church there were few if any of what we would call "full-time" or professional ministers. The apostles would perhaps correspond most closely with today's professional ministers. The New Testament primarily gives a picture of a volunteer ministry, such as the women who traveled with Jesus and his disciples and provided for them out of their own means (Luke 8:1-3), or Priscilla and Aquila, the couple who shared Paul's trade and assisted him in ministry (Acts 18:1-3, 18, 26). Like them, Paul was a tent-maker. Although, as an apostle, he had the right to be supported by the churches he served, Paul often chose to waive such support and provide for himself by practicing his trade (Acts 20:33-35; 1 Cor. 9:1-18).

The most common form of material support for ministers reflected in the New Testament was the food and lodging provided by Christians for apostles, itinerant prophets, and evangelists who visited their churches. This pattern was established by Jesus when he gave instructions to his disciples as he sent them forth on a mission. They were to travel lightly, take no silver or gold with them, and stay in only one household in any given town where they witnessed (Matt. 10:5-13). The latter instruction was intended to prevent their flitting from house to house in order to determine which had the best hospitality. This is the same sort of support implied in Paul's discussion of provisions for apostles in 1 Corinthians 9. It is also reflected in 3 John in connection with itinerant Christian evangelists. The Christians in the towns they visited were to provide them with food and lodging and sufficient provisions for them to travel to the next town on their itinerary.

Other texts in the New Testament attest some form of limited financial support for church leaders. For example, 1 Timothy 5:17-18 reflects some sort of material remuneration to faithful elders. Even this seems to have created problems. In the very next chapter Paul warns against those who would use religion as a means of gain (1 Tim. 6:5). By the second century, remuneration of Christian workers had been so abused that a handbook on church order from that period laid down strict guidelines for distinguishing true ("called") evangelists and prophets from those who were merely out for personal gain. Anyone who moved from the hospitality of one house to another was a false prophet. Anyone who appealed to a revelation from the Spirit in asking for food or material gain was likewise deemed false.[1]

In the New Testament, however, the general picture is one of the laity doing most of the ministry. The disciples were laity. Stephen and Philip were laity. Even Paul was a layman. Trained as a rabbi, he followed the Jewish pattern for teachers of the law. Rabbis were not paid for their religious teaching. They supported themselves with a trade, just as Paul did with his tent-making. Likewise, the earliest Christian churches seem to have been led by laity, much like the Jewish synagogues of the time. The development of a full-time, fully supported ministry was subsequent to the New Testament period, during which those who had special ministries were bivocational at most.

This is not to say that there were no special calls to the ministry. Although the language of calling was primarily used for God's general call of all the saints, there are significant exceptions. Paul, for instance, described himself as "called" to be an apostle (Rom. 1:1; 1 Cor. 1:1). In these instances Paul was obviously speaking of more than his general call into the body of Christ. He was speaking of his special call to be a witness to the Gentiles on behalf of Christ. Paul's was a very special case. His conversion and his call were of a single piece. He met Christ in a blinding vision on the road to Damascus, was led in total bewilderment into town, and awaited the coming of God's agent, Ananias. But note how Ananias not only baptized Paul. He conveyed at the same time that Paul would be God's chosen instrument, a herald to the Gentiles, to kings, and to the sons of Israel (Acts 9:15). For Paul, both calls came at the same time—the general call into the body of Christ and the special call to a specific ministry. Some today have a similar experience. Usually it is those converted in their adult years. They clearly feel a call to "full-time" ministry at the time of conversion. They are the exception. For most of us, the two callings are separate.

Even though the language of "calling" is not generally used in the New Testament for those who are called to a special ministry, the experience of receiving such a call is common. In the last section of this chapter we shall examine a number of these call experiences. But first we will examine the relationship of calling to gifts. Being called to a specific ministry and being specially gifted for a particular task often go together. In what sense do calling and giftedness go together?

CALLING AND GIFTEDNESS

In the earliest Christian churches "giftedness" seems to have been the all-important factor in congregational leadership. Members exercised their particular gifts, and the congregation acknowledged those gifts. There was a diversity of gifts in the congregation and, as Paul argued, the well-being of the congregation depended on all members exercising their diverse gifts. Problems developed when some members claimed that their particular gifts were more valuable or spiritual than those of others. This happened at Corinth, and so in his letter to them Paul insisted that all Christians have a gift of the Spirit (1 Cor. 12:4-11) and that the exercise of all gifts is essential to the well-being of the congregation (1 Cor. 12:12-26). In the course of his argument in 1 Corinthians 12, Paul gives two lists of these spiritual gifts (vv. 8-10 and vv. 28-30). A quick glance at the lists shows that some of the gifts have to do with teaching, some with witness, some with helping ministries, others with administration. Some are more obviously ecstatic, like healing or tongue speaking or the working of miracles. Others are less obviously Spirit-endowed, like helping others and serving as administrators. Paul insisted that all alike were gifts of God's Spirit whether they were outwardly more showy or not.

What does this have to do with call to ministry? Everything, for it shows that in the earliest churches, like the church of Corinth in the early 50s, the main ministry of the church was carried on by the members of the congregation. Each member exercised their own gift or gifts. One's particular ministry was determined by the gifts received from God's Spirit. God's calling for the particular service of each was determined by the gifts granted by God's Spirit.

Paul provided another list of God's gifts in his Epistle to the Romans. Written only months after 1 Corinthians, it is no surprise to find the treatment of divine gifts quite similar in the two epistles. In both Paul uses the analogy of the body to show that the well-being of the church, the body of Christ, depends on the proper exercise of the gifts of all its members. The lists of gifts in both epistles are also quite similar. The Roman list (12:3-8) includes prophecy, service, teaching, exhortation, contributing, leadership, and doing deeds of mercy. Some of the gifts are similar to those we associate with the professional ministry today, like prophecy (declaring God's word for a given situation), exhortation (preaching), and teaching. Others, like contributions and acts of mercy, we often associate with the laity. Paul made no such distinction in Romans, however. There was no professional ministry at this stage of the church's development. All members were gifted. Together they performed all the needed ministries for the congregation. All were called.

Ephesians, written some five to ten years after Romans, gives a somewhat different picture of God's spiritual gifts. The gifts Paul lists in Ephesians 4:11 seem to be more limited and more "full-time"—apostles, prophets, evangelists, pastors, teachers. Apostles were pioneer missionaries like Paul himself. They had a special calling from the risen Lord to witness where the gospel had never before been taken. Prophets were those who had a special spiritual endowment for discerning and proclaiming a word from the Lord. Philip had four daughters with this gift (Acts 21:9). He himself is designated as an evangelist (Acts 21:8). Evangelists could be either itinerant or established in one locale, as Philip seemed to have been in Caesarea. They were proclaimers of the gospel, just as they continue to be today.

The most intriguing endowment Paul listed in Ephesians is that of pastor-teacher. The term for "pastor" is the Greek word for shepherd, and Ephesians 4:11 is the only place where it is applied to Christian ministry. Elsewhere, it is used in the general secular sense of shepherd, or is applied to Christ, the Good Shepherd. In Acts 20:28 Paul refers to the Ephesian elders as "overseers" (or "bishops") of God's flock. That is probably the function of the "pastors" in Paul's Ephesian list. They were the overseers or ruling elders in the congregations. This probably is the closest equivalent in the New Testament to our role of the pastor of a congregation. In Ephesians 4:11 the pastor is linked to the term *teacher* to form the single entity "pastor-teacher," thus designating the major pastoral role as that of teacher. It is interesting to note that in the Book of James the only congregational leadership role which is specified is that of teacher (James 3:1ff.).

Ephesians falls halfway between the charismatic ministries of 1 Corinthians and Romans and the more fully developed leadership positions reflected in the Pastoral Epistles (1 and 2 Timothy, Titus). In the latter, congregational leadership is more formal, consisting of specific offices such as deacon and ruling elder (or bishop), each with well-defined qualifications, and each formally conferred by the laying on of hands. The Pastorals reflect churches coming of age, becoming more organized, and requiring more developed leadership. The overseers and deacons of the Pastorals were still basically lay leaders. Eventually, the overseers would develop into the professional ministry we have today.

Ephesians 4:11-12 is a crucial passage for showing the relationship between the general call of all Christians and the more restricted call of professional ministers. Let's take a closer look. When properly punctuated, the passage states that the more "full-time" ministers (the apostles, prophets, evangelists, and pastor-teachers) have as their primary function "equipping the saints for the work of ministry" (NKJV). All are called; all are ministers. But those with a special calling are to be leaders, equippers, and facilitators to assist all the members of the church in the ministries to which they are called.

THE CALL: SOME BIBLICAL EXAMPLES

In the Old Testament the idea of a call is generally associated with prophets. Priests served God by virtue of their birth. One was born a priest, but one was called by God to be a prophet. Of course, sometimes those of priestly birth received the prophet's call, as did Ezekiel in the Old Testament and John the Baptist in the New. There was no set pattern for a call. Some were called in a very dramatic manner, others much less so. Some were male and others female, like Huldah the prophetess, who had a major role in the reforms of Josiah (2 Kings 22:14-20). Some came from families of high status, like Jeremiah and Ezekiel with their priestly lineage. Others came from simpler backgrounds, like Amos the shepherd and dresser of sycamore trees (Amos 7:14-15). There were almost as many variations in calling as there were individuals who were called. The following are a few of the recurring elements in the biblical accounts of callings. They comprise only a sample. There is no attempt to be exhaustive.

The Dramatic Call

The Bible frequently depicts the call to a special task or witness in a very dramatic fashion. Often it is in the form of a theophany, a more or less direct appearance of God to the one receiving the call. God appeared to Moses in a burning bush which was not consumed (Ex. 3:1-6). Fire or smoke often accompanied theophanies. The temple was filled with smoke when Isaiah had a direct vision of God in his call experience (Isa. 6:1-8). He saw not only God's throne, but the winged seraphim who guarded it. Even more elaborate was Ezekiel's call at the river Chebar while he was in exile. This also was a vision of the divine throne room, accompanied by storms, four-headed winged beasts, and wheels within wheels (Ezek. 1).

The theophanic style of call is also found in the New Testament. Paul encountered Christ in a voice and a blinding light. For him, call and conversion occurred together (Acts 22:6-16). He experienced a confirmation of his call to the Gentiles in a subsequent vision of the Lord in the Jerusalem temple (Acts 22:17-21). One could also say that Mary received her call in the manner of a theophany, Gabriel serving as God's mouthpiece as he announced the divine child she was to bear (Luke 1:26-38). It could be objected that she was not called in the sense that Paul was called to be an apostle. Often, however, in the Bible, God calls individuals to specific tasks. Surely none was more significant than that of this "handmaid of the Lord."

Undeniably, the dramatic theophanic style of call is well-documented in the biblical record. Most of us, however, have no such experience. For many of us, the call has come more slowly, a growing conviction which developed over time. Sometimes it has even met our resistance. This too is a pattern which has its biblical exemplars.

The Reluctant Call

The role of the prophet was often a thankless task. The people did not want to hear God's judgment and thus rejected his prophets. Small wonder that many resisted his call. Jeremiah was among them. He often complained to God about the unpopular message God gave him to declare, but he could not hold it back. It was like an unquenchable fire, searing his bones until it came out (Jer. 20:7-10, 14-18). Jonah is perhaps the most glaring example of the reluctant prophet. In his case it was not the unpopularity of God's word with the people which he dreaded. It was, on the contrary, the success of the word which he feared. He was called to summon the enemy Ninevites to repentance. He didn't want them to repent. He wanted them to experience God's judgment, not God's mercy.

A more common biblical pattern of resistance to God's call was the feeling of unworthiness on the part of the one called. This is seen throughout Scripture. Moses resisted because he did not consider himself powerful enough or eloquent enough to be God's spokesperson, but God overcame these obstacles for him (Ex. 4:1-17). Isaiah protested that he was too sinful a person to speak God's holy words, but God assured him of forgiveness and of his worthiness by having a seraph touch his mouth with a live ember (Isa. 6:6-7). Paul likewise felt totally unworthy. How could God call him, the former persecutor of Christ's people? (1 Cor. 15:9-11)

This feeling of unworthiness is natural and healthy. The bottom line is that we are all unworthy of God's call, of his general call to salvation as well as his special call to service. By the miracle of God's grace we have been called, and by the same miracle of God's grace we will be enabled to fulfill the tasks to which God calls us. This is an essential element in any consideration of call. Left to our own resources alone, we are likely to fail. But, through God's grace we will succeed. Like Paul, when the going gets rough, we can turn to the one who called us and find our sufficiency in God's grace (2 Cor. 12:7-10).

The Family-Influenced Call

One of the most common biblical types of call is that in which the called person's family plays a major role. In many instances it is the child's mother or father who dedicates the newborn to God. The barren Hannah prayed to God for a son, promising to dedicate the child to God for all his days should God honor her prayer (1 Sam. 1). When Samuel was born she kept her promise, giving the child while still young to the care of Eli the priest. When only a small boy he had a dramatic call of his own in the temple where God spoke and appeared to him (1 Sam. 3). His own call was a confirmation of his mother's dedicating him to the Lord's service.

John the Baptist had a similar experience. Like Hannah, his father Zechariah and his mother Elizabeth were childless. Zechariah was a priest, and it was while he was serving at the altar in the temple that the angel Gabriel appeared to him and promised that a very special child would be born to his wife Elizabeth (Luke 1:5-23). At the child's circumcision on the eighth day after birth, Zechariah dedicated him to God's service in the *Benedictus*, his song to God (Luke 1:67-80). Surely, like Samuel, John must have had a call experience of his own that confirmed the promise of his father.

Many ministers have been strongly influenced in their call by their families. Sometimes parents have seen their child's response to God's calling as an answer to their own prayers. Often children who grew up in a ministerial household will follow in their parents' footsteps. This was my own experience, my father preceding me in the ministry. Nowadays I often have the joy of teaching students at seminary whose father or mother I taught in past years.

Unfortunately, sometimes the family has a negative response to their child's call. In a sense this happened to Jesus. His family attempted to pry him from his ministry and take him home when the crowds were accusing him of being beside himself (Mark 3:21). His brothers do not seem to have understood him or to have believed in him during the days of his ministry (John 7:5). Ironically, it is often the most dedicated families, the ones who are in church "every time the doors are open," who have the most problems with a child's call. They realize that the call is a high and holy experience. They just never thought their own child would "surrender to the ministry." They had counted on their son taking over the family business. They never dreamed their daughter would respond to a call to missionary service thousands of miles away. One needs a strong assurance of calling when meeting this kind of resistance. Hopefully, with time, the family will come to understand and affirm the call of one of its members.

The Community Call

Sometimes the faith community has a major role in encouraging one or more of its members to enter the ministry. Doubtless this was the case with many biblical figures. Timothy is a good example. The elders of the church seem to have recognized his "gift" and affirmed it by the laying on of hands (1 Tim. 4:14). Certainly his godly mother and grandmother had prepared the way for his subsequent ministry by embodying for him their own faith in God (2 Tim. 1:5). And surely Paul had a role in Timothy's later development as a leader by taking him on his journeys and serving as his mentor.

The Christian community can offer very significant support for the fledgling minister. I remember how my home pastor often had me preach and how the members would rave over the sermon and assure me I had a "natural gift." Now, when I look back at those sermon outlines I realize that some were pretty dreadful, and I appreciate all the more that community of faith that encouraged me in so heartily affirming my sense of call.

There have been instances in which a church asked one of its members to serve as their pastor, recognizing a special gift in that individual. Sometimes a church will have a remarkably large number of its members entering the ministry. One can usually trace this back to a pastor or youth director or to individuals in a congregation who have encouraged their young people to consider a career in full-time Christian ministry. When God calls someone to a full-time ministry, he calls them in the context of the entire community of faith. As we have seen, every Christian is called in the general sense. It is fitting for an evangelical seminary to require a church recommendation as part of a student's application. This is very much like the principle Paul established with the Corinthian charismatics. He admonished them that spiritual gifts were not a private affair but a community phenomenon. "The spirits of prophets are subject to the prophets" (1 Cor. 14:32). The same can be said for one's call. It is most valid when recognized and affirmed by the larger community of faith.

Of course, there are those exceptional occasions when a minister finds himself or herself at odds with the rest of the church, as was the case for many at the height of the civil rights movement in the late 1950s and early 1960s, when ministers who supported justice for African Americans sometimes clashed with their congregations. In those instances it is good to have mentors and a circle of peers in the ministry to whom one can turn. A strong sense of call and a clear conscience are essential in such situations. Paul found that out as he worked amidst the criticism of the problem-infested Corinthian congregation (1 Cor. 4:1-5).

The Redefined Call

If one follows the biblical account it becomes evident that calls are not set in stone. A prophet, for instance, is sometimes called to address a particular circumstance rather than to assume a permanent prophetic role. One finds individuals called to one ministry only to change to another. Stephen and Philip were originally called (very much in the community sense) to help distribute provisions to the Greek-speaking widows (Acts 6:1-6). Soon thereafter both appear in the role of evangelist.

Many seminary students experience redefinitions of their calls while in seminary. Many come to seminary without a clear focus on a specific ministry, and an assessment of their gifts often aids them in making such decisions. Helping in such choices is one of the reasons for having introductory classes such as a formation for Christian ministry course. Even after seminary and well into their careers, ministers find themselves reevaluating their specific form of ministry and often make changes.

The Misdirected Call

Sometimes a very real call experience is misinterpreted. A biblical example of this is the Gerasene demoniac (Mark 5:1-20). As a result of Jesus' having healed him, he concluded that he should join Jesus' band of disciples. Jesus told him to return to his home and friends. That was where his witness would have the greatest impact.

It isn't unusual for someone to have a very powerful spiritual experience that convinces them they are being called into a full-time ministry, when in fact they are being called to greater commitment in their present life situation. On occasion I have talked with seminary students who reevaluated their call and determined this was the case with them. Returning home, they have served in lay positions in their home churches with a renewed sense of commitment. Theirs was no less significant a call than that of others called to career ministries.

"BIBLICAL CALLING" AND YOUR CALL

It should be apparent by now that in many ways the biblical treatment of calling does not fit our stereotypes. The Bible reveals a rich variety of call experiences—some quite dramatic, others less so but just as real. Calling is an intensely personal matter. It is a mixture of God's Spirit, one's life-situation, and one's gifts. The most consistent New Testament treatment of call shows that all Christians are called. Some of us are called to leadership roles, to full-time ministries which have as their ultimate goal the equipping of others to discover and fulfill their calling. No one's call is static. It is a lifetime experience, always subject to revision as we are challenged anew by the Spirit of the One who called us first, when our Christian life began.

N o t e s
1. Didache, chap. 11.

F o r   F u r t h e r   R e a d i n g
Achtemeier, Paul J. "And He Followed Him: Miracles and Discipleship in Mark 10:46-52." *Semeia* 11 (1978): 115–45.

Droge, Arthur J. "Call Stories (Gospels)." *Anchor Bible Dictionary*. Vol. 1,

821–23. New York: Doubleday, 1992.

Kruse, Colin G. "Call, Calling." In *Dictionary of Paul and His Letters*, edited by Gerald F. Hawthorne, Ralph P. Martin, and Daniel G. Reid, 84–85. Downers Grove, Ill.: InterVarsity, 1993.

Schweizer, Eduard. *Church Order in the New Testament*. Studies in Biblical Theology 32. London: SCM , 1961.

Stagg, Frank. "Understanding Call to Ministry." In *Formation for Christian Ministry*, edited by Anne Davis and G. Wade Rowatt, 23–38. Louisville: Review & Expositor, 1981.

5

SPIRITUALITY AND SPIRITUAL GROWTH

DAVID S. DOCKERY
AND DAVID P. GUSHEE

I appeal to you therefore, brothers and sisters,
by the mercies of God, to present your bodies as a living sacrifice,
holy and acceptable to God, which is your spiritual worship.
Do not be conformed to this world, but be transformed by the renewing
of your minds, so that you may discern what is the will of God—
what is good and acceptable and perfect.
ROMANS 12:1-2, NRSVB

Few matters should be of more fundamental concern to you as a new seminary student than the issue of spiritual growth. It is no overstatement to assert that a continually growing spiritual life is the single most significant prerequisite for faithful conduct of the Christian ministry. Likewise, it is also not an overstatement to claim that a deteriorating or dead spiritual life is the single most lethal malady that can afflict the life of the Christian minister. Your level of spiritual health and well-being will affect every aspect of your character and every aspect of the conduct of your ministry.

For this reason, attention to spiritual development must lie at the heart of your daily life as a seminary student. This is the case regardless of whether such attention is a formal requirement in any particular course you might undertake in a given semester. Most seminaries and many Christian colleges offer courses in spirituality. At the Southern Baptist Theological Seminary (Louisville, Ky.), for example, significant attention to spiritual

David S. Dockery is President of Union University in Jackson, Tennessee.
David P. Gushee is Associate Professor of Christian Studies, also at Union University.

development is offered in the required "Formation for Christian Ministry" class, in another class called "Spiritual Formation," in a range of other courses, and through nonacademic means. Students are strongly encouraged (and sometimes required) to participate in such institutional opportunities for spiritual growth, but these cannot be understood as a substitute for one's own personal commitment to spiritual development. This commitment must be internalized and practiced in a serious, disciplined manner throughout the seminary years and on into ministry. We strongly believe that a fundamental goal of every student during these seminary years should be a consistent, growing, and increasingly mature spiritual life.

One reason to attend so closely to your spiritual life is because of what is happening in the churches you will be serving. The contemporary evangelical Christian scene is characterized simultaneously by a neglect of authentic and growing spirituality, on the one hand, and by an intense longing for a deeper relationship with God's Spirit, on the other. In terms of the former, some of our churches veritably reek of spiritual dryness, dustiness, death. Sometimes a church appears to be full of life, but this turns out to be little more than superficiality and busyness, both on the part of laypeople and ministers. This spiritual emptiness has resulted in Christian lives characterized by discouragement, frustration, and even problems of immorality that have brought disrepute on the gospel.

On the other hand, in many churches we can see hundreds seeking spiritual renewal. This search is being carried out in a confusing array of forms—fasting, meditation, retreats, spiritual directors, accountability partners, community and fellowship groups, men's meetings, women's home Bible studies, 12-step groups, and even the charismatic "signs and wonders" experiences. Baptist and evangelical magazines contain considerable discussion of such things as "prayer in the Spirit," "walking in the Spirit," "life in the Spirit," "baptism in the Spirit," "holy laughter in the Spirit," and even "being slain in the Spirit." One of our challenges in the years ahead will be to help Christian people distinguish between appropriate and inappropriate, biblical and unbiblical forms of spirituality. While that may be *our* priority, it is clear that the folks in the pews will want us both to incarnate a transparent and authentic spiritual life, and to instruct them in how to share in that kind of spirituality. Our people are hungry for authentic ministers of God, people who are visibly affected by their intimate walk with their Father in heaven. They will rightly have little patience with ministers who give no evidence of such an experience of God.

Some of the problems one finds today in the area of Christian spirituality can be traced to a faulty view of conversion. Others can be linked to our individualistic understanding of Christianity. Perhaps underlying these and other problems is the obvious lack among so many in our churches of a strong biblical and theological foundation for spirituality. We need a biblical theology for the spiritual life, and we need to teach it to those in our churches. After discussing relevant definitions related to spiritual development, we will offer a sketch of that biblical theology of Christian spirituality. Finally, we will conclude by looking briefly at some practical implications and applications.

SPIRITUALITY: SOME DEFINITIONS

The word "spiritual" is both overused and misused today. It seems that everybody wants to be "spiritual," and many can be found who offer some kind of "spirituality" for our time. Most major bookstores now offer extensive spirituality sections, with what one might with some understatement call a fairly wide range of approaches. Our first task is to define our terms well and ground them within sound Christian doctrine.

In Christian understanding, the word "spiritual" in any form simply means "deriving from the Holy Spirit."[1] Thus, "spiritual gifts" (Rom. 12:6-8; 1 Cor. 12–14; Eph. 4:11-13) are gifts given by the Holy Spirit for the building up of the church. Likewise, the term "spiritual life" refers to the Holy Spirit-given vitalization and continual revitalization of a believer's own spirit, or "heart" (Rom. 6:4; 7:6; Col. 3:10). "Spiritual vitality" is a phrase meant to evaluate the extent to which the believer, or body of believers, has been revitalized by the work of the Holy Spirit. A critical task of Christian ministers is to develop acute sensitivity to the level of spiritual vitality among the people with whom they minister (not to mention their own spiritual vitality!).

"Spirituality," in turn, is a word referring to the overall quality and nature of the Christian's spiritual life. It also may refer to one or more distinctive approaches to spiritual development that Christians have developed through two millennia of Christian experience. There are historical *traditions* of spirituality, some corresponding with classic denominational and theological categories (e.g., Catholic, Wesleyan, Reformed, and Anabaptist spirituality, etc.), and others crossing such lines.[2] This meaning of the term spirituality reminds us that while spirituality is a gift of the Holy Spirit, Christians are responsible for nurturing this gift to the best of their abilities. With the Apostle Paul, Christians affirm both that "God's love has been poured into our hearts through the Holy Spirit that has been given to us" (Rom. 5:5, NRSVB), and that it is our responsibility to cultivate that precious gift.

This point leads us to the term "spiritual development," the primary topic of this chapter. Spiritual development refers to the interaction of our efforts with those of the Holy Spirit in order to bring about strong and healthy Christian spiritual life in believers, congregations, and in the ministers who lead them. The term reminds us that the work of spirituality is never done. Instead, Christians are always responsible for the continual nurture and development of their spiritual lives. The hard evidence of centuries of Christian experience is that one's level of spiritual vitality does not stand still; one is always either progressing or regressing in the Christian spiritual life. "Grow or die" is an appropriate watchword of the spiritual life.

Having defined some key terms, let's look more closely at what the Bible teaches about the Spirit and the nature of the Christian spiritual life.

BIBLICAL AND THEOLOGICAL FOUNDATIONS

The biblical view of the spiritual life can best be summarized by the statement in 2 Corinthians 3:17, "Where the Spirit of the Lord is, there is freedom." Here we see three key concepts regarding the spiritual life: the Spirit, lordship, and freedom. The Spirit's activities so widely permeated the apostle's thought that in his writing there is hardly any aspect of Christian experience outside of the sphere of the Spirit.

Paul and other biblical writers were convinced that it was the responsibility of the Holy Spirit to draw attention to the glories of the risen Christ (1 Thes. 1:5; 1 Cor. 2:1-4) as well as to enable persons to respond to the message of the glorified Christ (1 Cor. 12:3, 13). The work of the Spirit brings about new life in Christ (2 Cor. 5:17). Through the redeeming work of Jesus Christ, God has graciously offered forgiveness to sinners and new, abundant life (John 10:10). It is the Spirit who enables sinful human beings to respond to this good news and to experience new birth (regeneration) and the beginning of this new kind of life (John 3:3-8).

The Spirit of God is not only active in revealing the gospel and bringing people to salvation, but is likewise involved in teaching believers, guiding them to further understanding and growth (sanctification—John 17:17; Eph. 5:26; Heb. 2:11). After receiving the gift of the Spirit, there is a capacity for understanding things spiritual that was previously denied (1 Cor. 2:10-16). It is important to be very clear that this new spiritual capacity is in fact a *gift* of unmerited grace and a result of God's redemptive work in our lives—not a reason why God should feel obligated to redeem us. It is the effect, not cause, of salvation. Our filial consciousness is directed by the Spirit who leads the children of God to cry out "Abba! Father" (Rom. 8:14-17; Gal. 4:6). Our minds, which were formerly hostile to God (Rom. 8:7) are renewed by the Spirit (Rom. 12:2). Our new values come through the leading of the Spirit and enable us to walk in the Spirit rather than to carry out the desires of the sinful flesh (Gal. 5:16; Rom. 8:4). The New Testament teaches that Christians are totally dependent on the empowering of the Spirit, demonstrating that the Spirit is utterly indispensable for Christian living and that it is impossible for any Christian not to possess the Spirit.

The Spirit makes it possible for us to pursue spiritual realities in our life (Phil. 3:10-14). "One thing I ask of the Lord," writes the psalmist, "this is what I seek: that I may dwell in the house of the Lord all the days of my life, to gaze upon the beauty of the Lord and to seek him in his temple" (Ps. 27:4). Jesus told the woman at the well that "God is Spirit, and his worshipers must worship in spirit and in truth" (John 4:24). The goal of all spiritual pursuit is to see Christ, an unclouded vision of him, to be like him, and to be with him. The vision of Jesus, which is the believer's present hope and future joy, has been called by Christians in earlier centuries the "beatific vision." To see Christ is to know him; to see him face to face will be to know him fully. No Christian spirituality is possible that is not rooted in the believer's daily experience of the cross and resurrection of the Lord Jesus Christ. For even he himself prayed to the Father for his disciples," that they may know you, the only true God, and Jesus Christ, whom you have sent" (John 17:3).

The twin goals of spiritual pursuit are seeing and knowing God. These will one day be brought into a glorious culmination in which seeing will be knowing. This is described by Paul in 1 Corinthians 13:12: "then we shall see face to face . . . then I shall know fully." The moving forward from faith to sight that will end our human pilgrimage—of which we experience glimpses now in prayer, Scripture meditation, worship, and obedience—inspire us further in our spiritual life. Christian spirituality is bound up with our spirits, our minds, our bodies, our entire being and identity in the deepest sense possible. The seeing and knowing of our Lord will one day instantly and utterly transform us to become like him; our bodies will be like unto his glorious body, and we will be, in a way incomprehensible to us now, like the One we are beholding (1 John 3:1-3).

Spirituality is vitally related to the idea of our union with Christ. The Apostle Paul used the idiom of dying and rising with Christ to express the truth of the believer's union with Christ in Romans 6:1-11. Jesus himself explained the source of his followers' spiritual life and means of living it out in the metaphor of the vine and branches in John 15. Believers are exhorted to "abide" in Christ, which implies a staying, a settledness. It equally speaks of total dependence on Christ. We are plagued with nagging spiritual homesickness when we do not choose this staying, this casting of ourselves upon God. We regain our spiritual equilibrium, even after falling into weakness and sin, by prompt, wholesale confession and repentance and by calling to mind that we are branches drawing our life from the only true Vine. These two passages suggest that we rest in the reality of our being crucified with Christ and of being participants in his resurrection life.

To abide in Christ is to abide in his Word and to let it dwell in us richly (Col. 3:16). We receive the Word of God implanted, which nurtures faith in us and is able to save our souls (James 1:21).

When we receive the Word mixed with faith, ready to obey, we are able to trust God for our spiritual growth and ultimate maturity and rest in him (see Heb. 4).

Resting does not imply a lack of responsibility. Having been liberated by Christ from the penalty of sin, believers are challenged to employ this freedom properly in every dimension of the Christian life. The process of spiritual growth—sanctification—involves the continual confession and repentance of any unholiness in a Christian's life, of any misuse of Christian liberty to satisfy unchristian sinful desires. "Mortification of sin" is the classic phrase used in Christian tradition to refer to this process of identifying, repenting, and "mortifying" (that is, killing), through the power of God, particular areas of sin. This process is inconceivable apart from a growing spiritual life. It is precisely through regular encounter with a holy God that areas of unholiness are called to our attention. Progress in the spiritual life naturally leads to progress in the moral life.

Responsible freedom includes a negative, as well as a positive, aspect. What Christian freedom does *not* allow is overstressed in more legalistic environments and understressed in more libertine settings. A biblical balance must be the goal for believers living in the Spirit. The New Testament teaches a rigorous self-discipline, self-control, and nonconformity with the world (1 Cor. 9:27; Rom. 12:1-2). Yet such disciplined nonconformity is not a worldly asceticism that appeals to human pride and attainment rather than trust in Christ and reliance on the Spirit. For example, in sexual matters, believers are certainly not to conform to worldly practices. Paul personally was celibate in sexual matters (1 Cor. 7), but only as a gift to promote the work of the kingdom, not as a tool to achieve greater spirituality or a virtue proudly trumpeted.

The relationship between spiritual and moral growth, and between spirituality and ethics, is a profound one. It is a relationship that includes but finally goes beyond individual self-examination and abandonment of individual vices, leading the spiritually and morally growing Christian into ever broader social concern and Christian social action.[3] Christian history regularly bears witness to the fruitfulness of a Christian spirituality that leads the Christian into such social engagement. Examples include the anti-slavery activism of committed nineteenth-century evangelical Christians like Charles Finney, as well as the activities of committed Christians who rescued

Jews during the Holocaust, their actions both motivated and sustained by their faith.[4] Ultimately, it is faithful obedience to Christ's law of love that takes us out of ourselves and into every arena of human need, seeking opportunities to obey him through loving others (cf. Matt. 22:34-40). It is clear that such love is not an emotion (though it may involve the emotions) but Christian concern in action. As we are reminded by the Apostle John, "Everyone who loves is born of God and knows God. Whoever does not love does not know God, because God is love" (1 John 4:7-8).

We recognize that spiritual maturity involves subjecting every aspect of our life to the Holy Spirit's discipline. We must even understand suffering as a spiritual discipline if we are to manifest its rich fruit in our lives. At this point spirituality becomes very "down to earth," far more than we would sometimes wish. Suffering is a discipline not that we choose but that God appoints for us, and one to which the Scripture speaks at length. The New Testament distills a theology of suffering that places it inextricably in a progressive and intensely practical development of the Spirit's fruit in our character—leading from tribulation to patience, perseverance, hope, and the shedding abroad of God's love in our hearts through the Holy Spirit (Rom. 5:1-5; 8:14-39). Thus life in the Spirit takes shape by the enablement which the Spirit provides for obedience in the midst of struggling and suffering.

Christians need a healthy appreciation of the obstacles to spiritual development. This awareness constitutes a critical element in any theology of Christian spiritual development. Paul wrote: "For our struggle is not against enemies of blood and flesh, but against the rulers, against the authorities, against the cosmic powers of this present darkness, against the spiritual forces of evil in the heavenly places. Therefore take up the whole armor of God, so that you may be able to withstand on that evil day, and having done everything, to stand firm" (Eph. 6:12-13, NRSVB).

This passage has implications that transcend the discussion in this chapter, but it also speaks in a very significant way to the issue of Christian spiritual development. Simply put, Christians must acknowledge that we face numerous obstacles to spiritual vitality and growth. In classic theological language, these obstacles are within us (the "flesh"), around us (the "world"), and among us/beyond us (the "devil").[5] In terms of the flesh (cf. Gal.

5:19-21; Col. 3:5-9), despite regeneration and the beginning of sanctification in our lives, Christians are still sinners (1 John 1:8-9). In terms of the world (John 8:23; 12:31), despite God's reclaiming of this rebellious world through Jesus Christ, it remains stubbornly unresponsive to God and often organizes itself in opposition to his will. In terms of the devil (Eph. 2:2; 6:12; Rev. 12), despite the victory won at the cross, "spiritual forces of evil" continue to wreak havoc, entities whose entire purpose is to thwart the will of God and deepen human alienation and misery.

"Modern" thinkers once believed it possible to understand Christian faith and human experience apart from these phenomena, particularly the demonic, a concept which seemed offensive to post-supernatural minds. However, the extraordinary evils of the twentieth century, in particular, have led to an unintended revival of biblical rather than Enlightenment sensibilities on this matter. On a smaller scale, every thoughtful Christian knows of these obstacles to spiritual development. Sometimes they seem to beset us, coming at us from every direction. One day it is the sin that is in us that rears its ugly head; the next, it is the sin that is in the world, and so on. The existence of these obstacles helps to make sense of a widely reported Christian experience: spiritual growth so often seems like sledding uphill, even when one wants desperately to grow as a Christian. Progress is not always constant or even particularly steady. Seminarians need a healthy appreciation for these obstacles, while celebrating the promise that "the one who is in you is greater than the one who is in the world" (1 John 4:4).

The Holy Spirit ultimately is made known as the power that creates openness for God, receptiveness in prayer, illumination in study, and enablement and victory in struggle. The Spirit is the "down payment" of future glory which will be inherited by believers in the eschaton. Until then, the community experiences life in a way that can be characterized as liberty. Paradoxically, liberty comes about through obedience, just as glory comes through suffering.

APPLIED SPIRITUALITY

We experience the Spirit primarily in prayer when we can call upon God in the words of the Lord's Prayer, "Abba! Father." The

Spirit provides divine enablement for the believer struggling in prayer (Rom. 8:26-27). The immediacy of devotion to God does not come forth from innate human capacity but from the Spirit. The Spirit brings to light an awareness that one has been accepted through the love of God, from which prayer springs forth. When the Spirit reaches to God's children, the love of God reaches out (Rom. 5:5).

We cultivate the presence of the Spirit in our lives through a variety of what historically have been called "spiritual disciplines." Our cultivation of these spiritual disciplines must result in all the spiritual graces in our lives, or it is of no effect. This is what it means in simplest terms for the Spirit of God to bear fruit in us. The uselessness and deadliness of spiritual exercise apart from Christian character, while hardly a popular sermon topic in our time, is one of the most relentless themes in Scripture. To emphasize this is not to detract from the great benefits, when rightly used, of the many historic disciplines—prayer, meditation, study, solitude, fasting, silence, simplicity, service, and others.[6]

Today some evangelical leaders are calling the churches to be much more open to appropriating certain ancient Christian spiritual disciplines, such as fasting, that in recent decades or centuries have been neglected.[7] Christian history has left us a rich legacy of practices designed to enhance the spiritual life and the Christian's relationship with God. These disciplines are not magic formulas or special elixirs guaranteeing spiritual growth. Instead, if practiced in a disciplined and intentional way, they can serve as useful tools, helping the Christian to move into the presence of God. When considering these spiritual disciplines, it is important to be open to practices which were not a part of our particular denominational or local church tradition as we first grew and developed in the Christian faith. Especially with regard to the spiritual disciplines, there is wisdom in diverse strands of the Christian tradition that all of us do well to consider.

Whichever disciplines are practiced, the spiritual life must be cultivated on a daily basis. We recommend that every seminarian spend a minimum of thirty minutes a day, on average, in fellowship with God. Just as tithing is best understood as coming "off the top" of income, rather than from whatever money might be left over after the bills are paid, the same is true of this daily appointment with God. It should make it onto your daily calendar with at least the same "unbreakability" as any other appointment. Of course, life sometimes presents emergencies that require us to make exceptions to this policy, but it is important to see to it that the exceptions do not become the rule. In seminary, as in ministry, there are always more demands on your time than there are hours in the day. The "tyranny of the urgent" always threatens to pull us away from the steady rhythms that sustain life, spiritual and otherwise.

Keeping a prayer journal often serves as an effective discipline for cultivating the spiritual life. In such a journal, barely articulated yearnings, fears, groanings, and prayers can find expression. As the years pass you then have in your possession a precious record of your pilgrimage with God. While this is a discipline of particular appeal to those who enjoy writing, it is valuable for any who will take it up. Many spiritual formation professors make journaling a requirement for students in their classes—in the hope that for some students, at least, journaling will become a lifelong practice.

We recommend the cultivation of an ongoing conversation with God rather than restricting that fellowship to a set period each day. Some who agree with this line of thought make the mistake of abandoning the fixed "date with God" altogether. Instead, add regular "breath-prayers" to that daily discipline. Be conscious of God's presence at every moment. One way to do this is to learn the joy of silence, into which God can speak and you can listen, or vice versa. Turn off the noise in your car, your room, your consciousness. Just because the opportunities for noisy entertainment are infinite does not mean that you must at all times avail yourself of one of them.

Build accountability into your spiritual life by developing at least one "spiritual" relationship. Find a Christian mentor or peer with whom to share your goals related to spiritual development, then ask him or her to hold you accountable for progress toward those goals. Meet with this person weekly, asking and responding to specific questions concerning your respective spiritual lives and practices in the preceding week.

Seminarians and ministers (and professors) face a unique challenge to spiritual well-being. Precisely because we handle holy things day by day we risk their desecration. The Bible can become a mere object of dissection, not the holy Book inspired of God. Worship can become an opportunity for grading techniques in music or preaching rather than communion with God. The community of faith can become a frustration and an object of derision rather than the people of God. The old truism, "familiarity breeds contempt," is the concern here. Prevention of such contempt is absolutely critical for your spiritual well-being, not to mention your ministry.

TWO PATHS TO TAKE

We find that most men and women who come to an evangelical seminary arrive "on fire for God," in the old expression. They have "left their nets" to follow God's call, sometimes at considerable sacrifice. They love God with all their hearts. They have an active spiritual life. They are here to be equipped for service.

Two paths can be taken upon arrival. One path involves the loss of that fire, that commitment, that sense of call, that desire to be equipped to win the world for Christ. No one comes here seeking to go down that path, but some travel it. It is not always clear how or why this happens, but it is clear that a lost or stillborn spiritual life during the seminary years is one key reason.

The other path is the one we hope you will take. That path involves an *intensification through training* of the fire, passion, commitment, calling, and desire to be equipped with which you arrived. The atmosphere that seminary faculty, staff, and administrators create on campus is obviously important in making this latter path a well-trod one. But ultimately you and only you are responsible for the state of your soul during the seminary years.

May God bless you richly as you seek to draw closer to him, now and all the days of your life.

N o t e s

1. Richard Lovelace, *Dynamics of Spiritual Life* (Downers Grove, Ill.: InterVarsity, 1979), 21.

2. For exploration of different traditions of Christian spirituality, see Donald L. Alexander, ed., *Christian Spirituality: Five Views of Sanctification* (Downers Grove, Ill.: InterVarsity, 1988); and Robin Maas and Gabriel O'Donnell,

Spiritual Traditions for the Contemporary Church (Nashville: Abingdon, 1990).

3. Lovelace, *Dynamics of Spiritual Life*, chap. 12; Kenneth Leech, *The Eye of the Storm* (San Francisco: HarperSanFrancisco, 1992).

4. Lovelace, *Dynamics of Spiritual Life*, chap. 12; David P. Gushee, *The Righteous Gentiles of the Holocaust: A Christian Interpretation* (Minneapolis: Fortress, 1994), chaps. 6–7.

5. Lovelace, *Dynamics of Spiritual Life*, chap. 3.

6. For discussion of the spiritual disciplines, see Richard J. Foster, *Celebration of Discipline*, rev. and exp. ed. (New York: HarperSanFrancisco, 1988); and Donald S. Whitney, *Spiritual Disciplines for the Christian Life* (Colorado Springs: NavPress, 1991), among other resources.

7. See Foster, *Celebration of Discipline*.

FOR FURTHER READING

Alexander, Donald L., ed. *Christian Spirituality: Five Views of Sanctification.* Downers Grove, Ill.: InterVarsity, 1988.

Foster, Richard J. *Celebration of Discipline*, rev. and exp. ed. New York: HarperSanFrancisco, 1988.

Kelsey, Morton. *The Other Side of Silence.* New York: Paulist, 1976.

Leech, Kenneth. *The Eye of the Storm.* San Francisco: HarperSanFrancisco, 1992.

Lovelace, Richard. *Dynamics of Spiritual Life.* Downers Grove, Ill.: InterVarsity, 1979.

Maas, Robin, and Gabriel O'Donnell. *Spiritual Traditions for the Contemporary Church.* Nashville: Abingdon, 1990.

Merton, Thomas. *Contemplative Prayer.* Garden City, N.Y.: Doubleday, 1969.

Whitney, Donald S. *Spiritual Disciplines for the Christian Life.* Colorado Springs: NavPress, 1991.

6

IDENTIFYING AND CULTIVATING SPIRITUAL GIFTEDNESS

GERALD L. BORCHERT

As I embarked upon theological education many years ago, I quickly learned that I could study all the biblical patterns for developing spirituality and spiritual gifts, but if I personally did not assume some responsibility for applying the knowledge of my head to my heart and life, I could easily become a barren tree, devoid of spiritual giftedness. My constant prayer in seminary, therefore, became "Lord, help me not only to graduate from this institution, but also to graduate with you." The honors and degrees that I received from several seminaries were not nearly as hard to gain as was a steady cultivation of my spiritual giftedness and my walk with the Lord who called me into ministry.

Let me, therefore, quickly warn you that the process of reflecting on biblical spirituality and the spiritual gifts will not be very productive unless your study involves your *whole life*. The gifts of the Spirit are not merely gifts for the head. Likewise, they are not merely "headless" gifts attached to emotion-driven bodies.

Gerald L. Borchert is T. Rupert and Lucille Coleman Professor of New Testament Interpretation at the Southern Baptist Theological Seminary, Louisville, Kentucky.

Spirituality and the gifts of the Spirit involve the totality of your personal being. Moreover, since you are unique, no one else's spirituality will be exactly like yours. Be careful, therefore, lest you make any human being the norm for your spirituality. This does not mean that you cannot find helpful models of spirituality, but it does mean that spirituality and the spiritual gifts are from God the Spirit and cannot be given by or borrowed from any human being. Furthermore, unless you covenant with God to make spiritual development a significant part of your ministerial preparation, you may find your faith and your ministry becoming an empty shell. The request of the disciples, "Lord, teach us to pray" (Luke 11:1), must be a lifelong petition of every minister.[1] That quest will involve learning to recognize the "gifts" or giftedness which the Spirit of God continually imparts to you as you walk daily with God. This chapter focuses on identifying and cultivating such spiritual giftedness as you prepare for Christian ministry.

GOD SEEKS US: FOUNDATION OF THE SPIRITUAL LIFE

Among the first lessons that we learn in the Bible concerning our spirituality is that in spite of our sinfulness God seeks us. God seeks us, even when we are not seeking God!

God's question to Adam, "Where are you?" (Gen. 3:9) is one that he actually poses to everyone. The starting point for understanding spirituality and spiritual gifts is not our search for God, but God's search for us. The Lord finds us in our hiding places just as he found the hiding Adam.[2] Moreover, God meets us as God met Moses—in our fears, failures, and attempts to escape the harsh realities of life. Indeed, the Lord challenges us to put off our shoes and discover the divine presence in the places where we least expect to find grace, such as in the secular contexts of life (Ex. 3:1-4).[3] If we are open we too may be surprised by God's presence in our routine daily activities. Thomas à Kempis, the medieval spiritual guide, wrote that he found God in the midst of washing pots and pans.[4] When I was in seminary, I also washed dishes for the seminary dining hall. I learned that God could meet me in that activity of life and not just in my Bible reading and devotional times. So too God wants to meet *you* as you go through your daily life. Spiritual sensitivity for ministry always begins when we hear the voice of God. The starting point is God, not us!

As ministers we may need to rediscover that starting point every so often, particularly when we have done something great for God (such as conducting a stirring revival) and we are tempted to think that spiritual strength revolves around us. Here we do well to remember Elijah. What person could have been more successful than Elijah, the prophetic victor at Mt. Carmel? He had demonstrated to everyone that Yahweh was in fact *God!* (1 Kings 18:39) Clearly Mt. Carmel was the peoples' test; but it was not yet Elijah's test!

Shortly after that event, the spiritual giant of Mt. Carmel was nothing but a fearful, disillusioned, and depressed fugitive who wondered if he could do anything for God or if there were any faithful people left in Israel—besides himself, of course (1 Kings 19:3-10).[5] Even though he had been serving God, he had forgotten the source of his spiritual strength. He was in danger of total collapse. Ask yourself: Where were his "spiritual gifts" then? Normally we think of spiritual gifts when everything is going well for us. In his post-success depression, Elijah had to hear God's reminder that his strength was not rooted in powerful demonstrations like earthquakes and the calling down of fire, but instead in the strange presence of the "silence" of God (a better translation than the "still small voice" [KJV], 1 Kings 19:11-12). Ministers worthy of their calling must grasp the power of silence and be able to recognize God not merely in times of success but also when things seem to be falling apart. This ability to recognize God is a fundamental "gift"! It is the basis of all spiritual gifts.

LEARNING TO THINK LIKE GOD

When one learns to listen and respond to God, then one may also learn how to think like God.

Jonah is a great example of *wrong* thinking. First, he did not want to listen to the call of God on his life. Then he tried to run from the presence of God and from his call to minister to those he considered below his dignity and unworthy of God's grace (Jonah 1:2-3). But he discovered rather forcefully that running from God was out of the question. Jonah had thought that God would certainly never follow him from the land of Israel onto the sea.[6] Many Israelites viewed the sea as the domain of evil, the dark realm that roars like a monster (cf. Ps. 46:3). Even early Christians did not expect the sea to be a part of the glorious hereafter (cf. Rev. 21:1).[7] While Jonah thought he could run from the presence of God, others in Israel were coming to realize that fleeing from God was impossible (cf. Ps. 139:7-9).

Did Jonah learn his lesson? When confronted with his problem, he became very "theological" and announced to the pagan sailors that he was a *servant of the God who made the sea* (Jonah 1:9). In his theological pride he hardly noticed his "status inconsistency" (not unknown in ministry)! Moreover, he thought his doom was sealed in the sea, but the God of grace gave Jonah a "gift"— the chance to amend his ways while in the belly of the fish. Jonah's poetic prayer (chap. 2), the spiritual highlight of the book, can serve as a model of confession and commitment to God in the midst of turmoil. But this preacher (prophet) demonstrated that *words* are not the test of spiritual authenticity. The merciful God delivered Jonah from death. Yet for all his apparent piety, Jonah was *not* a changed man!

There was no room for grace and love in Jonah, only judgment and condemnation on his enemies. Indeed, he was angry when God gave the gift of forgiveness and grace to Nineveh (4:1-3). The story ends with an unanswered question: Did Jonah *ever* learn to think like God? That question was directed to every Jew who read the book. Today it is also a question for you as a (future) minister. Do you operate in a spirit of condemnation and judgment on others who differ from you, or can you think the way that God thinks, in grace and love? The answer to that question is one measure of your ability to receive the gifts of the Spirit of God. Is grace just a theological idea for you, or is it a reality that transforms all of your relationships? This question is foundational to thinking like God and receiving the Spirit's transforming gifts.

The Pharisees of Jesus' day lived in the spiritual box of law and restricted grace (cf. Matt. 23:13-36). They believed that the only way Gentiles could receive the grace of God would be to become just like *them*. But in their sanctimoniousness they failed to understand that they too were in need of healing and reconciliation. So they judged people according to their constricted categories, not realizing that God desires that no one should perish but that all should come to repentance and receive the forgiveness of sins (2 Peter 3:9). The fact that not all people turn to God does not change the longing heart of God. To put it another way: God's grace extends far beyond human response.

If you seek to be a minister of the caring God, the Lord of the universe, you do well to have your mind stretched by God's grace. The Apostle Paul offers a good example of this.

When Paul met Jesus, his mind was stretched far beyond its former narrow confines. He was transformed by grace. As a result, Paul was able to articulate the good news of a gospel that sees everyone, both Jew and Gentile, as equally needy sinners to whom God's grace is equally available through Jesus Christ.[8]

Moreover, instead of condemning people, Paul learned to ache with God that people are perishing and not coming to Christ. He did not scorn or curse unbelievers but was himself willing to be cursed if he could thereby bring people to Christ (Rom. 9:3).[9] To think like Paul is to think like the radically self-giving Jesus. To think this way is nothing short of revolutionary.

DEVELOPING HUMBLE DEPENDENCE ON GOD

Receiving the gifts of the Spirit does not mean going into a closet, shutting the door behind you, and praying night and day until somehow God zaps you. Now, I am in no way denigrating the experience of spiritual retreats or time alone in prayer with God. Jesus himself went alone to pray on a number of occasions (cf. Mark 6:46; 14:32; Luke 6:12; 9:28; etc.). I am personally indebted to experiences of spiritual retreat and especially times of silence with God. The problem arises when one's relationship with God becomes the object of public display (cf. Matt. 6:5),[10] or when we begin to tell God how excellent our religious practice is in comparison to that of others (cf. Luke 18:10-12). Jesus utterly rejected such show as pseudo-spirituality. For him, humility before God, not showmanship, was essential (Luke 18:13-14).[11]

Jesus faced this very issue when he rejected the devil's temptation to throw himself down from the pinnacle of the temple in the sight of all the gathered worshipers. He would not abuse his relationship with God for show. All of us in public ministry must learn from Jesus to reject any spiritual showmanship as false piety that degrades our relationship to God (cf. Matt. 4:5-7; Luke 4:9-13). Humble dependence upon God is what God is looking for. It is the key to exemplifying the fruit of the Spirit (Gal. 5:22), which characterizes mature Christian living.[12]

LIVING WITH HOPE

Foundational to renewal and life in the Spirit is a genuine sense of hope. God is not dead![13] We may wrestle with death and disillusionment, but that is not God's problem. The resurrection of Jesus is a great *gift* to us from God and is our unqualified guarantee of hope. It is the hinge point of the Christian faith.[14] Without the resurrection of the Lord there would be no church, no seminary, no need for this chapter, and no salvation from sin for you or for me (cf. 1 Cor. 15:17). The resurrection of Jesus provides us with a vision of hope for our lives.

It is important to remember that the resurrection event is also tied to the gift of the Holy Spirit in the life of the believer. Like our experience of victory in Christ's death and resurrection, the coming of the Spirit in power is one of God's greatest gifts to us. You cannot buy it, as Simon the magician tried to do (Acts 8:9-24). It is a *gift!* And it is, as Jesus said to Nicodemus, a gift cloaked in mystery. Those who are "born of the Spirit" can never be fully understood by people of a worldly orientation (John 3:3-12).[15]

Because you cannot earn the Spirit, you cannot sell it like some product peddled door-to-door. If you try to profit by the gift or attempt to synthesize it with sin, you will soon discover your spiritual emptiness. The Spirit's presence in your life will either transform you or become a terrifying noose around your neck, judging your immoral actions and self-centered thoughts. Since the Holy Spirit demands fidelity, kindness, love, gentleness, and so forth (Gal. 5:22), the Spirit will hound you until you respond in truth or abandon the pretense of spiritual authenticity. Have you wondered why secret sin almost always seems to come out? The Spirit, as Jesus said, leads us into truth (John 16:12). His role is to show us the contrast between sin and right living and make clear to us the reality of judgment (John 16:8-11).[16]

To live with hope is *not* to adopt a "pie-in-the-sky" perspective! It is to live with the Lord who died for our sins. It is to experience the assurance that we can never be abandoned by Christ. It is to enjoy now the marvelous gift of peace that the world will never understand (John 14:18, 27).

GOD'S GIFTEDNESS AND THE SPIRIT'S GIFTS

Let us turn now to a discussion of the *charismata*, or gifts of the Spirit. I have deliberately delayed talking about spiritual gifts until first discussing the purpose of the "giving" God in the world. My starting point, as you have seen, is the caring God who is searching and working with us so that we can think and act differently from the world, in order that our motivations and goals will be conformed to those of Jesus who died and rose again to give us hope in the midst of a divided and hopeless world (cf. Phil. 2:1-11). This perspective should prevent us from becoming self-centered or self-serving in appropriating the spiritual gifts in our lives.

Such self-centeredness was the basic problem of the Corinthian Christians. Indeed, they were so driven by a "spiritual gift orientation" that they were ready to abandon Paul, who brought them to Christ, for the "super-apostles" (2 Cor. 11:5) who boasted about their spiritual gifts. This crisis forced Paul to talk about his spiritual status (2 Cor. 10:1-12; 11:6-7), but in so doing his focus never moved to himself; instead, it remained on Christ (10:5).[17] Paul recognized the folly and even danger of such talk and did so with regret and within strict limits (10:13-18). Soon his attention turned to his many troubles and God's all-sufficient grace to meet his need (12:7-10). Paul's example helps us to see that God's grace is given not because we are worthy, but because God cares for us and wants to make us strong where we are weak. There is no room for any boasting about our spirituality or giftedness.

Then what about gifts? They are *person-centered and purpose-driven*. God graces people and gives them responsibility at the same time. In the Old Testament, God's appearances in grace (theophanies) always came with a calling or a particular responsibility. Consider the experiences and calls of Abraham, Moses,

Joshua, Gideon, Samuel, Isaiah, and Jeremiah. Failure to fulfill the calling jeopardized the giftedness, as in the case of King Saul. The same is true in the New Testament. For example, the promise of Christ's constant presence with the church is set clearly within the commission for Christians to disciple all nations (Matt. 28:19-20). God graces us in order to help us accomplish his purposes in the world. If we fail to take our calling seriously, we risk the withdrawing of our spiritual giftedness.

Notice how in Ephesians the spiritual gifts are described in terms of people with particular tasks: apostles, prophets, evangelists, pastors, and teachers. These special gifts are given to minister to the people of God, that they might be firmly established in love, united, and able to resist all forms of evil (Eph. 4:11-16).[18] Likewise, in Romans, giftedness is outlined in purposive, person-oriented descriptions involving prophecy (bold speaking for God), self-giving service, teaching and exhortation, financial support of others, and merciful concern for hurting people (Rom. 12:6-8). All of these action-oriented descriptions are again set within the context of a humble, cooperative, loving, Christlike spirit in which pride and self-centeredness are completely rejected (12:3-5, 9-21).[19]

The great test of genuine spiritual giftedness is self-giving love. Nowhere is this more clearly articulated than in Paul's most detailed discussion of the spiritual gifts, in 1 Corinthians 12–14.[20] He begins the discussion by stating that he did not want the community to be "ignorant" of such gifts (12:1) and reminds them that ecstatic experiences—which were so important to the Corinthians—could easily be idolatrous (12:2). He argues that not everyone's spirituality is identical, but that the Spirit of God deals with everyone according to his or her individual personality (12:4-11). The gifts are not the same but are all given by the same Spirit for the good of the whole church (12:7, 11-12). Moreover, since Christians are different, God can use everyone in the church. We are not made in the image of each other! Therefore, we need to understand our interrelatedness and support one another both in times of suffering and achievement (12:26).

In this context Paul once again lists the gifts in terms of gifted persons, but he goes beyond apostles, prophets, teachers, miracle workers, healers, help givers, and administrators, and includes tongue speakers and their interpreters (12:27-30). The reason for such an addition is undoubtedly that the Corinthians considered the gift of ecstasy to be a test of superior spirituality. But this was not Paul's view. He prefers five words of clear instruction over "ten thousand words" in an unintelligible tongue (14:19). He does not forbid speaking in tongues. Instead he merely categorizes it at its best as a personal spiritual experience with little or no effectiveness in communicating the gospel (14:13-25). It is like the sound of a confused trumpet call in the midst of battle (14:8).

Paul's concern throughout his epistles is effective ministry in the context of love. This concern is the reason he inserts the great hymn of love (1 Cor. 13) in the midst of this major section on gifts. Love is *not* a specialized gift of the Spirit. It is the test of genuine spiritual giftedness. It is basic to all gifts. All ministers of Jesus must subject their lives to the test of love. The fundamental presumption of Christian service is love. This is not an ability to *talk* about love, but instead to exemplify love in all our work. Mere talk about love would be identified by Paul as a noisy cymbal (13:1) or worth nothing (13:2). Words are not the same as love (1 John 3:18). Ministers of Christ, who are usually so skilled with words, need to remember John's stark reminder that those who profess love for God and yet despise their brother or sister are liars (1 John 4:20). Lying is not from God, but from the devil (John 8:44).

CONCLUSION

My friend, being called by God to ministry means a whole new way of life. It means a new lifestyle of complete consistency between words and actions. It means an expectation that God will grace you with developing gifts for ministry. It means an acceptance of your responsibility before God for nurturing and using these gifts. It means an embracing of your uniqueness as a servant of Christ. It means a commitment to give the Lord your best in study, in faithfulness, and in caring for others. And finally, it means that God will continually surprise you with a growing sense of purpose and fulfillment as you discover and make use of the gifts he gives you for ministry.

May God bless as you identify and cultivate your spiritual gifts in a lifetime of ministerial service.

N O T E S

1. The response of Jesus in teaching his disciples the so-called "Lord's Prayer" (Luke 11:2-4) must not be understood merely as a formula prayer to be repeated word for word, but rather as a model of the way one should be praying to God. Prayers, like spiritual development formulas, can easily become empty acts and verbalisms. The quest is not for the formulas, but for the drawing near to God.

2. For a helpful discussion of the Genesis text, see Walter Brueggemann, *Genesis*, Interpreter's Bible Commentary, vol. 1 (Atlanta: John Knox, 1982), 40–54.

3. Cf. Roy L. Honeycutt, Jr., *Exodus*, The Broadman Bible Commentary, vol. 1 (Nashville: Broadman, 1969), 311–18.

4. Thomas à Kempis, *The Imitation of Christ*, trans. W. Benham (New York: P.F. Collier, 1909), 207–379.

5. For a helpful discussion concerning Elijah, see Norman Smith and Ralph Sockman, *1 and 2 Kings*, Interpreter's Bible Commentary, vol. 3 (Nashville: Abingdon, 1954), 148–67.

6. On Jonah, see Terence Fretheim, *The Message of Jonah* (Minneapolis: Augsburg, 1977) and Douglas Stuart, *Hosea-Jonah*, Word Biblical Commentary, vol. 31 (Waco, Texas: Word, 1987), 424–510.

7. See Gerald L. Borchert, "What Is God Doing in the Storm?" in *Following Jesus*, ed. W. Hulitt Gloer (Macon, Ga.: Smyth & Helwys, 1994), 7–11.

8. On Romans 1–3, see J.D.G. Dunn, *Romans 1–8*, Word Biblical Commentary, vol. 38A (Dallas: Word, 1988), 36–49, 145–83.

9. On Romans 9–11, see J.D.G. Dunn, *Romans 9–16*, Word Biblical Commentary, vol. 38B (Dallas: Word, 1988), 521–36.

10. See Robert A. Guelich, *The Sermon on the Mount* (Waco, Texas: Word, 1982), esp. 272–320 for the treatment of righteousness and prayer.

11. For a discussion of the Lucan story of the Pharisee and the tax collector, see I. Howard Marshall, *The Gospel of Luke* (Grand Rapids: Eerdmans, 1978), 677–81; and Robert H. Stein, *Luke*, New American Commentary (Nashville: Broadman, 1992), 447–52.

12. See Pamela J. Scalise and Gerald L. Borchert, "The Bible and the Spiritual Pilgrimage," in *Becoming Christian: Dimensions of Spiritual Formation*, ed. Bill Leonard (Louisville: Westminster/John Knox, 1990), esp. 31–45.

13. The "death of God" theologies were not, of course, really a reflection of God's "death." Instead they were a commentary on the state of institutional religious practices and on the purveyors of hopeless humanistic representations of their "gods."

14. See Gerald L. Borchert, "The Resurrection: 1 Corinthians 15," *Review & Expositor* 80 (1983): 401–13.

15. On Nicodemus, see Gerald L. Borchert, "John," in *The Mercer Commentary on the Bible* (Macon, Ga.: Mercer Univ. Press, 1994), 1050–51.

16. Ibid., 1070–74.

17. For a further discussion of 2 Corinthians 10–12, see G.R. Beasley-Murray, *2 Corinthians*, The Broadman Bible Commentary (Nashville: Broadman, 1971), 63–74.

18. Scalise and Borchert, "Bible and the Spiritual Pilgrimage," 37–42; see also Andrew Lincoln, *Ephesians*, Word Biblical Commentary, vol. 42 (Dallas: Word, 1990).

19. See Dunn, *Romans 9–16*, 718–56.

20. For further exposition of 1 Corinthians 12–14 see Gordon D. Fee, *The First Epistle to the Corinthians*, New International Commentary on the New Testament (Grand Rapids: Eerdmans, 1987), 569–713. Cf. Gordon D. Fee, *God's Empowering Presence* (Peabody, Mass.: Hendrickson, 1994).

FOR FURTHER READING

Bridge, Donald and David Phypers. *Spiritual Gifts and the Church*. Downers Grove, Ill.: InterVarsity, 1973.

Fee, Gordon D. *God's Empowering Presence: The Holy Spirit in the Letters of Paul*. Peabody, Mass.: Hendrickson, 1994.

Flynn, Leslie B. *19 Gifts of the Spirit: Which Do You Have? Are You Using Them?* Wheaton, Ill.: Victor, 1974.

Foster, Richard J. *Celebration of Discipline: The Path to Spiritual Growth*. San Francisco: Harper & Row, 1978.

Harbaugh, Gray L. *God's Gifted People: Discovering Your Personality as a Gift*. Minneapolis: Augsburg, 1990.

Hemphill, Kenneth S. *Mirror, Mirror on the Wall: Discovering Your True Self through Spiritual Gifts*. Nashville: Broadman, 1992.

Kinghorn, Kenneth C. *Gifts of the Spirit*. Nashville: Abingdon, 1976.

Leonard, Bill, ed. *Becoming Christian: Dimensions of Spiritual Formation.* Louisville: Westminster/John Knox, 1990.

Nouwen, Henri J. *The Wounded Healer: Ministry in Contemporary Society.* Garden City, N.Y.: Doubleday/Image, 1979.

Thielicke, Helmut. *A Little Exercise for Young Theologians.* Grand Rapids: Eerdmans, 1962.

Tournier, Paul. *A Place for You.* New York: Harper & Row, 1968.

———. *The Meaning of Gifts.* Richmond, Va.: John Knox, 1963.

7

HUMAN PERSONHOOD AND THE MINISTER

LEIGH E. CONVER

Perhaps you have wondered like Moses how God intends to utilize you in Christian ministry when you know that you are still "a work in progress." As evangelical Christians, we rely heavily on the work of the Holy Spirit to bring to completion the sanctification of each of our souls. Answering a call to Christian ministry is a commitment to following the Spirit's guidance not only in ministry to others, but in refining the vessel of our own lives as well.

MINISTERS ARE HUMAN BEINGS: A THEOLOGICAL ISSUE

We need to begin our discussion of the personhood of the Christian minister with some sensitivity to what Holy Scripture says about the subject. In Genesis we learn that humans were created to share with God in the appreciation of creation, to have fellowship with God, and to participate with God in the continuing

Leigh E. Conver is Professor of Psychology of Religion and Pastoral Care at the Southern Baptist Theological Seminary, Louisville, Kentucky.

work of creation through responsible care. Created in the image of God, humanity therefore possesses some of the reflections of God's nature, while at the same time, Genesis clearly states that humanity is not of the same nature as God. The sin of Adam and Eve was the desire to be as God rather than to enjoy their created nature as a reflection of God's image. Ministry challenges us to live effectively within both the limitations and the possibilities that being in God's image implies.

The New Testament asserts that in Christ the Old Adam has become transformed into the New Adam. One way of reflecting upon this transformation is to wonder how the essence of each human being has been transformed. Are the inherent personality traits of each new creature substantively different from the pre-converted person? Are the inherent gifts and talents transformed at the same time that the heart is exposed to God's redeeming love? Will temptation be experienced in different ways now that the Christian has accepted Christ as Lord and Savior?

Experiences of generations of ministers have confirmed what our natural conclusions are to these and other similar questions. Something is significantly different about the converted believer from the unbeliever! The goals of life, the priorities of our existence, and the meaning that each event of our life has for us are radically transformed in the process of conversion. And yet, the personality and identity of the Christian, though perhaps kinder and gentler than before encountering Christ, is essentially the same.

It appears that God has chosen to be revealed in and through the personalities of each of us. If you had taken a personality inventory before surrendering your life to Christ, and taken the same test several months after accepting Christ as your Savior, the same basic human personality would undoubtedly be detected by the inventory with perhaps some minor differences in degree in regard to some of your personality characteristics.

Rather, what the New Testament seems to suggest is that the Christian spends a lifetime in the process of discipleship and growth. In this fashion, the renewing of our minds into the likeness of the mind of Christ, is the ongoing work of the Holy Spirit within each of us. This process which many Christian traditions know as sanctification is the way in which we participate with

God in becoming all that we were created to be in Christ.

As ministers, like all members of the body of Christ, we have the privilege and challenge of guiding other believers along the same path that we are also taking. But wisdom teaches us that God's Spirit is at work within our personalities, transforming us into new beings in precisely the same manner as with each other member of the body of Christ. God's Spirit is alive within us, and being expressed through us, but the vessel of our personalities continues to be recognizable! Perhaps a helpful metaphor is found in wondering how the Holy Spirit is filling up the interior spaces that are structurally defined by our own personalities.

MINISTERS AS HUMAN BEINGS: A PSYCHOLOGICAL REALITY

If you accept the theological assumption that God's Spirit is expressing itself through the individual personalities of each Christian, then one important challenge in your formation as a Christian minister is the task of identifying the basic qualities of your own personality. Another way of thinking about this challenge is the process of embracing who you are as an instrument of God's ministry to others. Your experience of seminary will hopefully expose you to many opportunities of self-discovery and of sharing who you are with peers and professors as the primary way of learning how to share yourself as a tool of ministry to a broken world. Be careful to understand that this process of self-discovery and sharing is radically different from the rampant narcissism and self-aggrandizement of our world!

Rather, Christ's model of self-emptying sacrifice (Phil. 2) presumes an awareness of one's self and an appreciation of how to give one's self on behalf of others. The self-sacrifice we are considering is also more than an ascetic denial of a monastic retreat from the world. We are proposing that who we are in Christ can be of service and ministry to others by willingly giving of ourselves on behalf of the kingdom of God. This is more than self-denial. It is a special sensitivity in each situation of ministry to who we are and how we can participate with the Holy Spirit working through the vessel of our personalities, gifts, and graces for ministry in that situation.

PERSONALITY TYPOLOGY: MANY FACETS AND MANY INSTRUMENTS

There are many different personality tests and profiles available for the discernment and understanding of the characteristics of each personality. Some personality profiles pick up on weakness, pathology, and dysfunction and describe the test taker in terms of liabilities. Other personality profiles focus on learning styles and describe the test taker in terms of what variables that person finds easiest to assimilate in learning how to perform tasks. Other personality profiles focus on the inherent strengths and giftedness of the test taker, providing helpful insights about how that individual will function in normal life circumstances, as well as under situational stresses. In this chapter, we would like to introduce you to three of these personality profiles.

The Theological School Inventory
The Theological School Inventory (TSI) is a useful instrument for evaluating the strengths inherent in each student. It is especially useful because it may be taken at intervals during your education and would also be helpful at five- or ten-year intervals after you begin ministry. The TSI has been shown to be useful whether taken individually and discussed with a trained counselor or taken and discussed in a small group context. Typically, the scores of the TSI are reported to the student minister with statistical parameters that are able to show you how your responses compare to other test takers of the same sex, age-group, and ethnicity within your seminary, as well as in other North American seminaries who participate in the program.

The TSI is constructed mostly to enable the student to self-rate his or her self-motivation for ministry. A total of eighty-four points are distributed across seven preselected motivators: (1) *acceptance* of the influence and support of others, especially family, to become a minister; (2) *intellectual desire* to understand the deeper theological issues of the faith; (3) *self-fulfillment* as driven by your inner eagerness to become a minister; (4) *leadership success* in previous roles, especially in a ministry setting; (5) *evangelistic witness* indicated by an inner desire to lead people to Christ and his church; (6) *social reform* as a desire to be personally involved in the task of ridding society of injustice and evil; and (7) *service to persons* in terms of desiring to provide personal ministry to them in times of crisis such as illness, death, and personal problems. Other sections of the instrument focus on (1) the student's conceptualization of ministry calling, especially as it relates to hearing God's specific call for ministry; (2) the student's self-rating of skills considered useful in ministry; and (3) an estimation of the strength and definiteness of each student's current response to a call to be a vocational minister.

The TSI consists of 165 computer-scored questions and is constructed to provide valuable insight into the relationship of each student's self-personality assessment. Typically, group discussion of the TSI leads to a deeper appreciation of one's life story and sense of call into the ministry. It provides each student with the opportunity to share individual reactions to the test's assessment with his or her own personal growing sense of motivation to Christian ministry. If taken early in the seminarian's studies, the TSI can also provide a long-term reference in course planning while still in the seminary. It also is designed to help the student discern ways in which his or her gifts for ministry might be more successfully matched with one or more specific ministry vocations.

The Myers-Briggs Type Indicator and Kiersey Temperment Sorter

A second personality profile which can be helpful as you develop some insight into your personality typology as a minister is the Myers-Briggs Type Indicator (MBTI).[1] It is one inventory that is used, especially in its shorter version known as the Kiersey Temperament Sorter.[2] The MBTI and Kiersey tests are based on an understanding of personality that describes each personality by the use of four polarized spectrums: (1) extroversion vs. introversion, (2) sensing vs. intuiting, (3) thinking vs. feeling, and (4) judging vs. perceiving. Each of the four scales pick up on different ways that each of us is oriented toward the world, receive data about the world, make decisions upon that data, and prioritize our responses to each other.

Some persons are more extroverted than introverted; this describes their preference of pursuing experiences outside of themselves as opposed to the introverted preference for interior experiences. For the extroverted person, psychic energy moves from inside the self out into the world. For the introverted individual, psychic energy moves from outside of oneself into oneself. Introverts tend to be more reflective than active and extroverts tend to prefer activity over reflection.

The sensation and intuitive scales of the MBTI and Kiersey describe the process by which each of us takes in data from our experiences. The sensation or sensory oriented person defines reality on the basis of the five senses: sight, taste, smell, touch, and hearing define reality and therefore define what data is accessible for reflection. The intuitive person differs from the sensate person in that he or she also relies on a "sixth sense" and knows things about experiences before the sensory data confirms the truthfulness of these "gut hunches."

The thinking versus feeling spectrum describes how each individual makes important decisions. "Thinking types" make crucial decisions on the basis of analytical reflection upon the facts of the experience. "Feeling types" make decisions on the basis of what feels right in each situation and recognize that what feels right today may not feel right tomorrow. While trying to understand the difference between them, be careful to give thinkers the freedom to have emotions and feelers the freedom to use analysis as well. However, in the crucible of life's toughest moments, thinkers prefer logic and analysis and feelers prefer trusting what seems right for them in that moment.

Finally, the MBTI and Kiersey provide insight into issues related to preferences between self-discipline and spontaneity. The judging type describes individuals who value self-discipline and control and pace themselves carefully and efficiently to meet their goals on time. The perceptive types are individuals who value the experiential moments of opportunity inherent within each of life's experiences. Consequently, perceptive types are more interested in the quality of the experience they are having than they are in the timeliness of meeting deadlines and goals.

By combining the responses on each of the four scales, the MBTI yields a description like: INTJ or ESFP or any other combination of the four variables. The MBTI has a total of sixteen different typologies that can be produced giving each of us a different combination of the four spectrums of extroversion/introversion, sensing/intuiting, thinking/feeling, and judging/perceiving. By discovering your type on the MBTI, you will have a clear guide to help you understand how you will typically respond to life, make decisions, and prioritize your time. The MBTI also points out the value of people with different personality types working together and indicates some of the potential areas of difficulty each type may encounter with the other in a work situation.

Actually all of us possess the ability to function with any of the eight key concepts listed on the MBTI. However, the instrument is most helpful because it clearly shows our preferences. Some of us would *prefer* to be introverted, but if by necessity or by choice we must be extroverted, most of us can do so or, in time, learn to do so. This is the same with the other six indicators.

Such insights will prove invaluable as you learn about the different ways you respond to life, especially as a minister. In addition, learning about yourself through the MBTI will also provide you with a tool for pastoral assessment of the different types of people you will meet in ministry. It is also good to know that the sixteen possible types are all useful and valuable for ministry. God can and does use everyone who follows the call of Christ, whatever his or her personality type. This is probably the most valuable part of using an instrument like the MBTI.

The Enneagram

In pastoral care and counseling classes in your seminary, you may also learn about the Enneagram (pronounced: "any-a-gram," from the Greek *ennea* meaning "nine" and *gram* meaning "diagram").[3] The Enneagram is an ancient tool of pastoral assessment that is reported to have been handed down through oral tradition for centuries from teacher to disciple.

The Enneagram consists of a nine-pointed star within a circle. Each of the nine points (note the symmetry of a circle divided into nine equal parts) represents the characteristics of a unique personality type. Each point is clustered together with two other points to represent three "centers" of personality. First, it is good to know the Enneagram's identification of nine core "addictions" or "sins" (see diagram 7a on p. 114) corresponding to each of the nine types. These addictions/sins are the result of overuse of a particular Center of the personality, rather than a more balanced use of all three Centers of the personality. The Enneagram teaches

Core Sins and Addictions
Movement with the Arrows

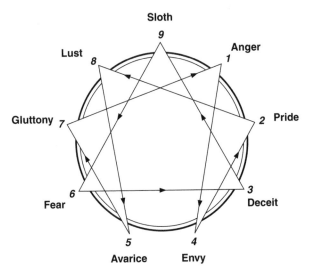

that through overuse, personality defenses become inflexible. They then become automatic and sometimes harden. In this way, what was in its purest form a spiritual gift becomes transformed into an addiction/sin. This process quickly becomes unconscious and, thereby, creates an illusion of reality that is self-perpetuating.

There are distinct similarities between the attributes of the three types that are clustered within what the Enneagram refers to as the "three Centers" of the personality. The three Centers are illustrated in the following diagram and represent the underlying use of one of the three functions of the personality: thinking, feeling, and doing (action). As can be observed by the following diagram (7b), the Center including the 8-9-1 types is oriented toward the function of action, the 2-3-4 types are oriented toward feeling, and the 5-6-7 types are oriented toward the function of thinking.

This concept of three Centers and their dominant function of thinking, feeling, or action helps us to understand why a person with a single type may relate to life differently than persons whose dominant function is represented by one of the two other Centers.

The Enneagram is also helpful in another way. Each of the nine types has a relationship with two other types on the Enneagram

The Centers

Action

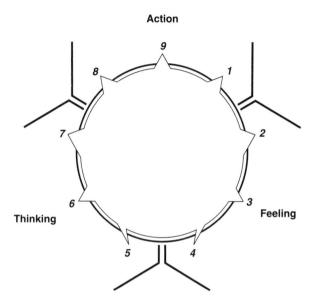

Thinking

Feeling

defined by the processes of integration (growth) and disintegration (stress or pathology). These relationships can be immediately identified by observing the arrows on the diagram that connect each of the nine points with two other points. Observation of the way people relate to others verifies the accuracy of the types which are so accurate they are predictable.

You will notice that by following the arrows and beginning with type 1, we observe the following sequences: 1-4-2-8-5-7 which defines the interrelationship of these six types through the processes of disintegration or regression under stress or due to personal pathology. For example, the type 1 regresses to take on the inferior qualities of the type 4. The type 4 regresses to take on the inferior qualities of the type 2. The type 2 regresses to an 8, an 8 to a 5, and a 5 to a 7.

Likewise, the central primary numbers at the points of 3-6-9 on the Enneagram are also interconnected by arrows which indicate their special relationship in times of integration or disintegration. The type 3 regresses to the inferior qualities of the type 9. The type 9 regresses to take on the inferior qualities of the type 6, and the type 6 disintegrates in the direction of the type 3.

It might be helpful to think of this disintegration as the

amplification of the inferior traits of a person's primary type with the inferior traits of the associated type following the direction of the arrows of the Enneagram. As evangelicals, we prefer to think of this disintegrative process of the personality under stress as representing how the unredeemed qualities of your primary typology join with the unredeemed qualities of another type during this process of disintegration.

The Enneagram reveals how growth and integration occur by observing the opposite interrelationships between the nine types. By moving against the direction of the arrows, we observe that in order to grow the type 1 needs to take on the positive qualities of the type 7. The type 7 grows through attempting to take on the strengths of the type 5, and the type 5 grows in the direction of the type 8. Type 8s become more like the strengths of the type 2 and so forth. Within the central triad of 3-6-9, the process of growth enables the type 9 to take on the strengths of the type 3, and the type 3 to strive for the strengths of the type 6. Finally, type 6 personalities may intentionally seek to emulate the strengths of the type 9 for growth.

Similarly, we might conclude that the redeemed qualities of your typology can be edified by the addition of the redeemed qualities of another type following the Enneagram's process of positive progression by moving against the direction of the arrows.

In this process of growth and integration, or in the reverse process of disintegration that has been described by the Enneagram, we may assume that strengths and weaknesses of each of the nine types are mirror reflections of the same essential dynamics. (Jungian psychology describes this dynamic in terms of the "shadow" side of every "ego.") In the Enneagram, this process of a natural polarity is more readily available to the observer when we speak in terms of the "strengths" and "weaknesses" of a particular personal dynamic. The "high and low" or "inferior/superior" or "redeemed and unredeemed" qualities of each type are also used by many redactors of the Enneagram to describe this essential process of polarity within each personality.

For example, using the type 1 for illustration, we note that the strength of this personality is frequently observed when in the name of "righteous indignation" the type 1 is energized to

**Spiritual Gifts and Virtues
Movement against the Arrows**

Peace
9
Justice 8
Righteousness 1
Joy 7
Love 2
Courage 6
Truth 3
Wisdom 5
Equanimity 4

**Core Sins and Addictions
Movement with the Arrows**

Sloth
9
Lust 8
Anger 1
Gluttony 7
Pride 2
Fear 6
Deceit 3
Avarice 5
Envy 4

prophetic acts of courage and mercy on behalf of those who have been victimized by injustice or evil. However, the dark side (shadow) or weakness of this type 1 dynamic is observed by understanding the core addiction or compulsion around the emotion of anger, which can become destructive bitterness and contempt in those persons who are out of balance, under stress, or pathologically fixated.

Hence, to appreciate the full implications described above around the processes of integration or disintegration, we need to look closely at how the Enneagram is defining the core addictions (sins) for each type, and appreciate the way in which each of these addictions/sins is expressed in both potential strengths and weaknesses within each type. The following diagram attempts to illustrate the strengths and weaknesses of each type.

There is another relationship between the nine types that is important to understand. The concept of "wings" is utilized to describe the process of incorporation of strengths/weaknesses that are characterized by another style on the Enneagram. This gives the Enneagram the opportunity to combine two separate types in ways that reflect the idiosyncratic interaction of the traits of both these types. Consequently, the Enneagram provides us with a descriptive array of seventy-two different personality types (i.e., you might be a type 3 with a type 7 wing).

You quite well may be interested to learn more about the Enneagram and your own personality type within this elaborate system of personality typology. You can pursue this further by reading some of the suggested resources in the bibliography at the conclusion of this chapter. Considerable research is being done on the use of the Enneagram as a viable tool for psychological diagnosis. However, whatever correlations that future empirical research will establish between the Enneagram and other contemporary forms of psychological diagnosis and assessment, there remains a uniqueness to this ancient system of particular interest to ministers and family counselors. The Enneagram provides a very sophisticated analysis of the human self that integrates both psychological insights and spiritual wisdom. Many psychologists of religion have seen correlations between various contemporary schools of psychology and spirituality, but the Enneagram has apparently integrated these insights for centuries. Imbedded within the concept of "core addictions or sins" is an understanding that the human person is made up of more than psychological characteristics, pathologies, or interpersonal proclivities.

The Enneagram understands each of these dynamics and identifies the way in which the inner spiritual essence of each person is outwardly manifested in personality, pathology, and interpersonal relatedness.The Enneagram assumes that spiritual maturity is essential to long-term psychological and relational health and provides a schema for understanding these processes. Furthermore, contrary to most contemporary schools of psychology and psychotherapy, the Enneagram presents a balanced view of what it means to be human by integrating both pathology and health within one system.

The Christian doctrines of conversion and sanctification are effectively delineated by the Enneagram since within each type there is a possibility of seeing how that type functions before and after redemption. Likewise, the interrelationship between the types suggests a process for spiritual growth in which movement toward affirming and internalizing the virtues of other types is described by the structure of the Enneagram.

SOME IMPLICATIONS OF NOT ATTENDING TO YOUR PERSONHOOD

Many successful ministers give testimony that personal under-standings of their own personality structures are in part responsi-ble for their successes as human persons. At the same time, many formerly successful ministers have left the ministry in disgrace and shame as a result of not taking seriously aspects of their per-sonhood which made them vulnerable to various forms of temp-tation. More than one congregation has suffered the disillusion-ment and betrayal of a pastor or staff member losing touch with the personal and professional boundaries appropriate to their role as ministers. Temptation toward sexual infidelity, greed and mis-use of money, and personal arrogance or pride are often aspects of the minister's personhood which, when unchecked, can under-mine any minister's effectiveness in a matter of a few careless minutes of impulsive behavior. Many seminarians feel offended by the suggestion that they might be vulnerable to the temptations of sexuality, greed, and pride and hide behind an innocent but false personal piety. These same ministers are frequently resistive to examining ways in which they might be helped to defend themselves before a sinful episode occurs, and some even resist assistance after being overtaken in a sinful event.

We acknowledge that one of the challenges and opportunities facing the minister is learning how to appreciate the full power of sexuality as a dimension of what it means to be human. Since God created us as sexual beings, we may conclude that sexuality is a dimension of God's image within humanity as well. Scripture teaches that sexuality within the sacred relationship of marriage is very satisfying and pleasing not only to the married couple, but also to God. It is through our sexuality and sensual pleasure that we participate with God in the ongoing (pro)creative activity of producing future generations.

However, the sexual power of attraction between persons must also be carefully controlled or it can lead to as much pain and disillusionment as it was intended for pleasure and love. All human beings are sexual and therefore all relationships are influ-enced by sexual responses. Between minister and parishioner, sexual attraction can also provide an opportunity for affirmation or for humiliation. However, sexual activity between a minister and parishioner is a breach of professional ethics and a painful betrayal for all parties (see chap. 10).

Because of the implicit power imbalance between minister and parishioner(s), the Christian minister must take special care to be sensitive to how the sexual dimension of the ministerial relationship is being processed. Frequently, emotionally impoverished and lonely parishioners entertain sexual fantasies about their ministers in which sexual behavior between the parishioner and the minister is seen as a way to fulfill desires for love, approval, attention, hostility, and empowerment. Ministers are warned to care for these parishioners with extraordinary concern and deep respect for the ways in which the power of their roles may be "valencing" relationships beyond the healthy well-being for either the pastor or the congregant.[4] Close working relationships and counseling situations are primary opportunities for even appropriate affection, support, and spiritual intimacy to be used as the setting for temptation. Unless the minister is sensitive to his or her own sexual needs and responses and unless appropriate professional etiquette, spiritual wisdom, and appropriate precautions are practiced, the relationship will likely be threatened by the potential for inappropriate sexual contact.

A good maxim to remember and affirm in close working or counseling relationships is that it is inaccurate to view sex between minister and parishioner as the private activity between two consenting adults! The power differential of the pastoral relationship removes any reasonable consideration of parity between the participants.

Greed is another acute temptation "waiting at the door" of the pastoral relationship. Ordination and consecration to ministry do not safeguard the minister from the temptation to exploit the pastoral relationship for personal economic gain. Unless ministers are knowledgeable about their own struggles with greed and take careful measures to keep it within bounds, they are vulnerable to the temptation to abuse the parishioner's trust and affections for personal and financial gain. It is inappropriate for a minister to accept expensive gifts and other "tokens of appreciation" from a well-meaning but overdependent parishioner. Group and/or congregational expressions of appreciation or acknowledgment of special milestones in the pastoral relationship are less likely to promote an abusive overindulgence of a personal relationship.

Pride is a difficult dimension of our personhood to separate from our pastoral calling. The very dimensions of personality that lend themselves to effective professional functioning can hide the temptation to pride. Self-assurance is but a small step from arrogance. Strong personality strengths can cover a narcissistic preoccupation with "me." Pride and narcissism are no respecters of persons. Strong theological convictions do not guarantee a congregation from the abuses of prideful pastoral leadership. The professional ministry is a natural opportunity for an unhealthy self not to be content with serving God, but to act like God. Only a genuine humility grounded in a painfully honest self-awareness can protect the minister and congregation from the subtle but terminal effects of submerged pride.

POSITIVE DIMENSIONS OF HUMAN PERSONHOOD FOR THE PRACTICE OF MINISTRY

We should not leave this discussion of the relationship of the personhood of the minister to the practice of ministry without affirming that in most instances, the ministry of each minister is enriched and enhanced by the same aspects of personhood. Our capacity for intimacy with parishioners provides wonderful opportunities to celebrate the gift of life and the gift of love we have received in Christ. Our natural talents become transformed by the Holy Spirit into spiritual gifts and graces to be used in the kingdom of God. Likewise, our families extend the impact of the ministry in ways that make us appreciative of these gifts as well.

Seminary is a wonderful time of preparation for ministry. Self-discovery and professional identity formation go hand in hand in this process of developing skills for future ministry. You are encouraged to take the gift of your humanness, especially the uniqueness of your own individual identity, as tools to be developed and appreciated with the same discipline as studying the body of divinity and of Scripture. Remember, your life may be the only Bible some people will ever read!

NOTES

1. See "Introduction to Type" by Isabel Briggs Myers, available through Consulting Psychologists Press, Inc., 577 College Avenue, Palo Alto, CA 94306. This test must be administered by someone who is an approved MBTI test evaluator.
2. David Kiersey and Marilyn Bates, *Please Understand Me: An Essay on Temperament Styles* (Del Mar, Calif.: Prometheus Nemesis, 1978).
3. Kathleen Hurley and Theodore Dobson, *What's My Type?* (New York: Harper, 1991), 3.
4. See the creative work of Marie Fortune in describing the relationship of power to the issue of clergy sexual misconduct.

FOR FURTHER READING

Beesing, Maria, Robert Nogosek, and Patricia O'Leary. *The Enneagram: A Journey of Self-Discovery.* Denville, N.J.: Dimension Books, 1984.

Bennett, J.G. *Enneagram Studies.* York Beach, Maine: Samuel Weiser, 1983.

Bergin, Eilis, and Eddie Fitzgerald, *An Enneagram Guide: A Spirituality of Love in Brokenness.* Dublin, Ireland: Twenty-third Publications, 1993.

Callahan, William J. *The Enneagram for Youth.* Chicago: Loyola Univ. Press, 1992.

Fortune, Marie. *Is Nothing Sacred?* San Francisco: HarperCollins, 1992.

Hannan, Peter. *Nine Faces of God.* Dublin, Ireland: Columbia, 1992.

Hurley, Kathleen V., and Theodore E. Dobson. *What's My Type?* New York: HarperCollins, 1991.

———. *My Best Self: Using the Enneagram to Free the Soul.* New York: HarperCollins, 1993.

Kelly, Mary Helen. *Skin Deep: Designer Clothes by God.* Memphis: Monastery of St. Clare, 1990.

Keyes, Margaret Frings. *Emotions and the Enneagram: Working Through Your Shadow Life Script.* Muir Beach, Calif.: Molysdatur, 1990.

————. *Out of the Shadows*. Muir Beach, Calif.: Molysdatur, 1988.

————. *The Enneagram Relationship Workbook: A Self and Partnership Assessment Guide*. Muir Beach, Calif.: Molysdatur, 1991.

Kiersey, David, and Marilyn Bates. *Please Understand Me: An Essay on Temperment Styles*. Del Mar, Calif.: Prometheus Nemesis, 1978.

Metz, Barbara, and John Burchill. *The Enneagram and Prayer: Discovering our True Selves Before God*. Denville, N.J.: Dimension, 1987.

Nogosek, Robert J. *Nine Portraits of Jesus*. Denville, N.J.: Dimension, 1987.

Palmer, Helen. *The Enneagram: Understanding Yourself and the Others in Your Life*. New York: Harper and Row, 1988.

Riso, Don Richard. *Discovering Your Personality Type: The Enneagram Questionaire*. Boston: Houghton Mifflin, 1992.

————. *Enneagram Transformations: Releases and Affirmations for Healing Your Personality Type*. Boston: Houghton Mifflin, 1993.

————. *Personality Types: Using the Enneagram for Self-Discovery*. Boston: Houghton Mifflin, 1987.

————. *Understanding the Enneagram: The Practical Guide to Personality Types*. Boston: Houghton Mifflin, 1990.

Rohr, Richard, and Andreas Ebert. *Discovering the Enneagram: An Ancient Tool for a New Spiritual Journey*. New York: Crossroad, 1992.

————. *Experiencing the Enneagram*. New York: Crossroad, 1992.

Tickerhoof, Bernard. *Conversion and the Enneagram: Transformation of the Self in Christ*. Denville, N.J.: Dimension, 1991.

Wagner, Jerome P. "A Descriptive, Reliability, and Validity Study of the Enneagram Personality Typology." *Dissertation Abstracts International* (1981), 41, 466A.

Zuercher, Suzanne. *Enneagram Companions: Growing in Relationships and Spiritual Direction.* Notre Dame, Ind.: Ave Maria, 1993.

———. *Enneagram Spirituality: From Compulsion to Contemplation.* Notre Dame, Ind.: Ave Maria, 1992.

For frequent listings/mailings about Enneagram workshops, tapes, videos, and current writing, you are encouraged to contact:

(1) Enneagram Resources, 12262 W. New Mexico Ave., Lakewood, CO 80228; Phone: 303-985-1889 (This is Kathleen V. Hurley's home number.)

(2) Enneagram Personality Types, Inc., 222 Riverside Drive, Suite 10E, New York, NY 10025; Phone: 212-932-3306 (This is Don Riso's company.)

(3) Clarence Thomson, *The Enneagram Educator* (quarterly newsletter), 115 East Armour Blvd., Kansas City, MO 64111.

8

THE CHURCH AND ITS MINISTRY

TIMOTHY P. WEBER

In the religious free-market system in which we live, "church" is becoming increasingly optional. Pollsters report that while interest in "spirituality" is high, many Americans are opting out of religious institutions. Their experience of the transcendent is individualistic and eclectic. Because religious choices are so numerous and personal freedom so highly valued, many people avoid organized religion and create their own faith out of the many kinds available. For a growing segment of American society, then, the church as a religious institution seems behind the times and even irrelevant to the spiritual quest.

Not everyone feels that way, however. Church remains the center of religious life for most people. Statistically, more Americans have church connections today than ever before. According to historian Martin Marty, when Americans decide to "get religion," most still go to the Yellow Pages first, where "churches" are listed between "chiropracters" and "cigars." Though loyalty to denominational labels is slipping, a majority of

Timothy P. Weber is the David T. Porter Professor of Church History at the Southern Baptist Theological Seminary, Louisville, Kentucky.

Americans believe that religion is best experienced and passed on in communities of faith. Thus anyone thinking about spending one's life in church leadership better have a clear idea of what the church is and what God expects of those who wish to serve it. In other words, two questions are crucial: What is the church? and What is the nature of the church's ministry?

DEFINING THE CHURCH

Throughout their history, Christians have defined the church in a variety of ways because of the complex picture presented in Scripture and the different historical contexts in which the church has existed. Thus we would do well to examine briefly some of the biblical and historical definitions of the church.

Biblical Images

Our word "church" translates the Greek term *ekklesia*, which is made of *ek* (out) and *kaleo* (to call), and means a public assembly or gathering of people.[1] It is used throughout the New Testament to refer both to local congregations of believers[2] and the one worldwide or universal church.[3]

The New Testament uses many images to describe the nature of the church. In fact, Paul Minear has counted about 100,[4] including the bride of Christ (Rev. 21), the salt of the earth (Matt. 5:13), a chosen people and a royal priesthood (1 Peter 2:9), ambassadors for Christ (2 Cor. 5:20), and temple of God (1 Cor. 3:16; 2 Cor. 6:16). But three capture best the church's nature: the people of God, the new creation, and the body of Christ.

The People of God. The notion of a special people of God is central to both Testaments. At the heart of this relationship is the concept of covenant, which is a solemn agreement between two parties. Though there are different kinds of covenants in the Scriptures,[5] in general covenants include both a promise and an obligation.

For example, God first established a covenant with Abraham: "I will make you into a great nation and I will bless you; I will make your name great, and you will be a blessing. I will bless those who bless you, and whoever curses you I will curse; and all peoples on earth will be blessed through you" (Gen. 12:2-3).

Israel's obligation to God can be seen in the covenant with Moses: "Now if you obey me fully and keep my covenant, then out of all nations you will be my treasured possession. Although the whole earth is mine, you will be for me a kingdom of priests and a holy nation" (Ex. 19:5-6). God affirmed the covenant to King David: "Your house and your kingdom will endure forever before me; your throne will be established forever" (2 Sam. 7:16). Later on, Israel's prophets used the people's covenant with God to judge their disobedience and call them to greater faithfulness. The Prophet Jeremiah predicted a day when God would establish a new covenant: "The time is coming, declares the Lord, 'when I will make a new covenant with the house of Israel and with the house of Judah. It will not be like the covenant I made with their forefathers when I took them by the hand to lead them out of Egypt . . . I will put my law in their minds and write it on their hearts. I will be their God, and they will be my people. . . . For I will forgive their wickedness and will remember their sins no more'" (Jer. 31:31-34).

The first Christians believed that they were this new covenant people. On the Day of Pentecost, Peter made a connection between the descent of the Spirit on the church and God's promise to the Prophet Joel. "In the last days, God says, 'I will pour out my Spirit on all people. Your sons and daughters will prophesy, your young men will see visions, your old men will dream dreams'" (Acts 2:17). Peter applied the words of Exodus 19 to believers scattered throughout Asia Minor: "But you are a chosen people, a royal priesthood, a holy nation, a people belonging to God, that you may declare the praises of him who called you out of darkness into his wonderful light" (1 Peter 2:9).

Paul believed that the church was joined to the old people of God "by faith." In his letter to the Romans, Paul cited Hosea's prophecy, "I will call them 'my people' who are not my people" (9:25), and argued that the Gentiles were like wild olive branches that God had grafted into the olive tree of Israel so that they could receive all of its promises and blessings (10:11-24). Likewise, in his letter to the Ephesians, Paul wrote that at one time Gentiles "were separate from Christ, excluded from citizenship in Israel and foreigners to the covenants of the promise" (2:12), but now they were "fellow citizens with God's people and members of God's household" (2:19).

The New Creation or Humanity. New Testament writers also portrayed the church as a new humanity, part of a new creation made possible through Christ's victory over sin and death. According to the Genesis account of creation and fall (chaps. 1–3), sin affected all parts of the created order. Consequently, God's cosmic plan of redemption involves the creation itself, which is currently in "bondage to decay" (Rom. 8:21). Along with the new heavens and new earth (Isa. 65–66; 2 Peter 3; Rev. 21), there will be a new humanity made up of those redeemed by Jesus.

This new humanity is currently under construction. According to Paul, Jesus is the last or second Adam through whom this new human race is being formed (Rom. 5:14-19; 1 Cor. 15:21-22, 45-49). Jesus' words to Nicodemus about the "new birth" (John 3) were echoed in Paul's words to the Corinthians: "Therefore, if anyone is in Christ, he is a new creation; the old has gone, the new has come!" (2 Cor. 5:17) Believers are new people because they have taken off the old nature and put on a new nature, "which is being renewed in knowledge in the image of its Creator" (Col. 3:9).

As a new humanity, Christians live by new rules. Those who have been "baptized into Christ" should no longer treat each other like they used to, when differences of race, class, and gender seemed so important. "There is neither Jew nor Greek, slave nor free, male nor female, for you are all one in Christ Jesus" (Gal. 3:28; also Col. 3:11).

The church is this new humanity, redeemed by Christ and being transformed by the Spirit. But as every student of church history knows, the church only approximates the new humanity at present. The final redemption of the cosmos is still future (Rom. 8); and the church is not yet what it will be (Col. 3:1-3). The church has often manifested the old nature, not the new. It has lived by—and sometimes even defended biblically—the "old rules" that enslave the old humanity. But through the grace of God and the power of the Spirit, the church demonstrates its identity as a new creation when it lives out the gospel in the world.

The Body of Christ. Paul's favorite image of the church was the body of Christ. He used this powerful metaphor to show the church's vital connection to Christ and the members' relationship to each other. By taking this metaphor seriously, one might say that in the church the risen and ascended Lord retains a physical presence on the earth. Through the Spirit, believers in Christ are baptized into his body (1 Cor. 12:13) and therefore carry out his mission in the world.

By calling Christ the head of his body, Paul underscored believers' connection to the Lord Jesus. Christ is the church's head because he has authority over all that is (Eph. 1:23), gave his life for the church as its Savior (Eph. 5:23), and is the beginning of a new humanity, the firstborn from among the dead (Col. 1:18). As Christ's body, the church is attached to the head and is helpless without it: "From him the whole body, joined and held together by every supporting ligament, grows and builds itself up in love, as each part does its work" (Eph. 4:16).

Paul also used the body metaphor to teach about the church's unity and diversity. Just as the human body consists of many different "members," so does the body of Christ, the church. "The body is a unit, though it is made up of many parts; and though all its parts are many, they form one body. So it is with Christ" (1 Cor. 12:12). In a healthy and well-functioning body, each part has its own important function to play. Just as it would be stupid to depreciate an arm because it is not an eye, or an ear because it is not a nose, so it would be foolish not to appreciate the diversity of the body of Christ. The church is diverse because God has distributed different spiritual gifts to the members "for the common good" (1 Cor. 12:7). Unless all the members are using their gifts, the body cannot function as God intended.

For Paul this understanding of the church undermined the human tendency to value people according to their exercise of power, wealth, or "standing." In Christ's body, no one is superior to anyone else, and no one is unnecessary. "Just as each of us has one body with many members, and these members do not all have the same function, so in Christ we who are many form one body, and each member belongs to all the others. We have different gifts, according to the grace given us" (Rom. 12:5-6). Unity *and* diversity are always present in the healthy body of Christ.

Four Historical Marks of the Church
When the early church first defined itself in creedal terms, it settled on four distinguishing marks: one, holy, catholic, and apos-

tolic.[6] These terms continue to teach valuable lessons about the nature and purpose of the church.

One. There is no suggestion anywhere in the New Testament that the church is anything but "one." In John's gospel Jesus said that there was one shepherd and one flock (10:16) and prayed to the Father that his disciples "may be one as we are one" (17:11). Paul taught that there is only one body of Christ, just as there is only one Lord, one faith, and one baptism (Eph. 4:4-6). Nevertheless, sometimes the church's unity is hard to observe. Even in apostolic times, its unity could be obscured by personal, racial, and theological factions; and in the twenty centuries since then, the church has divided into countless sects and denominations. What, then, can unity mean?

Unity does not mean uniformity. While there have always been sectarians who say "There is only one church of Jesus Christ and my group is it," other Christians have taken a different view: "There is only one church of Jesus Christ, but it is denominated—or named—in different ways." All who have been redeemed by Christ form the one church, even when they belong to different denominations and call each other by different names.

Of course, one would be naive to gloss over the many serious issues that have divided Christians: people who take the Scriptures seriously have often interpreted them differently and have followed their consciences in different directions. But the fact remains that it is God who creates the church, not Christians. Christ's work makes salvation possible; and the gift of the Spirit makes it a living reality. If Jesus says that the church is one, then it is, even when Christians make the unity hard to see.

Holy. If unity is hard to detect in the church, is its holiness any easier to find? Of course, it all depends on what we mean by "holy." Though we often use it this way, "holy" (*hagios*) in the New Testament does not mean sinless perfection. After all, Paul called the Corinthians "saints" and "sanctified" (1 Cor. 1) while they were guilty of everything from fomenting division to committing incest. In fact, all of the churches in the New Testament contained flaws of one kind or another. According to 1 John 1:8, no one in the church can say that he or she is without sin; and even the Apostle Paul freely admitted that he was far from perfect (Phil. 3:12) and that he still saw things "through a glass darkly" (1 Cor. 13:12).

At the root of *hagios* is the idea of being set apart for something special. The church's holiness consists of its being called out by God for special work—to share the gospel as his chosen people who are established in the truth and sanctified by the Spirit (2 Thes. 2:13-14). Martin Luther got to the heart of this paradox by saying that Christians are sinners and righteous at the same time. This is another way of saying that believers are holy because of what God has done for them even though they still struggle with sin and the demands of following Jesus. To say that the church is holy is to see it through the eyes of God's grace.

Catholic. Even though many Protestants think "Rome" when they hear "catholic," the word itself simply means "universal." Though the Greek word *katholikos* does not appear in the New Testament, by the second century, Christians were applying the term to themselves because it captured something crucial in the church's identity: that the gospel is for the whole world and the church's mission requires it to cross racial, cultural, and language barriers.

Jesus commanded his disciples to take the gospel to all nations (Matt. 28:19) and told them that after they received the Holy Spirit, they would be his witnesses to the ends of the earth (Acts 1:8). Unlike some early Christians who believed that the church needed to retain its original Jewishness to be authentic, Paul, Peter, Barnabas, and other missionaries to the Gentiles argued that the gospel must be communicated and lived out cross-culturally (Acts 15).

History shows that none of the other world religions is as widely disseminated as the Christian faith. None of the others has been able to "translate" itself so effectively among the world's various people groups. The church cannot be the church unless it is actively carrying out the catholic mission of Jesus in the world.

Apostolic. Paul stated that the church is "built on the foundation of the apostles and prophets, with Christ Jesus himself as the chief cornerstone" (Eph. 2:20). From the beginning, the church affirmed that its identity rested on the apostolic witness to the life and ministry of Jesus. In the formation of the New Testament canon, the church recognized this apostolic teaching as normative for its faith and practice.[7]

Most Christians during most of church history have believed it was vitally important to remain "apostolic" in one way or another. Some Christians, for example, base their "apostolicity" on a line of bishops that they can trace back to the first century. Others have argued that they are in an unbroken line of congregations reaching back to Jesus and the apostles. Still others assert that they are apostolic because they are simple "New Testament Christians" who use the Bible alone for their doctrine and church practice.

It is ironic that the desire to be apostolic has produced so much division over the centuries. Many of the arguments between Christians have had to do with what it means to be true to or consistent with apostolic belief and practice. Even in their divisions, the churches witness to their common commitment: to be authentic, the church in every age must base its identity, doctrine, and mission on the apostolic witness to Christ as found in the Scriptures.

THE CHURCH'S MINISTRY

The church's ministry is an enormously complex subject that we can only highlight here. We shall look at two basic questions. The first question is, "What is the church's ministry?" that is, "What is the church supposed to do?" The second question is, "Who are the ministers?" with emphasis on "Who is supposed to do it?"

The Scope of the Church's Ministry

A summary of the range of the church's ministry can be seen at the end of Acts 2 where we learn that the first church was involved in four activities after the Day of Pentecost. Believers studied the apostles' teaching, worshiped regularly, fellowshipped often, and evangelized enthusiastically (2:42-47). Probably most of what the church calls ministry falls into one of those four categories. Though they are all distinctive, none is completely separated from the others. For example, devotion to the apostles' teaching—the church's teaching ministry—impacts the church's worship, which is to be done "in spirit and in truth" (John 4:24). Similarly, in order to evangelize effectively, the church needs to keep its message straight. Fellowship occurs in all aspects of the church's life: sharing in baptism and the Lord's Supper; serving those in need both inside and outside the church; conducting special programs for youth, families, singles, or senior adults; participating in Sunday School classes; singing in the choir; and the like. Worship provides the renewal of spiritual capital that is needed for the church to accomplish all of its other tasks.

Put in another way, the church's ministry should give close attention to three closely related dimensions: orthodoxy, orthopraxy, and orthopathy.[8] Orthodoxy (right praise/belief) relates most directly to the church's teaching ministry, but it also ties into its worship. The Christian faith is not whatever one wants to make of it. It is rooted in the person and work of Jesus Christ, the divine Word of God who became flesh (John 1). Paul put it this way: "For what I received I passed on to you as of first importance: that Christ died for our sins according to the Scriptures, that he was buried, that he was raised on the third day according to the Scriptures, and that he appeared to Peter, and then to the Twelve" (1 Cor. 15:3-5). In its manifold ministries, the church must pass down what it received and be faithful to the Scriptures in its teaching, preaching, and witness.

As crucial as orthodoxy is for Christian ministry, it is not the church's only concern. Orthodoxy (right thinking) needs to be joined to *orthopraxy* (right practice). This is James' point: "faith by itself, if it is not accompanied by action, is dead. . . . Show me your faith without deeds, and I will show you my faith by what I do. You believe that there is one God. Good! Even the demons believe that—and shudder" (2:17-19). Correct doctrine without Christian deportment is not enough.

Just as Christians sometimes have disagreed on definitions of correct belief, they have also struggled to define correct behavior (all the "shoulds" and "shouldn'ts" that some Christians love to argue about). But orthopraxy is about more than lifestyle questions; it has to do with following Jesus in the way we pray, worship, and witness; run our businesses and our families; care for those in need; practice the spiritual disciplines; treat our enemies as well as our friends; and deal with conflicts. In other words, if orthodoxy is about confessing our faith, orthopraxy is about our Christian character and how we live.

Orthopathy (right affections) is also needed for effective Christian ministry. Alongside doctrine and doing, there must be devotion, a vital love of God—and a sincere humility toward others—that energizes and brings integrity to Christian life and ministry. Some Christians think they must choose between "head" and "heart" religion, between a religion based on "truth" and one based on "experience." But this is a false dichotomy. Without orthopathy, orthodoxy is "dead" and orthopraxy is hypocritical. Paul makes the point clearly: "If I speak in the tongues of men and of angels, but have not love, I am only a resounding gong or a clanging cymbal. If I have the gift of prophecy and can fathom all mysteries and all knowledge, and if I have a faith that can move mountains, but have not love, I am nothing. If I give all I possess to the poor and surrender my body to the flames, but have not love, I gain nothing" (1 Cor. 13:1-3).

Christian ministry needs all three "orthos" to maintain its integrity and to fulfill its calling. It does not have to choose between them or prioritize them in order to give one more attention than the others. Believing, behaving, and loving are indispensible in doing Christian ministry.

The Variety of Christian Ministers

Who is responsible for the church's teaching, worshiping, fellowshipping, and evangelizing? To whom does the church's ministry belong? Christians have provided different answers to those questions, depending on their doctrine of the church and their view of ecclesial authority.

Numerous traditions insist that their view of the "ministry" (and church government, for that matter) is straight out of the Scriptures. But the precise nature of church "offices" is difficult to discern. The New Testament mentions many different kinds of leaders: apostles, prophets, teachers, miracle workers, healers, tongues speakers and interpreters, administrators, evangelists, pastors, overseers (bishops), elders, and deacons (1 Cor. 12:28; Eph. 4:11). But can we say with assurance which were actual offices and which were merely functional roles?

Most scholars conclude that there were only two offices in the earliest congregations: a teaching office (described variously as overseer or bishop, elder, pastor) and a serving office (deacon). Though the titles themselves may indicate something of what these leaders did (overseers direct and administer, pastors "shepherd" their flock, deacons "wait tables"), nowhere in the New Testament are there clear-cut job descriptions. The most extensive passages on church leaders (1 Tim. 3; Titus 1) are actually about character qualifications more than the specific tasks they perform. To be sure, overseers/elders are not to be recent converts and must be able to teach well, but the rest of their qualifications are mandated elsewhere of all believers.

In short order, the overseers (elders/pastors) bore responsibility for teaching, the discipline process, guarding the congregation against false teachers, and performing the sacraments or ordinances. Leaders served with one ultimate goal in mind: "to prepare God's people for works of service, so that the body of Christ may be built up until we all reach unity in faith and in the knowledge of the Son of God and become mature, attaining to the whole measure of the fullness of Christ" (Eph. 4:12-13). One thing seems certain, nothing in the New Testament exactly corresponds to the role expectations of the pastoral office as presently understood and performed in North America.

Likewise, it is impossible to be definitive about local church structures in the New Testament era. Some scholars have discerned a process of institutionalization at work in the apostolic writings—a movement from loosely organized "charismatic" congregations (1 Cor.) to more formally structured ones with clear lines of authority (1 Tim., Titus). Yet well into the second century the structure of local churches varied widely. For example, at about the same time that Ignatius described churches with well-developed hierarchies of bishops, elders, and deacons, the author of the *Didache* addressed churches in which bishops and deacons still had less authority than itinerant prophets. Though models of church government we see today—congregational, presbyterian, and episcopal—are certainly hinted at in the New Testament, none is fully developed there. They take shape over time.

There is both a positive and negative side to the historical development of church structures and offices. On the negative side, it appears that Christians have often borrowed freely (and uncritically?) from prevailing notions of order and authority around them. Thus the church has at different times patterned itself after imperial, monarchical, feudal, military, democratic, and, more recently, business or corporate models. Sometimes church leaders have forgotten that whatever form the church or their offices take, there are certain biblical "givens" concerning the way Christian leaders operate. According to Jesus, "servant-leadership" is the norm. "You know that the rulers of the Gentiles lord it over them, and their high officials exercise authority over them. Not so with you. Instead, whoever wants to become great among you must be your servant, and whoever wants to be first must be your slave—just as the Son of Man did not come to be served, but to serve, and to give his life as a ransom for many" (Matt. 20:25-28). In the end, Christian leadership is fundamentally moral and relational, which means that "it is a balanced combination of oversight (1 Tim. 4:11-13; 6:17-19; Titus 3:9-11) and example (1 Tim. 4:12; 6:6-11; 1 Peter 5:1-4)."[9]

On the more positive side, flexibility in understanding both church structures and offices means that the churches have been able to make necessary adjustments to conduct their mission in the world. Those who believe that the Bible contains only one pattern of church order might disagree, but it seems that a more flexible approach has produced an amazingly diverse array of church, "parachurch," and lay ministries that have enabled the church to carry out its mission in creative and effective ways. In some quarters, it has meant the welcoming of women into positions of church leadership.[10] Even in churches that maintain a more hierarchical view of leadership, views of Christian ministry are expanding in ways that reflect the Bible's teaching that the church is the body of Christ and it is the Spirit who distributes gifts to its members.

CONCLUSION

As the Christian church faces the twenty-first century, it will encounter a number of new challenges. Christians from the Northern Hemisphere will have to come to grips with the realization that the center of gravity in the Christian movement has shifted to the Southern Hemisphere, whose people will increasingly come to dominate the world's Christian community. Christians will also have to come to terms with the exploding urbanization of the world's population, as well as the growing racial and cultural diversity within their own societies. Likewise,

Christians will have to decide what to do with religious pluralism and the pervasive consumerism of a worldwide market economy.

The history of Christianity is the story of met challenges, as well as missed opportunities. The resources available to past generations of Christians are still available today—the mission of the resurrected Lord, the presence and power of the Spirit, the authoritative guidance of the Scriptures, and the involvement of participants in the new humanity in whose hands the church's ministry ultimately belongs.

N O T E S

1. For an in-depth study of *ekklesia*, see K.L. Schmidt, *"ekklesia,"* in *Theological Dictionary of the New Testament*, ed. Gerhard Kittel (Grand Rapids: Eerdmans, 1965), 3: 501–36.

2. See Matt. 18:17; Acts 15:41; Rom. 16:16; 1 Cor. 4:17; 7:17; 14:33; and Col. 4:15.

3. See Matt. 16:18; Acts 20:28; 1 Cor. 15:9; and Eph. 1:22.

4. Paul Minear, *Images of the Church in the New Testament* (Philadelphia: Westminster, 1960).

5. See the helpful chart and description of three types of covenants (royal grant, parity, and suzerain-vassal) in the notes on Genesis 9 in *The NIV Study Bible* (Grand Rapids: Zondervan, 1985), 19.

6. These terms can be found in the creeds produced by the councils of Constantinople (A.D. 381) and Chalcedon (A.D. 451).

7. *Apostolicity* seems to have been the most important criterion for inclusion in the New Testament canon. Evidently, to be considered apostolic, a book had to be written by an apostle or a close associate of an apostle. See F.F. Bruce, *The Canon of Scripture* (Downers Grove, Ill.: InterVarsity, 1988).

8. I am adapting the insights of Steven J. Land, who first applied them to the distinctives of Pentecostal spirituality. See Stephen J. Land, *Pentecostal Spirituality: A Passion for the Kingdom* (Sheffield, England: Sheffield Academic Press, 1993).

9. D.A. Carson, "Church, Authority in," in *Evangelical Dictionary of Theology*, ed. Walter A. Elwell (Grand Rapids: Baker, 1984), 230.

10. Bonnidell Clouse and Robert G. Clouse, eds., *Women in Ministry: Four Views* (Downers Grove, Ill.: InterVarsity, 1989).

For Further Reading

Baptism, Eucharist and Ministry, Faith and Order Paper #111. Geneva: World Council of Churches, 1982.

Dulles, Avery. *Models of the Church*. Garden City, N.Y.: Doubleday, 1974.

Grenz, Stanley J. *Theology for the Community of God*. Nashville: Broadman and Holman, 1994.

————. *Created for Community: Connecting Christian Belief with Christian Living*. Wheaton, Ill.: Victor/BridgePoint, 1996.

Küng, Hans. *The Church*. Garden City, N.Y.: Doubleday Image, 1976.

Leonard, Bill. *The Nature of the Church*. Nashville: Broadman, 1987.

Minear, Paul. *Images of the Church in the New Testament*. Philadelphia: Westminster, 1960.

9

VOCATIONAL OPTIONS IN MINISTRY

DORIS A. BORCHERT

Baptists and other evangelical Christians are certain of one truth about full-time employment for ministry: the local church is the heart of ministry; it is the centerpiece of God's plan and strategy. Indeed, whether the worship of God's people and their education in faith was conducted in small "house church" groups or in the greatest church buildings or cathedrals, the local, face-to-face congregational organization of believers has been vital for the survival of the gospel of Jesus Christ. In all cultures and in every century the local church has been central to the Christian faith. At this writing, it seems to be crucial to the continuing survival of the community of Christ's disciples as we await his second coming.

With every passing generation, new ministry opportunities have been developed in local churches. Why, then, should you or I look in any other place than the local church for a place of ministry? The answer to that question has a lot to do with the subject of this chapter. My first purpose in writing is to encourage you to consider the growing variety of ministry opportunities in the local

Doris A. Borchert is Associate Professor of Christian Education at the Southern Baptist Theological Seminary, Louisville, Kentucky.

church. You may not be acquainted with some of them. Those of you who have felt the tug of God's Spirit calling you into ministry may well believe you do not possess sufficient gifts, talents, or skills useful for vocational ministry in the churches. As you read through this chapter with its catalog of ministry opportunities, perhaps the tug of calling may change to the excitement of real identification with a clearly defined ministry in a local church.

A second reason for writing this chapter is to describe the scores of vocational ministry opportunities that exist outside the local church. Just as is the case within the local church, ministry opportunities continue to multiply in stateside and overseas ministry placements largely supported by but carried on outside the boundaries of the local church. Many of you who have answered God's call to ministry are yet not clear about the kind of ministry in which God can best use you. As you read these pages, you may be stimulated to focus on one or more of the new-to-you ministry placements described here. Others of you who have just about decided God cannot use you in vocational ministries may be startled to read about a ministry role or position for which you are already largely qualified.

When I began as a young seminarian, my catalog of vocational choices in ministry seemed to be quite limited. Pastors, missionaries, educational directors in local churches, church musicians; all of these I knew about, but I was unaware of other options. Since that time, other options have developed. The following listing of ministry positions, roles, or tasks may lead you to consider a new and more focused way to fulfill your stewardship of time and talents as you serve God through vocational service. As you read along, I encourage you to ask yourself the question: "Am I doing my part to discover all the areas where God may wish me to use my talents, gifts, and energies?"

LOCAL CHURCH MINISTRIES

During the twentieth century, church staff ministries have been enlarged through an increasing number of specializations. In addition to the senior pastorate, positions as ministers of education, recreation, music, and youth have emerged as viable vocational goals. Larger churches have created part-time and/or full-time ministry positions for ministers of children, senior citizens, college-aged students, and ministers of administration and finance. For church expansion and growth, ministries of evangelism, outreach, and church planting have evolved. The influx of non-English speaking immigrants from Mexico, Cuba, Puerto Rico, Southeast Asia, Korea, Africa, and South America stimulated local churches either to establish language group churches within their own buildings on a shared space arrangement or to provide alternate space in buildings owned by the church close by. Bilingual Americans often served as ministers in these churches. In addition, ordained Christian ministers who arrived with the immigrant communities were frequently called to serve the newly created congregations. Perhaps God could use you in such ministries.

Innovative church planting methods have created other ministry positions. For example, many churches follow the New Testament challenge to spread the gospel into all the world by establishing new congregations using their own fellowships of believers as resources. Laypersons as well as college and seminary trained ministers have felt called to participate as vocational ministers in just such ministries.

Local churches have also taken to heart the gospel's urging to teach and proclaim family values and to minister to family members struggling to live as Christians in the ever-changing American culture. Family ministers, ministers of counseling, social work ministers, and pastoral care ministers have often been found as staff pastors in local churches. In order to put spacious and expensive church educational buildings to use on other days than on Sunday, large numbers of churches have established day-care facilities, preschool classes, and kindergartens. Many cities and counties with large populations have witnessed the establishment of full-ranged elementary and secondary schools. Principals and other administrators as well as teachers in these schools, free from sterile state laws which ban religious instruction and prayer, are considered to be ministers of their local congregations. They certainly provide a ministry to the children under their teaching. This includes children from families of believing parents and from the wider community itself. Frequently, the general education in these schools is somewhat superior in academic quality, traditional ethical training, and general discipline and deportment. As a result, these Christian schools become educational placements of choice for discerning citizens who are able to enroll their children in them. Much valuable ministry is provided by churches through such schools, and many educators are given opportunity to use their vocational training in education as a direct ministry of the church.

Other local churches take to heart the need of all of the citizens of their communities for the gospel. Specialized ministries are organized in the local churches to reach the affluent, educated, and otherwise comfortable families. Other churches have a heart for the inner cities where crime and violence negatively impact children and youth and where rampant sin and neglect continues to destroy the fabric of the rare traditional as well as the nontraditional families who live there. The people living in poverty pockets throughout local church areas are mostly neglected, but sometimes enjoy the compassionate witness of local congregations who take Jesus' ministry to the poor seriously. Of course, churches still mount a witness to the ethnic well-to-do citizens, but more than likely a minister who feels a specific calling of the Lord to minister to such populations is necessary for such ministries to take place. Many of these ministries are conducted by ministers trained in church social work. Their training prepares them to minister in poverty bound areas, both urban and rural, in ways to both be advocates for the residents and to empower them to discover and use their God-given gifts for more fruitful and productive lives. Skilled also in the art of soul-winning, family ministry, "congregationalizing," and church planting, social work ministers have a valiant record as missionary witnesses to the dispossessed.

For the most part, local churches in the United States will remain small to medium sized in the near future. Nearly 90 percent of Baptist and other evangelical churches have membership rolls listing fewer than 1,500 members. The remaining churches are part of the growing megachurch phenomenon. Churches with more than 1,500 members fit into the "mega" category. These burgeoning churches are in the process of designing new, innovative forms of ministry vocations. This is especially true in the task of nurturing *disciplers* as well as *disciples*. Ministers with seminary training are presented with a wide array of pastoral opportunities in local churches with this kind of goal for ministry.

DENOMINATIONAL MINISTRIES

Many churches have made denominational alliances with other congregations holding similar beliefs and understandings about what it is to fulfill the Great Commission. Together in smaller geographical areas, in state or multistate conventions, or in nationwide conventions or associations, churches have banded together to launch ministries they could not fully staff or fund alone. These groups of churches have established institutions such as Bible schools, colleges, and seminaries. Many Christians called to ministry have found their vocational selves fulfilled by serving as administrators, professors, recruiters, foundation executives, and support staff in these institutions of learning.

Orphanages and foster-home facilities dot the American landscape. These facilities, many with Christian origins, have been in great demand in ministering to children and other family members in a variety of ways since the middle of the nineteenth century. Formerly providing custodial care for orphans, these institutions play a vital part in supplementing state and federal programs for the care of and the adoption of children. Family advocacy and counseling is usually available through these institutions. Positions for social work ministers, house parents, chaplains, and a variety of other ministries continue to be available within such institutions for ministers.

In cities, across rural America, and especially in areas such as poverty bound Appalachian communities, on Native American reservations, and in disadvantaged population pockets across our great land, good samaritan ministries known by dozens of names have been established and supported by the churches. Education, health care, distribution of basic goods and services for life such as food, clothing, and medicines, as well as innovative social ministries have been provided in the name of Jesus Christ to large populations unable to secure such things for themselves. Christians who have begun life in such places and who are now trained as ministers are readily accepted as ministers by the people and are usually in great demand.

Hospitals and health care institutions have also been established by conventions and associations. While a few Roman Catholic hospitals existed on the North American continent before 1776, they were built in large numbers in the 1800s. Strangely enough, many Catholic hospitals are inviting evangelical ministers to join their chaplaincy departments, a ministry opportunity not known to many and an excellent opportunity to be a gospel witness to hospitalized patients and to the health care workers as well.

Protestant hospitals began appearing in the late 1800s and in accelerated numbers with growth spurts after the two World Wars. Christians who are educated as physicians, nurses, and other medical personnel have been grateful for opportunities to care for patients in institutions whose whole existence is based upon and supported by evangelical faith. Specialized chaplaincies were created and ministry training programs were established in such hospitals. Schools of nursing and a variety of medical technologies were established in denominational hospitals. Some are affiliated with universities and other institutions of higher education in order to provide faith-based environments for learning in the medical and other healing professions. Such institutions today still require ministers with Christian faith and specialized training who can be part of an "educational team" for the training of ministers. When thoroughly trained, they have opportunity to minister to persons in the health care traumas of injury and illness as welcomed members of the health care team. In addition, medical professionals and hospital administrators are now seeking ministers trained in Christian ethics, especially medical ethics, to consult with them or to be chaplain consultants to assist in ethical policy setting as well as day-to-day ethics issues arising in the course of health care.

When individuals or entire families discover themselves to be in need of competent counseling regarding their relationships, they may be surprised to discover their area religious hospitals provide quite competent outpatient counseling ministries. This is especially valuable when the hospital also has access to a broad network of helping professionals of many healing disciplines and a spiritually compatible hospital environment for inpatient care when necessary. One may find religiously trained professing Christians educated and practicing in the mental health care disciplines in nonchurch-sponsored placements throughout your community. However, it is wise to consider preparing to mount such a ministry in placements where the counselors serve under the guidance and sponsorship of a church with its pastor, deacons, or overseers. If you have gifts and skills for medical or mental health care vocations, such a training pattern may quite well be just what God has in store for you.

Probably one of the most under-considered ministry options, until recently, is in the area of publication and media ministries. Literature production for use in Bible study, Sunday School curricula, church training, discipleship training, spiritual growth, theological education, and a variety of ministry tasks such as missions and evangelism are frequently not recognized as a ministry. Such literature creation and distribution is a vital ministry in and of itself.

Some denominational groups enlist many hundreds of employees with a variety of editing, printing, and production assignments. These same groups often employ many theologically educated, ordained ministers for use in their literature ministries. The Southern Baptists, for example, have employed nearly 300 ordained ministers to work in their printing and other media ministries. Other smaller groups may choose between denominational and independent Christian publishing houses for their literature. These groups who serve your own denomination would certainly be open to ministers of your group in a wide variety of vocational positions.

With the rapid explosion of media technology, Christian ministers with any of the many skills in broadcasting through radio or television facilities are constantly needed. Accomplished and gifted program designers, script writers, and program personalities of many kinds are in some level of demand. Technicians, talk-show hosts, fund raisers, and support staff are needed to sustain these ministries.

Book writing, editing, and production within and outside denominational settings are ministry areas of vital importance among Christians today. The demand for solid Christian literature for young people who read elementary primer books and for others who read the most comprehensive adult volumes seems to be increasing. Denominational and independent Christian bookstores which dot the landscape are struggling to provide books able to meet the demand of seekers hoping to understand the gospel better. Christians who are hungry for understanding of spiritual things are purchasing books from Christian bookstores in unprecedented numbers. Some of the authors of this literature have been so helpful to their readers that they have become household names across the nation and beyond. More technical books about Scripture and theology are also in great demand. Christians are seeking increased awareness and literacy related to the faith. The authors and publishers of today have a great calling and a greater challenge from the Lord to provide adequately for these needs. Retail outlets for these products require knowledge-able Christian owners, managers, and sales assistants to see this kind of work as a ministry in order for it to achieve its maximum value. One local bookstore manager pointed out that using his talents and abilities in a denominational or other religious setting was one way in which he could repay, out of gratitude, his denomination for the thirty years of spiritual, emotional, and financial support he had received from its programs. If you have any such talents, gifts, and sense of internal calling to be involved in such a ministry, it would be well to seriously consider whether God may be calling you to prepare for this field.

SPECIALIZED MISSIONS AND EVANGELISM MINISTRIES

For generations, evangelically minded Christians have held the calling to mission service to be among the highest kind of spiritual calling. To be invited by God to participate in a ministry so clearly identified as a "Great Commission" ministry is considered to be a humbling as well as a spiritually thrilling call.

International Missions

As the twentieth century draws to a close, the openness of nations around the world to overseas missions from the United States appears to be narrowing in some places but increasing in others. By mid-century, rising nationalistic feelings in third-world nations supported the preservation of their own national religions. In nations and areas where Christians had already maintained a missionary presence, mission activities have been or have begun to be transferred to indigenous believers. However, missionaries with enabling, empowering, and equipping skills are always in high demand. Teaching a Christian believer of another culture, language, or race to spread the gospel is still needed. In many places, missionaries are in even higher demand than before.

In any event, this kind of ministry is hard. To leave father and mother, houses and lands, and all that is familiar to journey to a totally different culture in which to live is an enormous challenge. However, God still calls to such places. Christian ministers still accept such callings. Perhaps such a ministry is awaiting you, in the providence of God.

Christians who have special skills and training in medicine and agriculture have always been welcomed in disadvantaged nations of the earth. Today, such skills are still in great demand. Literacy workers, businesspeople, and engineers are just a few of the skills where in practice missionaries meet people's vital needs and participate in ongoing "lifestyle evangelism." They are also usually acceptable as "direct personal witness-evangelists" in the host countries where they labor in ways missionaries prepared only as evangelists may be denied visas.

North American Missions

Stateside ministries are also important. With the massive waves of immigration in the twentieth century and the high reproductive curves of the newcomers to our shores, winning these persons to Christ is vital. When they arrive, they have many needs. Baptists and other evangelicals have several ways to meet those needs and, in the process, to witness to and win to faith in Christ those who are helped. The growing number of ethnic evangelical churches in the United States give testimony to the vitality and viability of the Christian gospel for these people. Many young persons called as ministers have unique language skills, ethnic backgrounds, and deep longings to lead their people to faith in Christ. Who will address the needs of this vast harvest in the name of the Lord if the native Christians do not respond in some numbers to such a challenge? Some denominations maintain a "home mission" or "North American" missionary program of their own. Persons needed in such endeavors include researchers skilled in the art of tracking societary trends and discovering with careful definition why, from the human side, success is occurring. They are also trained to spot the places where there is little or no success in "Great Commission" ministries and to develop theories and/or programs to carry the gospel to such neglected places. Research ministers and strategists are needed to continue such ministries.

A mandate for "home mission" boards exists to assist the individual state conventions or local associations of churches to carry forth ministries they have begun or wish to begin. This includes many ministries listed already in this chapter, but requires persons able to travel and consult with the local churches or groups of churches as they carry forth their ministries. Consultants can provide helpful tips and information about "proven" approaches and share new or creative insights from other churches currently attempting to do similar things. Their value as a source of inspiration is evident. They also serve as a link between the current church with whom they consult and the other churches with whom the consultant has talked recently.

OTHER STRATEGIC MINISTRY VOCATIONS

Seminary education prepares ministers with basic learning in biblical, historical, theological, and practical disciplines; and this learning can be translated into many different kinds of ministry. Among the more visible in our culture are the following tasks, roles, or vocations.

Bi-Vocational Ministers

Many of the vocations described above must be lifetime, full-time ministries to achieve excellence and maturity. However, that pattern is not the only kind of ministry available to those preparing to minister in the twenty-first century. The first prominent bi-vocational minister was the Apostle Paul. The New Testament describes this itinerant missionary/evangelist as a "tent-maker," a believer who earned his bread in a secular industry while he worked at his "calling" as a minister.

The history of the church has seen hundreds of examples of bi-vocational ministries, but all follow the standard model of the Apostle Paul: (1) earning support by direct labor in a secular vocation, (2) beginning a ministry to establish believing communities, (3) increasingly accepting support by believers who wish to free the minister for full-time ministerial work.

The tasks of church planting (starting) as well as church reclaiming (rejuvenation of plateaued churches) cry out for bi-vocational ministers. Whether working in a local community job, establishing a small business to serve as an economic launching pad for ministries, or remaining in one's present vocation and reaching out through any of a variety of ministries could place one in the ranks of bi-vocational ministers.

Specialized Ministries

Most military services still require chaplains; for example, the army, navy, and air force. Local fire and police departments and community health care institutions frequently need replacements for their retiring chaplains or are open to establish new ones in response to initiative-taking ministers. Full-time or bi-vocational ministers may apply for such positions.

Hospital chaplains are vital to the holistic care the medical professions speak so eloquently about. Secular counseling centers, and more recently psychiatrists and clinical psychiatrists, are inviting theologically and clinically trained ministers to participate as pastoral counselors in their practices. Local churches, denominations, evangelistic associations, and other parachurch ministry groups sometimes seek biblically based, theologically sound, and clinically trained ministers to join their teams for ministry to their own staff ministry families and to the converts who turn to them for care.

Family life teachers and educators are desperately needed in local churches to assist pastors in the task of family life and value education. In too many places those who have seen the vision of the deep need for such education are not sufficiently educated to do the ministries. Seminary trained ministers with specialized Christian family life education are in a position to provide such ministries. Especially is this true with the growing Christian day school movement sponsored by churches. Ministers who are knowledgeable and caring can provide Christian values education for teachers in the schools, teachers in the Sunday Schools, and for church staff ministers themselves.

Camping and resort ministers are priceless and supportive gifts to other ministries. Meeting people in the relaxed times of their lives with wholesome and holistic gospel witness is a ministry task a wide variety of "called" ministers of God may fulfill. Permanent managerial and custodial workers to sustain religious conference centers are unique ministers. Spiritual life ministers who establish retreat centers and who are gifted in the deeper arts of spiritual discernment, prayer, and soul care provide havens of rest and good enough holding environments for troubled and despairing Christians.

Parachurch ministries such as Young Life, Campus Crusade for Christ, InterVarsity Christian Fellowship, and the like are evangelistic and discipleship ministries geared to meet younger persons at the crucial life-changing times of high school and college. When seminary trained ministers serve in such placements and when they are networked with supportive local churches with their mature ministers, such parachurch ministries can be a valuable asset to the gospel calling to minister to everyone in every stage of life.

Baptists and other evangelicals have long mounted student ministries for the same populations—high school and college-aged young people—through college/university campus ministries, student fellowship organizations, and youth ministers. And, of course, ministers who heed the call to academia provide witness and wisdom in college, university, seminary, and Bible school setting. They give themselves to scholarship so that their teaching might be comprehensive, enabling, and equipping for those future ministers who study in their classes. Sometimes bivocational, professors may teach as their main vocation, but also be involved in interim pastorates, church planting, Bible conferences, and other ministries which require their own specialized training and experience.

CONCLUDING REMARKS

This chapter's listings are far from exhaustive, but offered with the hope that you have been stimulated to consider praying about a wider variety of options for ministry. In addition, there are increasing numbers of ministers who as they mature in life experience two or more indelible invitations to serve Christ in vocations different from their first such calling. Perhaps your own calling to ministry is not fully settled as yet. That is not unusual. Many students arrive in seminary with no direct vocational calling but to a life of ministry. Thank God for the Holy Spirit whose part-time job is to nurture us to fulfill our various callings and from time to time even to take up different and frequently more dangerous tasks. However, when God does call you in an indelible way to serve him, celebrate your good fortune. Spend your youth in a ministry wisely in the center of God's will, and then your midlife and older days will be filled with the good things of life. May God bless you as you study, graduate, and depart to serve.

F o r   F u r t h e r   R e a d i n g

Allen, Katherine B. *Laborers Together with God*. Birmingham, Ala.: Women's Missionary Union, Southern Baptist Convention, 1987.

Best, Harold M. *Music through the Eyes of Faith*. San Francisco: HarperSan Francisco, 1993.

Bosch, David J. *Transforming Missions*. Maryknoll, N.Y.: Orbis, 1991.

DuBose, Francis M. *The God Who Sends*. Nashville: Broadman, 1983.

Dudley, Carol S. *Building Effective Ministry: Theory and Practice in the Local Church*. San Francisco: Harper & Row, 1983.

Gangel, Kenneth O. *Feeding and Leading: A Practical Handbook on Administration in Churches and Christian Organizations*. Wheaton, Ill.: Victor, 1984.

Harris, Maria. *Fashion Me a People: Curriculum in the Church*. Louisville: Westminster/John Knox, 1989.

Hessel, Dieter T. *Social Ministry*. Philadelphia: Westminster, 1982.

Husted, Donald Paul. *Jubilant II: Church Music in Worship and Renewal*. Carol Stream, Ill.: Hope, 1993.

Miles, Delos. *Evangelism and Social Involvement*. Nashville: Broadman, 1986.

Montgomery, Felix E. *Pursuing God's Call: Choosing a Vocation in Ministry.* Nashville: Convention, 1988.

Pazmiño, Robert W. *Principles and Practices of Christian Education: An Evangelical Perspective.* Grand Rapids: Baker, 1992.

Shurden, Walter B. *Not a Silent People: Controversies That Have Shaped Southern Baptists.* Nashville: Broadman, 1972.

Sullivan, James. *Baptist Polity: As I See It.* Nashville: Broadman, 1983.

10

CLERGY SEXUAL MISCONDUCT: A CRISIS IN MINISTERIAL ETHICS

DAVID P. GUSHEE

Imagine the following scenario. You are a forty-five-year-old seminary graduate with fifteen years of pastoral experience. By any standard, you have had a fabulously successful start to your ministry. Besides the universal praise of the four churches you've served, you have made it big on the preaching and evangelism conference circuit. With your church's indulgence you've been gone ten weeks a year doing that. Your wife and children have graciously supported you in this aspect of your ministry. You have also earned high praise for two books: *How to Grow a Wilting Church* and *Integrity in Christian Ministry*. Your files contain two other signed book contracts; long ago you deposited the generous advances that came with those contracts. You have been on Christian radio programs many times. Most preachers in your denomination have begun to recognize your name. Some have even envied you. You've noticed—and tried not to enjoy the feeling too much.

Why is it, then, that at this very moment you are sitting alone

David P. Gushee is Associate Professor of Christian Studies at Union University, Jackson, Tennessee.

on a tattered couch in a cheap hotel room half-watching an "I Love Lucy" rerun on a fuzzy TV? Why are you staring at letters from your two publishers, informing you of the cancellation of your book deals and demanding that you return your advance money? Why are you looking at a letter from Smith, Jones, & Wu, announcing your wife's intention to file for divorce and summoning you to a meeting next week to discuss the terms? Why are your feet tired from waiting all day in the unemployment office to collect your check? Why is there a message on the answering machine from your twelve-year-old daughter, saying, "Why did you do this to our family, Daddy?" Why are you the subject of a lawsuit from a man you have never met?

Why all of this calamity? Because three weeks ago you had sexual intercourse with a woman you had been counseling. You were discovered. The news became public. And now your entire life has collapsed around you.

Welcome to the crisis of clergy sexual misconduct.

DEFINING THE PROBLEM

"Clergy sexual misconduct" is a term used to describe any form of sexual malfeasance, wrongdoing, or misbehavior on the part of a person serving in a recognized ministerial capacity. This term is to be preferred to certain commonly employed alternatives, such as "sexual dalliance," which carries a too playful connotation, "sexual indiscretion," which does not do justice to the seriousness of the offense, and "sexual failure," which sounds like a sexual function problem. "Clergy sexual abuse" is another phrase which appears frequently in the literature to denote any and all forms of clergy sexual misconduct; while I will argue that any sexual malfeasance on the part of a minister certainly is an abuse of the pastoral office, I prefer to restrict the term "clergy sexual abuse" to undeniably exploitative (not to mention illegal) behaviors such as rape and sexual contact with minors.

The very need to make such distinctions reminds us of the sordid fact that clergy sexual misconduct today comes in a variety of forms. Some of these include:

1. *Child sexual abuse*—whether heterosexual or homosexual molestation, the latter, according to recent revelations, a particu-

lar problem among Roman Catholic priests in recent decades.

2. *Coercive sexual contact*—attempted or actual forced sex, one of the offenses of the now infamous "Peter Donovan," the pseudonym for the sexually predatory minister discussed in Marie Fortune's book, *Is Nothing Sacred?*[1]

3. *Sexual harassment*—verbal, visual, or physical contact with a coworker in ministry implying or demanding inappropriate sexual response, especially where this expectation is tied to continued employment or advancement in the workplace.

4. *Consorting with prostitutes*—paying money for promiscuous sexual relations, the alleged offense that rocked the ministry of televangelist Jimmy Swaggart in the early 1990s.

5. *Undue familiarity*—any form of inappropriately intimate verbal, emotional, or physical relationship between a minister and someone other than his or her spouse.[2]

6. *Inappropriate verbal comments*—statements intended to titillate, arouse, or flirt with a member of the same or opposite sex with whom one has contact in ministry.

7. *Inappropriate physical touch short of intercourse*—such as kissing, "full-body" hugs, hair-stroking, genital fondling, and so on.

8. *Sexual intercourse with a person outside of the marriage covenant*—an offense against ministerial ethics whether the minister is single or married (the latter, of course, also constitutes adultery), whether the partner is of the same sex or the opposite sex, and whether the partner is within or outside of the congregation.[3]

The evidence reveals that for the great majority of ministers it is items 5–8 that constitute the greatest threat. Certainly there are a handful of pedophiles, pederasts, rapists, and sexual predators lurking in our churches. Ministers with such disastrous problems need the same kinds of radical intervention that anyone else with such tendencies would need. But for most ministers, it is items 5–8 to which attention must be paid. I intentionally listed them in ascending order of seriousness, because most ministers who find themselves involved in sexual intercourse outside of marriage (item 8) do not *begin* there. They drift into "sexual-boundary violations" in incremental steps, steps that they frequently do not even notice as they are happening.[4] Two studies of ministers conducted in the 1980s found that 12 percent self-reported sexual intercourse with someone other than their spouse during their years in ministry, but that 33–37 percent admitted inappropriate sexual behavior short of intercourse.[5] The 33 percent become the 10 percent if their downward spiral into sexual misconduct is not halted. This chapter is written to help prevent you from joining the 33 percent; or if you are in that number, to help keep you from tumbling into the 10 percent. It is never too late to change course and save your ministry from ruin.

CAUSES OF CLERGY SEXUAL MISCONDUCT

Stanley Grenz and Roy Bell have written, "Clergy sexual misconduct knows no theological or ecclesiastical boundaries. . . . No pastor dare claim that he is immune from temptation merely because of the orthodoxy of his theology or the structure of the church he serves."[6] Grenz and Bell are right, and their comment points us to the right beginning for discussing the causes of this problem.

The root cause of clergy sexual misconduct is the stubborn sinfulness of the human heart, including the heart's resistance to the Spirit's work of sanctification. "Behold, I was brought forth in iniquity, and in sin did my mother conceive me" (Ps. 51:5, RSV). To the veteran Sunday School attender this explanation will come as no surprise. But you might be surprised at how infrequently human depravity is explicitly named in discussions of this crisis. Only the "sin hypothesis," though, ultimately can account for behavior on the part of Christian ministers that is so destructive, so unfaithful and, to put it plainly, so stupid. As I continue to ponder this problem I am drawn back to classic currents of the biblical witness—such as the Genesis account of the Fall, in which Adam and Eve just could not resist the *one* thing God said was forbidden (Gen. 3); Proverbs, with its clear warnings against the slippery slope into sexual seduction and its depiction of the outcome of such sin—death (cf. Prov. 5:1-23); and Ephesians, where Paul declares, "We are not contending against flesh and blood, but against the principalities and powers, against the world rulers of this present darkness, against the spiritual hosts of wickedness in the heavenly places" (6:12, RSV). Clergy sexual misconduct is so insidious in its development and so wretched in its consequences that one rightly sees sinful hearts manipulated by Satan's wiles as the root cause.

In the therapeutic age in which we live, however, we are not content merely to name sin as the cause and leave it at that. No, we want to know about the *psychological dysfunctions* and other hidden causes of inappropriate, unacceptable, and immoral behavior. On balance, this is probably good. Abundant literature now exists which explores the psychological dynamics of the "at risk" minister, one likely to be susceptible to a slide into sexual misconduct.[7] While no single pattern has been identified, several warning signs or "indicators" can be named. I find it helpful to break these indicators down into problems that anyone could have, on the one hand (let's call these Group A), and problems inextricably related to the ministerial role, on the other (Group B).

For Group A, the following list of warning signs/indicators can be adduced:

1. *Deteriorating or neglected marriage relationship.* A chronically or temporarily poor marital relationship can lead to susceptibility to sexual misconduct.

2. *Loneliness.* Persons lacking outlets for meeting their social and emotional needs, especially if they are single or if their marriage relationship is deteriorating, are sometimes vulnerable to sexual misconduct.

3. *Stress.* Abnormal stress and/or poor stress management can leave people weakened and susceptible to immoral behavior.

4. *Attraction to another person.* While most contemporary Christian psychologists and ethicists describe feelings of sexual and/or emotional attraction to persons other than one's spouse as natural and inevitable, such feelings can become problematic if allowed or encouraged to flourish (cf. Matt. 5:27-30), especially if sexual and/or emotional needs are currently unmet.

5. *"Midlife crisis."* This is the everyday term for the severe crisis of values and identity, and shaking of commitments to spouse and family, that occurs so frequently among adults today (in the North American setting, at least).

6. *Psychological dysfunctions.* Ministers whose upbringing was marred by addiction, abuse, divorce, or other unhealthy experiences are afflicted by the same kinds of difficulties others face in similar circumstances. Grenz and Bell point to such problems as fear of intimacy, unrealistic expectations of marriage, addictions, low self-esteem, the need for approval, and the desire to rescue

other needy people as among the consequences of particular family dysfunctions.[8]

7. *Overall lack of moral and spiritual maturity.* Fidelity to one's marriage vows, and to biblical sexual ethics, is not always easy. Many Christians simply lack the spiritual and moral steadfastness to keep these commitments and adhere to biblical norms in this dimension of their life, while others have been seduced by the culture into a questioning of the norms themselves.[9]

It is important to note the social/cultural pressures at work here, as well as the individual and psychological factors. Indeed, they are inevitably related, for all of us swim around in a cultural and social context that profoundly affects our perceived internal psychological attitudes, moods, and feelings. Put plainly, North Americans live today in a cultural setting that creates many of the psychological pressures mentioned and which simultaneously lacks the moral consensus about sexual behavior that would deter people from responding to such pressures through sexual misconduct.

Perhaps of greater interest for our purposes are those causes or indicators of clergy sexual misconduct that are related particularly to the nature of the ministerial role. Our Group B list of these causes could be developed as follows:

1. *Power, trust, and the ministerial role.* Ministers have a subtle but enormous power in that they are frequently perceived as authoritative representatives of God and as mediators of divine truth and healing—even if they would be reluctant to describe themselves in such exalted terms. To an extent, all professionals who are trusted with matters of intimate personal concern by their clients share a similar kind of power, as Peter Rutter has pointed out,[10] but the religious nature of a minister's work adds a uniquely potent and intense dimension to that power. This power is easily abused. Research reveals that it is also easily sexualized, from either the minister's side or that of the counselee, client, or congregant.[11]

2. *Blurring and ignoring of ministerial boundaries.* Wayne Oates and Samuel Southard point particularly to this concern, discussing the ways in which ministers sometimes violate important boundaries of touch (e.g., hugging), time and place (e.g., a "counseling" appointment late in the evening alone in the counselee's home),

initiative (e.g., frequent calls at private times, perhaps intended to be clandestine), gifts, language, and so on.[12] Ministers are alone among helping professionals in generally having permission to *initiate* contact with "clients." This freedom places an enormous concurrent responsibility on the minister to guard his or her boundaries.

3. *Counseling dynamics.* Trained psychologists and pastoral counselors long have been aware of such dynamics as transference and countertransference in the counseling relationship and have been cognizant of the importance of developing and maintaining an appropriately limited intimacy. Local church ministers are generally less well-trained in counseling and are thus more susceptible to the problems these relatively inevitable dynamics can create. In one study, counselees constituted 17 percent of the sexual partners of clergy who admitted sexual misconduct.[13]

4. *Lack of supervision and accountability.* Whereas professional counselors and therapists are required to remain under supervision as long as they continue counseling, ministers—especially in decentralized, local church polity structures—often lack such mechanisms of accountability. Thus they frequently have no one in place to whom they can confide their own feelings of attraction to another or their sense of anxiety about a developing ministerial relationship—and no one to help address such issues with them.[14]

5. *Burnout or desire to leave the ministry.* The widely noted phenomenon of ministerial burnout has now been linked to the problem of clergy sexual misconduct.[15] On the one hand, ministers sometimes drift into affairs because of a search for affirmation and emotional warmth within a brutal or conflicted congregation; on the other, ministers at times behave in an immoral fashion to force a congregation to dismiss them and thus put them out of their (ministerial) misery once and for all.

6. *Group A patterns with a ministerial spin.* Those readers with some ministerial experience will have noticed that our Group A list looks an awful lot like the life of many ministers. A demanding church and a driven pastor quietly conspire to work the minister ninety hours a week, causing the inevitable personal stress and neglect of the marital relationship. The busy pastor may see people all day long but still long for intimacy, especially if home is an unhappy refuge. Finally, the demands of ministry have squelched

the minister's devotional life and hindered his or her walk with God. All of these factors can set the minister up for a clergy "midlife crisis" with disastrous consequences.

PREVENTION: SOME PRACTICAL STEPS

I hope that the discussion thus far has been sufficiently sobering enough to make you eager to turn to a consideration of practical steps that can help prevent clergy sexual misconduct. I will conclude this chapter with several suggestions along these lines, drawn from my own personal practices as well as the literature on the subject.

The first step in prevention is to acknowledge that yes, this *can* happen to you. Because we are all sinful human beings, we are all vulnerable. We must not let pride and a false sense of imperviousness to sin mislead us. Scripture regularly warns us against such spiritual and moral complacency—"If you think you are standing firm, be careful that you don't fall" (1 Cor. 10:12)— and calls us to a vigilant watchfulness when it comes to sin: "Sin is crouching at the door; and its desire is for you, but you must master it" (Gen. 4:7, NASB).

A second element in prevention is attention to one's spiritual and emotional health and well-being. Too many ministers are so busy *doing* that they spend no time thinking and feeling. I am continually amazed at the unreflective way many ministers live their lives. One way to reflect is through the discipline of journaling. I have kept a regular prayer/reflection journal since high school, and I find my journaling time to be of critical importance in restoring my equilibrium and equipping me to meet the demands of my ministry. When I teach classes in Formation for Christian Ministry or Spiritual Formation I always require my students to keep a journal. I have been surprised at how many students find this an entirely new exercise. Remember that clergy sexual misconduct usually results from a drift into boundary-crossing behavior that the minister *does not know is happening at the time*. This egregious lack of self-awareness is much less likely to exist if self-examination is built into the regular rhythms of one's life.

Self-awareness is aided profoundly by involvement in one or more accountability relationships. I have come to believe that every minister needs at least one person of the same sex to whom they can tell *everything* without fear of rejection or other fallout. Today the term "accountability partners" is frequently used to describe the type of relationship I have in mind. The idea is to be engaged in a relationship with a fellow Christian in which together you establish the highest standards of personal moral conduct, commit to living in accordance with those standards, and directly hold one another accountable for doing so. Conversations that occur weekly (ideally) include opportunity for intensive discussion of both partners' fidelity to their commitments, undergirded by prayer for one another. I have found my participation in such a relationship in recent years to be tremendously edifying (and fun). While the term "accountability partners" may be new, this model of mutual accountability is as old as the New Testament (Matt. 18:15-20). It also finds echoes in church history in relationships that developed in monastic life between the novice monk or nun and his or her abbot or abbess. The concept of a "spiritual director" is also related. The model I favor is less hierarchical and more of a peer relationship. However accountability is structured, though, the critical point is that the minister must not try to be a "lone ranger"—a sure recipe for burnout, or worse.

Of course, deepening your self-awareness and developing accountability relationships must be augmented by other forms of what I like to call "self-care."[16] Every living thing that God has made requires some appropriate form of nourishment to survive. Human beings, as the pinnacle of God's creation, have a complex set of "nourishment" needs. We need adequate food, sleep, exercise, and medical care; we need sufficient relational interconnectedness to feed that God-given aspect of ourselves. We need intellectual stimulation, aesthetic pleasure, and emotional support; we need opportunity for celebration and relaxation. Above all, we need a living and vital relationship with our Lord Jesus Christ. Ministers are notorious for neglecting some or all of these aspects of self-care as they labor so intensely in their vocations. The problem is that any living thing that goes without nourishment dies. The term "burnout" nicely communicates the "fried" heart, soul, mind, and body of the minister who fails to care for himself or herself over the long term. I have seen all too many seminarians with early symptoms of burnout. The habit of self-care must begin during the seminary years, or it will probably never begin to take hold in one's life.

A number of practical "rules of thumb" have been suggested for handling relationships with the opposite sex in ministry. Christian writer Jerry Jenkins has argued that any marriage needs "protective hedges" built around it; plant those hedges and one can forestall not only sexual misconduct but even the appearance of impropriety.[17] The same is all the more true when it comes to ministry. The debate in informed evangelical circles today does not concern whether or not such hedges should be planted, but—to continue the metaphor—how far away from the "house" they should be planted and how high they should grow. In other words, the issue is the balance between sealing oneself off from danger, on the one hand, and preserving space for authentic and caring ministry for all God's children, on the other.

For example, some ministers and churches have concluded that it is unwise for male clergy to do any solo counseling with women whatsoever. Those taking this approach have several options for how to proceed—involving qualified pastors' wives in counseling women, adding a female minister to the staff whose job includes handling such situations, bringing in a third person to any counseling done with a member of the opposite sex, training mature Christian women in the church for same-sex counseling (cf. Titus 2:3-5), or simply referring women congregants to counselors outside the church.

Others who have addressed this sensitive counseling issue have concluded that this kind of hedge marks an unhealthy and unnecessary truncation of one's ministry. They propose procedural safeguards that will allow opposite-sex counseling to occur, such as: leaving the office door ajar, closing the door but installing a glass insert to prevent total privacy, making sure that another person is always in the building during counseling (and telling the counselee that this is so), and never doing visitation alone. Evangelist Billy Graham adopted related guidelines early in his ministry, such as never riding in a car with a woman alone, and never eating a meal alone with a member of the opposite sex, including one's secretary.[18] Most experienced ministers seem to have developed some rules of thumb for handling these issues, though these guidelines vary.

CONCLUSION

It is important that you consider seriously the tragedy (and travesty) of clergy sexual misconduct and that you build into your ministry the kinds of "hedges" that will be most likely to help prevent disaster.

But as you do this, please remember that rules alone cannot save you. Our ability to rationalize the violation of rules is part of what it means to be a sinful human being. Write good rules, and keep them. But also build into your life those practices and habits that will keep you spiritually, emotionally, relationally, and morally alive. Above all, lean on Jesus Christ.

"Now may the God of peace himself sanctify you entirely; and may your spirit and soul and body be preserved complete, without blame at the coming of our Lord Jesus Christ" (1 Thes. 5:23, NASB). May it be so, indeed.

N O T E S

1. Marie M. Fortune, *Is Nothing Sacred?* (New York: HarperCollins, 1992).

2. This term is borrowed from Peter Rutter, *Sex in the Forbidden Zone* (New York: Fawcett Crest, 1989), 27.

3. This list is heavily influenced by that of Lloyd Rediger, "Clergy Moral Malfeasance," *Church Management* (May/June 1991): 37–38. Of course, a wide range of other forms of sexual sins could be cited. For another list, see Stanley J. Grenz and Roy D. Bell, *Betrayal of Trust: Sexual Misconduct in the Pastorate* (Downers Grove, Ill.: InterVarsity, 1995), 39.

4. T.G. Gutheil and G.O. Gabbard, "The Concept of Boundaries in Clinical Practice: Theoretical and Real Management Considerations," *The American Journal of Psychiatry* 150, no. 2, 188. Cited in Wayne E. Oates and Samuel Southard, "Understanding and Responding to Clergy Sexual Misconduct," *Journal of Family Ministry* 8, no. 2 (1994): 5.

5. "How Common Is Pastoral Indiscretion?" *Leadership* 9 (Winter 1988): 12–13; Richard A. Blackmon and Archibald D. Hart, "Personal Growth for Clergy," in Richard A. Hunt, et al., eds., *Clergy Assessment and Career Development* (Nashville: Abingdon, 1990), 39.

6. Grenz and Bell, *Betrayal of Trust*, 39.

7. The best single book on this dimension of the problem is Rutter, *Sex in the Forbidden Zone*, cited previously.

8. Grenz and Bell, *Betrayal of Trust*, 47–52.

9. In a similar vein, Oates and Southard argue that *commitment*—to God, one's ordination vows, and one's marriage—is the core ethical issue involved in clergy sexual misconduct. Oates and Southard, "Understanding and Responding to Clergy Sexual Misconduct," 15–16.

10. Consider Rutter's now-famous definition of "sex in the forbidden zone"—"Sexual behavior between a man and a woman who have a professional relationship based on trust, specifically when the man is the woman's doctor, psychotherapist, pastor, lawyer, teacher, or workplace mentor" (*Sex in the Forbidden Zone*, 25).

11. See Fortune, *Is Nothing Sacred?* Grenz and Bell, *Betrayal of Trust*, chap. 4; Karen Lebacqz and Ronald G. Barton, *Sex in the Parish* (Louisville: Westminster/John Knox, 1991), chap. 4.

12. Oates and Southard, "Understanding and Responding to Clergy Sexual Misconduct," 5–6.

13. "How Common Is Pastoral Indiscretion?" 12.

14. See Oates and Southard, "Understanding and Responding to Clergy Sexual Misconduct," 6.

15. Grenz and Bell, *Betrayal of Trust*, 54–55; Oates and Southard, "Understanding and Responding to Clergy Sexual Misconduct," 9–10.

16. For another perspective on what "self-care" can mean see, Ray S. Anderson, *Self-Care: A Theology of Personal Empowerment and Spiritual Healing* (Wheaton, Ill.: Victor/BridgePoint, 1995).

17. Jerry B. Jenkins, *Hedges: Loving Your Marriage Enough to Protect It.* (Brentwood, Tenn.: Wolgemuth & Hyatt, 1989).

18. Cited in Joe E. Trull and James E. Carter, *Ministerial Ethics* (Nashville: Broadman & Holman, 1993), 88.

FOR FURTHER READING

Fortune, Marie M. *Is Nothing Sacred?* New York: HarperCollins, 1992.

Grenz, Stanley J., and Roy D. Bell. *Betrayal of Trust: Sexual Misconduct in the Pastorate*. Downers Grove, Ill.: InterVarsity, 1995.

Jenkins, Jerry B. *Hedges: Loving Your Marriage Enough to Protect It*. Brentwood, Tenn.: Wolgemuth & Hyatt, 1989.

Lebacqz, Karen, and Ronald G. Barton. *Sex in the Parish*. Louisville: Westminster/John Knox, 1991.

Mace, David, and Vera Mace. *What's Happening to Clergy Marriages?* Nashville: Abingdon, 1980.

Oates, Wayne E., and Samuel Southard. "Understanding and Responding to Clergy Sexual Misconduct." *Journal of Family Ministry* 8, no. 2 (1994): 4–19.

Rutter, Peter. *Sex in the Forbidden Zone.* New York: Fawcett Crest, 1989.

Trull, Joe E., and James E. Carter. *Ministerial Ethics.* Nashville: Broadman & Holman, 1993.

PROFESSIONAL
FORMATION
AND TASKS OF
MINISTRY

11

CHURCH MINISTRY LEADERSHIP[1]

WALTER C. JACKSON

Christ is every Christian's Leader,
and you begin ministry by becoming a leader.[2]
EARNEST WHITE

INTRODUCTION

Who among us can define ministry leadership? Most of us can describe it to suit ourselves, but no one has been able to find a working definition satisfactory to all Christians. However, all of us know good leadership when we see it.

Ministry Leadership Patterns
Leadership is at least a functioning quality of a minister's active self. When people gather within a congregation, denomination, or religious institution to follow their minister eagerly, when the people and the institutions grow and develop, and when they accomplish important things for the Lord's work, we proclaim that we see leadership in action. We see ministry leadership when the goals and mission statements of God's people become the ongoing accomplished results of those involved and especially so when the accomplishments are achieved through activities com-

Walter C. Jackson is the former Lawrence and Charlotte Hoover Professor of Ministry at the Southern Baptist Theological Seminary, Louisville, Kentucky.

patible with our biblical faith. And, much to our surprise, when we do see what we recognize as leadership, it consists of different combinations of activities, characteristics, and strategies in different places. Leadership, then, is many different things exercised by different people and in different situations.

A *working definition of ministry leadership* is:

> the ability to inspire and to bring people to faith in Jesus Christ; to enrich and disciple them as whole persons into whatsoever the Lord has commanded, and to lead them to achieve the goals of ministry assigned by Jesus Christ to the church.

Christian ministry leaders are empowered to use every knowable leadership and management strategy ethically appropriate for each particular ministry setting and to rely upon God and discerning Christian wisdom for the strategies to design, equip, empower, and accomplish Christ's desires for His disciples. That mission related to the gospel has a twofold emphasis—the achievement of mission goals on the one hand; and the care, growth, and personal enrichment of the Christians in both leader and follower positions on the other hand.

Secular Leadership Patterns

Scholars of other disciplines such as business, education, law, medicine, engineering, sociology, architecture, and government each have their own carefully worked out theories of leadership. Even there, however, we find different definitions, goals, and descriptive acts called leadership. Part of the confusion is the inability or the unwillingness of the various authors to differentiate clearly between leadership and management, between leadership and supervision, between leadership and productivity. This confusion is also evident in writings about ministry leadership as well. Neither ministers nor any other leadership professionals have the luxury of finding one simple pattern of leadership for all persons or all occasions. So much has to be learned that ongoing and continuous study seems to be the way to become and remain competent in a leadership position.

A general working definition of secular leadership is fairly simple to sketch in general.

Leadership is the capacity to achieve results through interaction (relationships) with others; it is a process in which one person influences others so as to achieve the desired goals while giving careful attention to each separate context.

Secular leadership is largely task-oriented, but in many places it considers benefits for the workers an important part of the leadership task.

LEADERSHIP IS ESSENTIAL FOR MINISTERS

Leadership, in any case, is not optional for a minister. If you are a minister, you are already a leader. Believers look to you, a minister, as if God has already given you the gift of leadership. In whatever way you speak, act, or teach, that will be considered leadership activity by your parishioners. Everything about you, who you are and how you behave, is factored into the way people see you as a leader.

If you wonder whether your leadership abilities are adequate to the test, there is good news for you. Leadership is largely a learned art. You can begin wherever you now are and grow into leadership. The truth of the matter is that God can use every type of person and personality style for successful ministry leadership and, in fact, has called you into the ministry because your own present and future leadership abilities are worthy tools for use in ministry service. Adequate leadership does require a basic level of giftedness. Some leadership placements require different levels of leadership competence and experience, but most of what is necessary for ministry leadership can be learned by everyone.

Your present leadership abilities and your future promise as a leader are important to the work of the Lord. But you do have some choice in the matter. The major choice you have is between (1) whether you will work prayerfully and consciously at the task of learning and growing as a leader or (2) whether you will ignore learning about ministry leadership. Those practicing ministers who choose the second option quickly reach a plateau in ministry effectiveness. Those who have chosen not to grow have mostly stagnated in a place far below their ministry potential. Many of them survive in ministry by surrendering leadership functions to other persons. On the other hand, those who have selected the first option have embarked on a lifetime of study and growth, but report having ever widening opportunities for ministry service.

This chapter is a brief introduction to the subject of ministry leadership. Its goals are at least four in number. The first goal is to encourage you to reflect on your past experiences under the leadership of others. They are among the primary data necessary for your growth and development as a leader. The second goal is to encourage you to reflect upon the characteristics of a leader and especially on your own leadership gifts. You may not have made a list of the leadership characteristics producing excellence, but you will more than likely be pleased to learn that your own thoughts, efforts, and dreams of leadership may well reveal you to possess the raw materials of leadership excellence in abundance. A third goal is to inform you of some introductory sources of leadership theory, learning, and growth in an effort to stimulate you to make ministry leadership a continuing area of prayerful study and growth. Finally, the fourth goal of this chapter is to challenge you to become intentional and disciplined in your task to become an ever improving leader for Christ.

REFLECT ON YOUR LEADERSHIP MEMORIES

All of you have been followers at one time or another. You have memories of good leadership events, and possibly some memories of poor leadership. Some of your leaders have been excellent in many ways, but the same leaders may have been weak if not incompetent in other areas of leadership. Whatever your experiences, your memories provide you with a ready fund of leadership awareness, leadership examples, and leadership challenges.

As you reflect on your own memories of leadership, do you wonder why so many ministry leaders seem to begin well but are soon surrounded with followers who have hard feelings toward each other? Why do the loyalties of their followers harden in some ways that close other people out? Why do the strong members in the group seem to take sides in petty ways, causing divisions between themselves and other followers? Do you have an awareness of these things in general? These behaviors are symptoms of a dysfunctional pattern in a leadership group. Such incompetence gives aid and comfort not to mention delight to the forces of evil who do not wish the kingdom of God to grow and succeed.

Hopefully, your memories are filled with examples of successful and harmonious experiences with leaders who seemed to know the best goals to pursue, the most attractive ways to enable their followers to work together, and when to push for success or to spend more time in preparation before launching out. Take time now to rehearse in your mind or jot down on paper some successful ministry leadership events which you have observed or of which you were/are a part. What caused them to be so excellent? Besides getting the task accomplished, did the Christians involved as followers grow spiritually? Were their personal gifts and personalities nurtured by being part of the group?

Do the same exercise recalling one or more of your poor experiences with ministry leadership. What caused them to be so bad? Why were the failures so pain filled? The answers to these questions along with the testimonies of your experiences will make wonderful "grist" for the conversational mill of your supervisor-led peer discussion.

REFLECT ON LEADERSHIP CHARACTERISTICS

One strong set of contemporary leadership theories insists the secret to successful leadership lies in the personal characteristics or "traits" of the leader. There is wide variety of agreement on which "traits" are to be included as valuable, but the differences largely fall on which "traits" are most important. The following is a basic and representative list. They are possessed by most of us in some measure or other. None can be completely ignored. All, however, are gifts of God able to be exercised with discipline by ministers committed to develop leadership personalities acceptable to God and Christians who seek a ministry leader.

Trust speaks of a leader who enjoys the confidence of the followers. Trust must be earned over time, although some followers "give" trust to a ministry leader from the beginning, only to loose it if the leader gives reason to doubt. A trusted leader is one whose reliability in word and deed is well known to the followers; indeed, it is a mark of pride for them to tell their neighbors that their minister is trustworthy.

Integrity speaks of a leader's loyalty to principle even when disloyalty would bring personal gain. Christian integrity is seen in believers who strive to follow the teachings of the New Testament. A person of integrity does what is honest and truthful because he or she is habitually honest and truthful by internal nature. A leader of integrity is like an Israelite without guile.

Loyalty speaks of a leader who is faithful, especially to Jesus Christ, to friends, and to the causes of the kingdom of God. Durability and unchangeability are principle ingredients in loyalty. The disciples who followed Jesus and who did not leave him, he called his "friends." A loyal Christian friend "sticks closer than one's nearest kin" (Prov. 18:24, NRSVB). The Christian leader will be steadfast and faithful to those enlisted as followers in just such a manner.

Compassion speaks of a leader who is sensitive to the pains, needs, and celebrations of other people. This leader has an internal drive to alleviate suffering or to offer companionship to the celebrating ones. A compassionate Christian is considered to have a heightened ability and willingness to listen to, to care for, and to respond to others in helpful ways.

Courage speaks of a leader who has fortitude and resilience and who possesses mental and/or moral strength to confront trouble, danger, or evil with tenacity and forcefulness. A courageous Christian is one who will steadfastly confront overwhelming challenges to the faith with resolution, although is often seen as stubborn by detractors of the faith.

Strong system of values speaks of a leader who possesses a deep commitment to cherished values deeply within his or her person. A leader with a strong system of Christian values will exercise justice, honesty, truth, righteousness, faith, hope, and love in ways to enhance both the leadership tasks and relationships with those who follow.

Competence speaks of a leader who has achieved a self-conscious use of gifts, talents, skills, and abilities and especially the ability to know much about how to conduct himself or herself as a leader of others. The specific collection of abilities needed for the role or task to which the competent leader has made a covenant to fulfill are functioning at a high degree of proficiency.

Persuasion speaks of a leader able to enlist the eager assistance of others for the task. A Christian leader will be ethically aware to enlist others with appropriate tactics of persuasion, ones that will enrich the followers as well as achieve the accomplishment of goals or tasks.

Intelligence speaks of a leader who possesses an advanced ability to learn, understand, and reason, one who can apply knowledge to a situation in a creative way and transfer knowledge from other fields of learning appropriately so as to solve current although unrelated problems. A Christian leader is not arrogant or boastful of his or her learning, but uses it so as to accomplish the tasks assigned in a most efficient manner.

Imagination speaks of a leader who has the ability to visualize methods to achieve a goal or complete a task which are unavailable to the usual five senses. The Christian leader especially can visualize ways to accomplish personal growth and development, spiritual enrichment, as well as task completion in ways frequently not considered by others. Sometimes the solutions seem "off the wall" to those of us who cannot see what the leader sees, but the resourceful leader has a high degree of imagination reliability.

Memory speaks of a leader who has good recall of the lived-in past and who exerts energy to learn from people with longer memories. The Christian leader who cultivates memory will remember details; recall names, persons, and places with high level accuracy; and will invest time to study available sources to discover the history of the ministry in which he or she is currently involved.

Vision speaks of a leader who can construct a future from the raw material of the present that is useful and motivating to the minds and hearts of the followers. A Christian leader will seek a vision filling full the hopes and dreams of the people, but with a sufficiently practical flair as to make the vision attainable in incremental steps so as to inspire confidence with each successive step along the way.

Physique speaks of a leader who is basically healthy in mind and body; such a person cares for the bodies, minds, and spirits of followers in respectful ways—ways to preserve their energy, vigor, and the ability to function. The way you use your physical selves is an indicator of your ability to make use of assets which might come into your hands as a leader. Dexterity and coordination are important, personal good health, and mental alertness is quite important. The most valuable part of physique management is to do whatever is necessary to become comfortable with the body God gave to you.

Persistence speaks of a leader who is not a quitter. A Christian leader is so convinced of the value of his or her constituency, as well as the goals to which the group has committed itself, that he or she will continuously persevere.

Urgency speaks of a leader who has learned the single leadership characteristic that is so vital for leadership success that only minimal success will be possible without it. The Christian leader with the characteristic of urgency has a vital sense of timing. Schedules are met on time or ahead of time. Goals are designed in sequence and are met in a timely way. When emergencies arise, they are addressed quickly. Decisions to be made today are made today. Neglect is the enemy of leadership. A momentarily forgotten person is, in their own eyes, an abandoned person. A Christian leader will pay attention to a lot of things, but will have a sense of urgency concerning all things.

These are a few of the often mentioned characteristics. There are many more, ones you can list for yourself. As you reflect upon your own leadership characteristics, be assured that Christian followers expect their leaders to possess these and others in a high degree of visibility. Of course, no leader can measure up to such standards 100 percent of the time. When your activities breach one or more of these characteristics, you will do well to seek out the follower(s) affected, to make your apology, and to seek reconciliation. You may well discover grace and forgiveness in the most unlikely places.

An attitude of *willingness to learn about yourself* can be a contagious characteristic that will translate positively to your followers. They may quite well begin to imitate your own *openness to grow and change*. When that happens, both you and your followers will have entered upon an often unspoken covenant toward excellence in the faith, certainly a covenant of excellence in relationship to each other as well as to God.

REFLECT ON SOURCES
OF LEADERSHIP THEORY

A third goal of this chapter is to inform you of some introductory sources of leadership theory, learning, and growth in an effort to stimulate you to make ministry leadership a continuing area of prayerful study and growth.

Old Testament Leadership Indicators

The Old Testament records stories of dramatic leaders whose gifts and methods were useful to the tribes of Israel in their process of becoming a nation. The Hebrew *patriarchs, judges, priests, priestesses, kings, and prophets* each in turn exerted formative leadership on the nation. They left indelible patterns and images as leadership models for subsequent generations. Mostly, people filling these roles were forthright men and women who directed the Hebrew nation through the difficult years of organization and progress. Their authority was derived from a series of "theophanies," or divine appearances, in which the very presence of God was experienced by them. In the exchange, they acknowledged God as their leader. Hebrew leaders accepted certain directives *from* God; and made certain covenants *with* God on behalf of the people.

The stories of these leaders and their historic dealings with God were recorded in an ever growing group of sacred writings. Eventually, the custodians of the Scriptures declared themselves to possess exclusive rights and authoritative interpretations of the sacred writings. They continually promoted themselves as divinely appointed leaders.

Times were often difficult, and leader-types tended to be called forth in reaction to pressing national needs. While the leaders who emerged were in many ways shaped and "bent" in the direction of their times and culture, the Hebrew leaders were apparently evaluated by their contemporaries, as well as their historians, by two major canons: (1) their faithfulness to the nation's covenant with God, and (2) their obedience to a personal code of righteousness consistent with the religious traditions and teachings of the holy writings of Israel.

As with many aspects of Hebrew theology, positive success of leadership outcomes was taken to reflect the blessings of God.

Lack of success in leadership outcomes was taken to reflect the punishments of God. Successful leaders were followed; unsuccessful leaders were abandoned. The criteria of judgment of outcome success, however, was often indistinguishable from secular canons of judgment.

A religious assessment of Old Testament Hebrew ministry looks carefully at each leader's intent to guide the nation in the direction of its task to represent and do the work of God as His "chosen people." From the nation's earliest beginnings, Israel and its ministers, whatever they were called, were to be "people chosen and called into the service of a larger purpose than the achievement of their (own) highest well being. . . . Part of Israel's ministry to God is to articulate, in words and actions, the intention of God for everything that is."[3] Israel is to do this in the context of a covenant relationship which God offers to Israel and its leaders; and, through them to the human race. "God's style of relating," however, "is marked by covenant love, covenant justice, covenant truth, covenant 'delight in the other.'"[4]

In brief, the leaders of the nation were to keep their part of the covenant by being the messenger servants of God. They were to proclaim Yahweh to be the powerful, caring creator God of all that is; of their nation, to be sure, but to all families of heaven and earth.

In the process of the history of Israel, however, its leaders and citizens became increasingly self-centered. They became embroiled in the tasks of self-definition, self-preservation, and self-perpetuation. Like other nations, they established themselves as temporal lords with kings, national bour.daries, taxes, armies, and the trappings of a people whose self-vision as a servant people to all humankind was submerged, unable to be fulfilled as an historical reality. The promise of Israel's leadership role as servant messenger of God was relegated to a future, messianic era, a prophetic hope kept alive in the hearts of devout believers but only as "lip service" in the goal planning sessions of its prominent leaders.

New Testament Leadership Indicators

Jesus is every Christian's leader.[5] The gospels present him as the final, full revelation of God. "I am in the Father and the Father in me" (John 14:10, RSV). "I and the Father are one" (John 10:30). "I am the way, and the truth, and the life; no man comes to the Father, but by me" (John 14:6, RSV).

Yet, with such overwhelming leadership credentials, Jesus insisted he had come as servant, not as overlord. "The Son of Man came not to be served but to serve" (Matt. 20:28, RSV). Jesus is portrayed as servant many times in the gospel narratives, but with exceptional clarity in the John 13:1-20 account of his washing the feet of his disciples. In Luke 22:25-27 Jesus clearly addressed the pattern of leadership his disciples were to follow as well as the pattern they were to avoid.

> The kings of the Gentiles exercise lordship over them; and those in authority over them are called benefactors. But not so with you; rather let the greatest among you become as the youngest, and the leader as one who serves. For which is the greater, one who sits at table, or one who serves? Is it not the one who sits at table? But I am among you as one who serves.

The servant motif as a leadership style was certainly portrayed clearly in the New Testament.

But that was not the only leadership style exhibited by Jesus as reflected in the gospels. Jesus also was decisive in giving directive commands. He commanded demons to depart from those whom they tormented, he ordered a tax collector down from his perch in a tree, commanded a rich man to sell all his goods and give to the poor, he declared the sins of others to be forgiven, and he healed many who suffered from a variety of diseases. In addition, he commanded boisterous winds and waves to be still, he scolded the Apostle Peter for patronizing him, yet gently chided Judas for betraying him with a kiss. In his most celebrated act of violence, he energetically attacked the temple priest-merchants who had, in Jesus' phrase, turned "my Father's house into a market" (John 2:13-16).

Jesus' most outstanding act of leadership, however, was in his death on the cross. The purpose of the gift of his life was, in part, to take the lead to communicate God's message to all humanity; to decree with unmistaken eloquence the extreme limits to which God has gone to bear responsibility for the sins of us all. And, in the same set of writings, the evangelists remind us of Jesus' message, "If anyone will come after me, let him deny himself and take up his cross, and follow me" (Matt. 16:24, RSV).

The message of Jesus about leadership is clearly able to be discerned, but enormously difficult to imitate. One is to serve God by being a servant leader among people; a communicator for God to all who are available to listen. And, as the Apostle Paul may be interpreted to say in his letters, Christian ministry leadership "can only be validated as such when it is devoted to the service of God, and the eventuation of the gospel of God, understood as the 'word of the cross,' in the world. Such a ministry is not to be judged by how much it 'achieves,' but by how well it serves to monitor and maintain faith's vital signs in the body of Christ."[6]

As in the days of his earthly ministry, the leadership challenge of Jesus continues to be the simple command, "Follow me," or, more simply, "Come." The greatest temptation for Christians in leadership positions throughout the centuries has been to replace Jesus and to be self-serving rather than representing him at every opportunity. The temptation to portray yourself in tones of greatness just because you happen to be a minister of the gospel of Jesus Christ is one of the most constant temptations of Christian ministry leadership in the latter part of the twentieth century.

Contemporary Leadership Indicators

Contemporary Christian ministry leaders are faced with a situation nearly unprecedented in the history of the faith. Rapid broad-coverage audio and audiovisual communication mated with highly developed public relations skills have made possible the development of religious leadership "personalities" for immense audiences. Latent dependent desires in human hearts have proven to be tractable to Christian leadership images. Large followings of devotees bestow popularity, wealth, and political influence—both religious and secular—upon leaders with the "correct" image projections. To cast one's ministry in a way to capitalize upon this kind of preference is a large temptation for ministers today.

Power, youthfulness, and certitude are characteristics of preference in Western civilization. Weakness is frightening, aging is terrifying, and uncertainty is unacceptable. Leaders promising to dispose of fear and terror, reduce uncertainty, and project stability in the name of religion are leaders of preference. Religious "super-leader" personalities are able to be developed, are successful when measured by the standards of the culture, and remain a temptation as a ministry image of choice by increasing numbers of ministers.

Servant leadership, as portrayed in the gospels, is difficult to maintain in a climate where increasingly larger segments of the Christian population prefer "super-leader" styles. This is especially true where employment decisions are made by persons demanding such "super-leader" styles—even in ministry situations incompatible with such a style. The contrast becomes even more evident when "servant-leader" styles ignore and even avoid the more gospel-compatible dimensions of the "super-leader" style.

In the present climate, it is important for ministry students to learn as much as possible about the theories, styles, and strategies of leadership in courses designed for such a study. However, it is worthwhile to consider a few of the following foundational or elemental principles of leadership. They are included here as a tip of the iceberg sample of much there is to be learned.

Leadership Posture

The first such elemental principle relates to leadership posture. From what position does the minister lead? Does the leader lead routinely from an awareness of strength and power? When you lead from strength exclusively, you lead from the position that you know everything there is to know, that you know every method applicable to every situation and, what is more important, that you know which is the best method to select at every time and place in which you hold leadership. When you lead from strength, the people are required merely to follow your will. If you lead in this fashion, you posture yourself as an invulnerable person leading the vulnerable ones.

On the other hand, do you lead from an awareness that you too participate in the weakness of the human race? Do you have the ability to offer your gifts and talents for leadership in a way that includes the gifts and talents of other Christians? Can you use your energies to bring about a consensus—through some spiritual methodology—so you include the congregation in the ministry? Are you willing to risk vulnerability as you lead—to lead from a sense of weakness and not a sense of power? If so, you lead as a human among humans with a special commission from God to lead.

Leader's Perception of Followers

A second elemental principle is the perception on the part of the leaders of those who follow. In the middle 1960s, Douglas McGregor advanced his well known "Theory X and Theory Y" understanding concerning motivation and leadership.[7] His theory X leaders defined followers as those who evade exertion and work, persons preferring to avoid responsibility, who possess little individual ambition, and who desire security as their first priority. In order for theory X leaders to move persons toward achievement of goals, they believe followers must be directed, controlled, coerced, and threatened with punishment. Otherwise, they believe, no gain will be accomplished. His theory Y leaders believe work to be a normal human endeavor—as natural as play and rest. When committed to an objective, people demonstrate self-direction, even self-sacrifice. The level of commitment usually determines the level of energy available for the task. McGregor reports theory Y leaders to believe that, under certain conditions, humans even seek responsibility. Leaders do not have to produce all of the insights for leadership. Actually, followers may demonstrate a wide variety of creative, imaginative, and ingenious ideas worthy for inclusion in a leadership plan. Theory Y leaders believe only a small portion of any person's potential energy and leadership abilities are activated and used. True leadership includes the art of using increasing portions of the underutilized potential possessed by followers.[8]

A leader with perception X as a guiding understanding would be free to exert external pressure on his or her followers without restraint, all the while believing the cause of ministry leadership was being well served. A leader with perception Y would sense the need to develop leadership skills in his or her followers, giving them a firm basis upon which to anchor their various commitments. Constant growth in discipleship and increasingly more refined tools for followers to make Christlike decisions would be the concern of this type of leader.

Leader's Perception of Goals

Another elemental principle of leadership relates to the overall goal of leadership. Is leadership best used to produce a product, service, or a program? Or is leadership best used to nurture and develop the persons involved in the endeavor under the leader's tutelage? Maybe some combination of these two elements would make a better goal for ministry leadership?

Another model called the Management-Grid was developed by Robert Blake and Jane Mouton. In their model, they identify five major leadership styles.[9] Their work uses the strength of leader preferences to favor "production" or "persons" as the measure of a leader. They use a scale of one to nine to calibrate preferences. A 1–9 leader (low on production, high on people) is considered a "Country Club Leader." Such a leader favors caring for people's needs well in advance of dealing with achieving goals or being productive. A 9–1 leader (high on production, low on people) is considered a "Productive Pusher." Such a leader favors turning out the work and meeting production quotas with little attention to the persons involved as followers. A 1–1 leader (low on people and production) is considered a "Do-Nothing Leader." Such a person functions with a laissez-faire game plan giving attention only to the most necessary items of leadership—and then in a reactionary fashion. A 5–5 leader (medium high on both persons and production) is considered an "Organizational Man." Such a person does not want to offend the people, nor to offend the managers of production. This leader wants to be scrupulously fair in all things. A 9–9 leader (high in both areas of production and persons) is considered a "Team Builder." Such a person is highly motivated to care for persons, but is equally dedicated to achieve the goals and be efficient in productivity.

Brooks Faulkner has translated this grid into a pastoral leadership assessment tool labeling the 1–9 as the "Country Club Pastor," the 1–1 as the "Impoverished Pastor," the 5–5 as the "Middle of the Road Pastor," the 9–1 as the "Task Master Pastor," and the 9–9 as the "Equipping Pastor." He includes a brief questionnaire in his book *Getting on Top of Your Work* in order that you may test yourselves on leadership style in relation to your higher preference for production or for persons as you lead.[10]

In a similar fashion, Ernest White has diagrammed a "Christian

Leadership Grid" on a twelve point scale using "Servanthood" and "Authority" as his dual polarities.[11] His five styles are the "divine authoritarian leader" (12/1), the "submissive-servant leader" (1/12), the "passive paralytic leader" (1/1), the "people-pleaser leader" (6/6), and the "body leader" (12/12). His discussion is quite relevant for the development of your personal idea of leadership style for ministry.

Leadership Based on Congregational Needs

Robert Dale has taken a different approach. By placing emphasis upon the mission of a congregation or group of Christians, Dale has developed a congregational leadership model which seeks to emphasize the needs of the membership. Your leadership style as a minister is to be evaluated first, in terms of your active or passive methods and second, in terms of your positive or negative involvement. An additional measurement device is to gauge the leader's "emphasis on membership needs" in comparison with "emphasizing congregational mission."[12] In Dale's conceptualization, there are an unlimited number of leadership options within his format, but "four mainstream possibilities" serve as examples: The *catalyst* leader is active/positive with a good balance at the point of integrating "mission and morale." Catalysts are active, flexible, and durable (long-range). The *commander* leads with an active/negative style which communicates clearly the expectation that the follower follow the leader exactly; commanders are often negative and autocratic. The *encourager* leads with a passive/positive style emphasizing personal relationships rather than the mission. And the hermit is a passive/negative leader who is uncomfortable with both relationships and productivity; hermits frequently withdraw from others allowing lay leaders or other self-starters to take initiative. The hermit leader herself/himself becomes most exclusively vulnerable if the organization stagnates around the ministry leader's inactivity.[13]

Leadership Covenant

A final elementary leadership principle relates to the covenant between the people and the minister-leader. Perhaps the most interesting pair of judgment tools related to ministry leadership was originated by polarizing the terms *transactional* and *transfor-*

mational.[14] This set of characteristic leadership patterns is based on (1) a transaction as an exchange between leader and people in which value is exchanged from both sides, but no essential changes are made in either the leader or the followers; and (2) a transformational leader style as aiming to transform the followers (and the leader) in the direction of increased Christian values, meaning, and actions—to a higher level of human conduct, action, and thought.[15]

Can you as a minister of the gospel establish a purely transactional covenant with a congregation and remain true to your calling? Can you establish a purely transformational covenant with a congregation and still be in touch with the humanity of its membership? And how, if at all, can you blend both elements into a covenant able to honor your call to ministry and your call to care for these people? The matter of greatest importance is that you become quite clear *before* you pledge to begin a ministry which type of covenant your followers believe they have made with you. Many churches will tell you they want to change and grow. However, when the new converts begin to swell the membership you discover them to be telling you that you have brought in the "wrong kind of people" or "too many people" in order to mask the pain they feel at having to change. Be sure to look for the hidden as well as the visible covenants your people make with you as you surrender to their particular call for ministry leadership.

Reflect on Becoming a Disciplined Ministry Leader

When I was in transition between grammar school and junior high school, I remember a particular terror-filled summer. How could I survive in that place of advanced learning? What must an ex-sixth grader do in a crowd of seventh, eighth, and ninth grade giants?

About mid-August, a neighbor friend who was making his transition from the junior high school I would attend to the city high school the same fall told me a secret. I received his message as a wonderful gift from God. He told me something like:

> The only difference between people is how much you know and how much you can do. Those who know the most and who do the most are always among the best.

I took heart, and much of the terror gave way to determination. I was a new Christian, had been baptized only the previous March, and already I had found a desperate need for the Lord. I would trust God to walk with me into this threatening new society with faith and would work to develop every gift, talent, blessing, and skill God had given me. I pledged to know as much as I could learn, and to do the most I could do, and all the while to trust the Holy Spirit to guide me and bless me.

The only difference between you and other leaders, especially in the secular workplace, is your calling in Christ, *and* how much you know and how much you can do. God leads, uses, and loves us all, but only you can decide how much you will know and how much you will learn to do as a leader.

Begin with a commitment to become a more competent leader for Christ every day. Observe a leader. What happens to the people led? What seems to be the *discipleship value* for them? Observe the leader's stated mission. Is the preparation, follow-through, and evaluation visible? What seems to be the result in terms of disciple growth or task achievement? Return to the Bible and read its pages with a desire to learn from the leadership strategies of the people God used in their day. Make a list of leadership awareness derived from the great characters in Scripture. Observation and reflection on the Bible improves even the best leader.

What leadership characteristics are visible as the leaders you observe go about each leadership action? You can begin your observations and draw your conclusions by observations in your local church, in your educational institution at large, in your classrooms, and in student-led activities. Any place where leadership is exerted, pay attention to it. Keep a learning log about it, and do not neglect to study yourself as leader. This last item is really the most important. The leadership characteristics listed in this chapter are only introductory. What are the others—especially the deeply spiritual ones—you can discover in the Bible, in your studies of seminary courses such as church history, evangelism, history of missions, church and community, pastoral care, theology, and others? Make a list of those characteristics that come most naturally for you, and give thanks to God for them. What are the characteristics most difficult for you? What must you do to practice them so diligently that they are more easily a part of what you do in ministry leadership? Remember, practice with reflection improves even the best leader.

Be sure to enroll in classes or seminars on leadership theory, administration, management, and supervision as they are available. Anything you can learn in these areas will provide you with leadership competence. Because everything does not proceed smoothly in most churches, it is important to discover and practice the patterns of conflict management, small group process leadership, responding to difficult persons in the church, and grief theory related to institutional failure or less than expected outcomes as well as on occasions of death and bereavement ministry. Systems theories, change theories, transition stage theories, theories of functional and dysfunctional groups, and some knowledge about personality health and/or dysfunction are data bases advanced Christian leaders need to have in their awareness. Apply what you have learned in your ministry opportunities. Practice and reflection improves even the best leader.

Observe covenants. Most or all of their parts can be divided into transactional and transformational categories. Be faithful to the covenants you have made, or be sure to renegotiate if you wish or intend to change any features of the covenant. Two-way covenants are superior to one-way covenants. Strive for mutuality and openness in covenants. Remember, practice improves even the best leader.

Make a fearless inventory of your own leadership history. When did you lead? How did you lead? What would you do differently and/or better than at that time? Accept leadership opportunities as they come. Accept only the ones you have time to accomplish. Remember you have only one time to make a first impression; only one time to initiate leadership with new people, in a new place. Reflect on what you did. Evaluate yourself. Meditate and pray about those events, and start a habit of personal meditation and prayer for each act of leadership you will ever perform. Make your leadership activity an offering of worship and service to God. As a minister, that's what it is whether you acknowledge it or not.

What did you do well? Plan to do those things again. What did you neglect? Plan not to forget those kinds of things again. What errors or blunders did you make? Make amends. Plan not to make those errors again. Also, allow yourself to feel the blessing of a request for a repeat performance; accept the invitation and do an even better job the next time. Invite a friend to give you an honest critique to check out your own impressions. Where possible, have a trusted, mature minister become your mentor. You can really establish your own leadership curriculum, learn how to do more things, and do more things better.

Decide whether your current leadership projects require 9/9 or 5/5 leadership strategies. Be intentional about the way you lead. Remember, practice improves even the best leader.

Decide whether your leadership attitudes match the X or Y theory of leadership. Which style does your leadership practice reflect? Which is your goal for your own preferred or dominant style? Again, practice moves toward perfection.

> The only difference between people is how much you know and how much you can do. Those who know the most and who do the most are always among the best.

But that is so much to learn, you say. Not much if you only have to learn one thing a day. Even to learn 300 things a year, one each day with 65 days off, would be a massive gain.

Do you think God has called you to any task that is easy?

N O T E S

1. Gratitude is expressed here for permission granted by the editorial board of the *Review & Expositor* for the liberal use of materials included in this chapter previously published under the title, "The Minister As Leader" in *Formation for Christian Ministry*, ed. Anne Davis and Wade Rowatt, Jr.

2. Ernest O. White, *Becoming a Christian Leader* (Nashville: Convention, 1985), 5.

3. James A. Wharton, "Theology and Ministry in the Hebrew Scriptures," in *A Biblical Basis for Ministry*, ed. Earl E. Shelp and Ronald Sunderland (Philadelphia: Westminster, 1981), 44.

4. Ibid., 53.

5. White, *Becoming*, 5.

6. Victor Paul Furnish, "Theology and Ministry in the Pauline Letters," in *A Biblical Basis for Ministry*, ed. Earl E. Shelp and Ronald Sunderland (Philadelphia: Westminster, 1981).

7. Douglas McGregor, *Leadership and Motivation* (Cambridge, Mass.: M.I.T. Press, 1966), 9–10.

8. Ibid., 14–20.

9. McGregor, *Leadership*, 15–20; Brooks Faulkner, *Getting on Top of Your Work* (Nashville: Broadman, 1973), 43–45.

10. Faulkner, *Getting*, 140–44.

11. White, *Becoming*, 29–34.

12. Robert D. Dale, *Ministers as Leaders* (Nashville: Broadman, 1984), 15–27.

13. Ibid.

14. Speed B. Leas, *Leadership in Conflict* (Nashville: Abingdon, 1982), 27–37.

15. Ibid.

F O R   F U R T H E R   R E A D I N G

Bennis, Warren. *Why Leaders Can't Lead*. San Francisco: Jossey-Bass, 1989.

Biersdorf, John. *Creating an Intentional Ministry*. Nashville: Abingdon, 1976.

Clinton, J. Robert. *The Making of a Leader*. Colorado Springs: NavPress, 1988.

Dale, Robert D. *Ministers as Leaders*. Nashville: Broadman, 1984.

————. *Pastoral Leadership*. Nashville: Abingdon, 1986.

Finzel, Hans. *The Top Ten Mistakes Leaders Make*. Wheaton, Ill.: Victor, 1994.

Leas, Speed B. *Leadership and Conflict*. Nashville: Abingdon, 1982.

Oates, Wayne E. *The Christian Pastor*. 3d ed, rev. Philadelphia: Westminster, 1984.

Shelp, Earl E., and Ronald H. Sunderland, eds. *The Pastor as Servant*. New York: Pilgrim, 1986.

————, eds. *A Biblical Basis for Ministry*. (Philadelphia: Westminster, 1981.

Stacker, Joe R., and Bruce Grubbs. Authors and Compilers. *Shared Ministry*. Nashville: Convention, 1985.

White, Ernest O. *Becoming a Christian Leader*. Nashville: Broadman, 1985.

12

WORSHIP LEADERSHIP

CRAIG A. LOSCALZO
AND
LLOYD L. MIMS III

When a scribe asked Jesus which commandment was the most important, Jesus replied, "The first is, 'Hear, O Israel; the Lord our God, the Lord is one; you shall love the Lord your God with all your heart, and with all your soul, and with all your mind, and with all your strength.' The second is this, 'You shall love your neighbor as yourself.' There is no other commandment greater than these" (Mark 12:28-31, NRSVB). Citing the *shema* passage from Deuteronomy 6:4, he insisted that the first commandment was to love God with one's whole being—heart, soul, mind, and strength. From its context in Deuteronomy, however, this commandment is not merely a call for personal piety. Herein lies the clarion call to God's people, Israel, to worship. At the heart of their corporate understanding existed the driving compulsion to love God first.

Above all else, worshiping God remains the central and quin-

Craig A. Loscalzo is Pastor of Immanuel Baptist Church in Lexington, Kentucky, and **Lloyd L. Mims III** is the Dean of the School of Church Music and Professor of Church Music at the Southern Baptist Theological Seminary, Louisville, Kentucky.

tessential task of the people of God. Ultimately, the motivation to love God with all our heart, soul, mind, and strength should be the force that drives us to corporate worship. No other task of the church exceeds the importance of worship. However, one of the most confusing aspects of corporate gathering among evangelicals has been the equating of evangelism with worship. Both ministries are important in God's work, yet they are not the same. Baptists were a driving force in the evangelistic meetings that spread across this continent in the last two centuries. Camp meetings, brush arbor revivals, and protracted meetings brought a large number of people into the kingdom. When the revival ended and people built houses of worship, they continued to worship in the manner of those evangelistic meetings, attempting to re-create their fervor and spirit. Unfortunately, they seldom learned the true discipline of corporate worship to help them grow beyond the infancy of their salvation experience. At their best, the contemporary forms of worship that have arisen in recent years have helped move many churches from formal evangelistic meetings to Spirit-led worship. In a discussion about worship leadership, remember this key factor: above evangelism, before caring ministries, ahead of missions, in front of church growth, comes the church at worship.

GOD AS THE FOCUS OF WORSHIP

The worship of God demonstrates the most important characteristic of God's creatures. Scripture tells us the heavens declare the greatness of God and reveal God's handiwork day by day. All creation proclaims the supreme value and worth of almighty God: the trees praise God with their beauty and grandeur; the animal kingdom praises God through beauty and coordination. Scripture reminds us that even the rocks would cry out the greatness of God. Humans, however, having experienced the Eden of God and the fall of humanity, have a choice in worshiping God—a choice of worship or neglect. Those of us who have allowed God's grace to reconcile us to a state of communion with God have the supreme opportunity of worshiping God with a doubly grateful heart—grateful for creation and grateful for salvation.

God is the focus of our worship. Did you expect to read anything different in a chapter on "Worship Leadership"? A minister preaching a children's sermon described an object and asked the children to guess what it was: "It's small and furry, and has a bushy tail. It climbs trees. In the fall it collects nuts and stores them for the winter months." At this point in the description, a child raised her hand and quipped, "I know the answer's Jesus, but it sure sounds like a squirrel to me!" In a chapter on worship, we just know the answer is *God* without giving the matter a second thought. Yet, one wonders if God really is the one to whom we offer our deepest commitment when we gather under the banner of worship.

Is the repetition of announcements—clearly printed in a bulletin—worship? Is worship the promotion of a church program or a denominational offering? Is the sermon a part of worship? What about clapping following the choir's rendition of "How Great Thou Art"? Is applause part of the worship of God or merely cheerleading the choir? Such practical questions prod the heart of a sound theology of worship.

The term *worship* comes from the Anglo-Saxon *weorthscipe*, meaning to assign ultimate value. Hence, worship is the ascribing of ultimate worth to God. When we talk of worship, we presume God to be the recipient of our praise and adoration. All that we do and say when a congregation gathers should be done and said in remembrance that we have gathered to offer our best selves to God. One definition of faith says, "Faith is giving all that I know and understand about myself to all that I know and understand about God." Shifting the saying slightly, could we say worship *is giving all that we know and understand about ourselves to all that we know and understand about God?*

A model of worship, often attributed to the Danish philosopher Søren Kierkegaard, sees the congregation as the actors, the worship leaders as prompters, and God as the audience.[1] This model suggests that we prepare corporate worship with God as the one who will receive our worship. All that we say and do comes together as a living offering to God (see Rom. 12:1-2).

The purpose of worship is not to please or entertain a congregation. When a congregation's wishes and whims dictate the hows and whys of worship, it is time to reevaluate our worship practices. Please do not hear us suggesting that the congregation's concerns about worship are not important. In fact, the opposite is true; we believe the congregation is a vital part of worship, but as *participants in*, not *recipients of*, worship.

CORPORATE WORSHIP IS PARTICIPATORY

When people gather for corporate worship, are they an *audience* or a *congregation?* In colloquial expression an audience is a group of listeners or spectators. We think of an audience watching a film or a play, or listening to a symphony. But in most cases we do not expect an audience to take an interactive part in what they view or hear, certainly not to the extent of helping create the event. Since the name we give to something sets the tone for how we view and understand it, we prefer to call the gathered people at worship a congregation. These people are not an unrelated group of persons attending a civic event as an "audience"; they represent an assembly of believers, related as brothers and sisters in Christ. Through their heritage in Christ, they meet together to recall their common experiences—joys and sorrows, successes and failures—and to celebrate their partnership in the gospel with Christ. No mere audience claims such linkage. This *koinōnia* emerges as people gather and become a *congregation.*

Worship demands participation on the part of all worshipers. Too many worship services revolve around the worship leaders. The ministers read all the Scripture lessons, recite all the prayers, and voice all the concerns. In some cases, worship services become another form of entertainment—sanctified with Jesus language—but entertainment nonetheless. No wonder many people sitting in the pews feel like an audience; they have no expectations placed on them to participate. Hence, people leave the church on Sunday evaluating the performance of the preacher and musicians. Have we created Sunday morning Siskels and Eberts, acting more like critics of a film than participants in a worship event? The question Christians should ask following worship should not be directed at the preaching or the musicians. There is one critical question: *God, was my worship pleasing to you today?*

Again referring to Kierkegaard's model, we can say that the worship leaders prompt the congregation, who become active in worship. At this point, Fred Craddock's contemporary definition of worship is extremely helpful: to worship is "to narrate in word, act, and song the community's memories and hopes, glorifying the God who redeems, enables, and sanctifies."[2] In this definition, the congregation constitutes the narrators, who glorify God through word, act, and song. Such is the end of our worship.

What are some practical ways participation can be accomplished? The gift of music is an integral part of corporate worship, enabling and enhancing all of the elements of the service. Music is produced by congregational singing, choirs, soloists, ensembles of various sizes, and instrumentalists. It is used in virtually every portion of the service to enhance and underscore the spoken words of worship. In admonishing the Corinthian church about the use of tongues, Paul also gives valuable insight into the use of music in worship: "I will sing with my spirit, but I will also sing with my mind" (1 Cor. 14:15). Music in worship should be uplifting, inspiring, and even filled with emotion at times. Yet it must also be filled with cognitive images that expand our understanding of who God is and what work he has for us in the kingdom. There must be a balance between emotion and cognition when we use music in worship.

Congregational singing remains a common form of participation in worship services. Yet as worship leaders we should not presume that the congregation knows they worship God when they sing. Help them to see explicitly that their singing is an offering to God. When they sing the great hymns of faith, make sure you draw their attention to the richness of the lyrics and the texture of the melody. When they sing choruses of praise, make sure you help them see and hear that their voices offer worship. Help them experience faith through their singing.

The human voice is undoubtedly the best instrument of praise God gave us. We can use it to join in singing the hymns of our faith, the moving gospel songs of our tradition, the energizing praise and worship choruses of contemporary worship, or the simple songs of quiet devotion. When we unite our voices with those of like mind and heart—a congregation—the praise of God seems to increase exponentially. Nothing can match the great singing of a large body of people in an acoustically resonant room praising God in congregational song.

For lack of a better term, we tend to classify music sung by a select part of the congregation as "special music." Frequently a choir presents such music, but it is quite common for a soloist to sing this as well; even a small group or a vocal ensemble may fulfill this function. Different worship styles elicit different types of special music. Liturgical and traditional services frequently utilize sacred choral works or vocal solos of composers throughout history; contemporary services usually use music written within the last five to ten years. One of the complications facing the use of music in the church lies in the confusion of Christian worship with Christian entertainment. The Christian entertainment field has produced a large number of artists who provide wonderful diversions for believers who seek alternatives to the world's pleasures. Although Christian entertainers usually work hard to give God the glory in their presentations, going to a concert or listening to a recording is not the same as participating in corporate worship. Too often, well-meaning church soloists try to re-create a musical setting by a Christian entertainer only to spend more effort mimicking the entertainer than using his or her gifts to praise God. This is not to say that the Holy Spirit does not intercede when we lead in worship, but it does mean that we must be careful to offer our best gifts to God when we offer corporate worship leadership.

Instrumentalists also have a gift to give in worship. Not only do they effectively accompany the human voice but they also provide music to inspire us to worship. Frequently, what they play helps us call to mind words that form our praise; sometimes their playing helps us to focus our emotions and our spirits more than our minds. Instrumentalists spend countless hours in their preparation to share in worship; too often we take them for granted.

The praise of God is an important element in corporate worship. It usually prepares us for all the other elements of worship that follow. Usually one or more worship leaders are visible to engage the congregation in this important act. This may be a minister of music, the organist, the pastor, or some other person. Whoever leads this part of worship needs to be dynamic, gifted with an engaging personality, authentic and not artificial. The right words must be said, yet too many words defeat the purpose of the element of praise to follow. The visage of the leader must be pleasant and inviting. In some circumstances, the leader may lead without physical movement, using only facial encouragement and vocal strength.

Public prayers are an important part of corporate worship. We use prayers for various elements of the service. At the beginning we prepare for worship in private meditation. We extend prayers of praise for God's presence to surround us and uplift our worship. We confess our sins and ask for forgiveness. We offer our gratitude for God's blessings and dedicate our gifts to God's service. We pray for the sick and bereaved, and we pray for the lost people in our midst. One of the parts of worship we often call a prayer is the benediction; however, the benediction is actually a blessing given by the minister on the people for service, not a prayer to God. When we pray in a personal way (as Jesus taught, "in our closets") we use the pronoun "I." However, in corporate worship, when we are praying on behalf of all God's people, it is important to use the pronouns "we" and "us." Such usage enables all listeners to become more actively involved in the prayer time rather than merely listening to someone else pray.

Printed prayers or confessions of faith that a congregation reads in unison provide excellent resources for participation. Responsive readings and Scripture readings presented by a variety of church members—including children and senior adults—offer the congregation visible participation in the worship event. When it is appropriate, ask members of the congregation to share their testimonies; not merely what God has done for them in the past but how God is moving in their lives now. Also, do not be afraid of silence as a group's response to the awesome presence of God in worship.

Evangelicals have always prided themselves on being a "people of the Book." One of the important aspects of worship is the public reading of Scripture. Many churches follow a lectionary to assist with the systematic public reading of the entire Bible in corporate worship over a three-year period. In such churches an Old Testament lesson and a New Testament lesson are read each week; usually the sermon of the day is based on one (if not both) of these passages. It is unfortunate when the public reading of Scripture is relegated to a single proof text for a sermon. Hearing God's Word in its fullest form is an important aspect of corporate worship. Some churches have begun the practice of dramatized presentation of Scripture where stories are told as conversations and poetry is heard with emphasis. A recent publication of the *Dramatized New Testament*[3] assists in the presentation of Scripture in this manner. (For more help in the matter of worship planning resources, see the suggestions for further reading at the end of this chapter.)

WORSHIP NURTURES THE CHURCH

When a worship service ends, the key question should be, *Have we, corporately and individually, encountered God?* The church in worship finds itself uplifted, empowered, motivated to love one another, and prompted to love the world because it has met and honored her Lord. When a congregation humbly meets God—in prayer, adoration, and submission—they are changed. Having met God, we can no longer view injustice with a fleeting glance. Having met God, we begin to live now in terms of a kingdom ethic. Having met God, our church agenda is shifted from inside to outside. Like a cool drink after a long walk, worship quenches the thirst of the church that truly worships God. Jesus said, "You shall love the Lord your God with all your heart, and with all your soul, and with all your mind, and with all your strength" (Mark 12:30, NRSVB). Nothing else can so transform the church, nurture its ministries, and revitalize its fellowship as the encounter God makes available to us through worship.

As a result of worship, the church finds itself empowered to move beyond its walls, finding its neighbors and loving them. That, after all, was Jesus' second word: "You shall love your neighbor as yourself" (Mark 12:31, NRSVB). Yes, the worship of God prepares the church to meet the world.

DIVERSITY OF WORSHIP DIALECTS

The manner or style of worship is a matter of personal choice, often shaped by corporate traditions. Some persons feel they can best worship God through a life of monasticism; others attempt to worship primarily through works and good deeds. Evangelical Christians, however, have always believed strongly in the importance of corporate worship, and they have fought governments and other powers to defend their right to worship God as they choose. The rise of denominations has not only been a phenomenon of theology but also of worship practices.

As persons preparing for ministry, we have brought with us a variety of worship patterns and traditions. Some of us have known only formal worship. Others of us have known only free and spontaneous worship. In the practice of these and other patterns of worship we have experienced a variety of musical languages as well. Some of us have known only a traditional form of historic church music; others have known only a diet of gospel songs and "southern gospel" music; still others have known only "contemporary Christian music" in worship. Many of us have worshiped in places where a mix of all these forms has characterized our corporate worship services.

This diversity of worship patterns and variety of musical dialects has recently begun to cause tension and strife within some evangelical churches, including our own Southern Baptist Convention. Persons with sincere beliefs feel that one worship/music form or the other is not appropriate for corporate worship. Yet just as God is worshiped by all living beings in a variety of ways, so too can Christians come to worship God in any number of authentic patterns with voices united in many different ways. Ministry preparation brings responsibility for each of us to learn ways of corporate worship other than the ones with which we have grown up. God will call us to ministry opportunities in varieties of settings throughout our lives; to be able to feel comfortable in all of these settings means that we must learn to appreciate the various ways of experiencing corporate worship and to see the authenticity of each pattern.

Southern Baptists, for example, have employed a wide variety of forms of worship since their early days. The Charleston tradition and the Sandy Creek tradition[4] are two key models that have shaped formal patterns of Baptist worship as well as more charismatic types. While some congregations were focusing on stateliness and order in worship, others were zealous in their attempts to highlight the ardent revivalistic nature of worship. Thom Rainer, in his book *Great Awakenings,*[5] argues that evangelical churches will move into the twenty-first century with a variety of worship patterns and musical dialects. Some churches will worship in liturgical styles, some in contemporary styles, some in traditional styles, and many in "blended" styles. Since ministers move from one placement to another at least once in their careers, it is important to be able to adapt to other patterns of worship so that God's work can be accomplished without *worship stress* in the minister's life. To understand these different patterns one must experience them with some frequency. Ministry preparation requires exposure to various styles and forms of worship, and persons engaged in that preparation are encouraged to seek out such varied experiences.

No matter what its style, format, or dialect, authentic corporate worship of God (as taught in Isa. 6:1-9) will include the following elements: praise of God, confession of sin, assurance of pardon, presentation of gifts for God's kingdom, the public reading of Scripture, the preaching of the Word, the opportunity for response to God's Word, and the blessing of God's people for service in the world.

PREACHING AS A WORSHIP EVENT

Though exceptions occur, preaching normally takes place within a context of worship. That being the case, ministers should carefully examine their theology of preaching in terms of its role as a worship element. Not too many years ago, one could hear Baptist worship services described as a dichotomy between a *singing* service and a *preaching* service. People considered singing or the "song service" preliminary to the "preaching service." Everything that happened before the sermon merely got the congregation warmed up for the real worship service, "the preachin'." Even a cursory study of Baptist liturgical practices would bear out this observation. Though this mind-set still holds in some parts of the country, Baptists have been developing a healthier and more holistic understanding of worship, one that recognizes the importance of the entire liturgy. As worship leaders, we must teach our congregations the importance of each of the elements of worship, their interrelatedness and differences, and how each helps us offer glory and praise to God. Hence, preaching is an important aspect of a worship service, but its importance does not devalue the significance of prayers of confession, songs of praise, or verbal declarations by the congregation of God's majesty, love, and grace.

Preaching invites people to encounter God. When we preach, if people remember our sermons, but do not meet God, then we have failed. Too often, preachers build sermons with flashy titles, catchy alliterative outlines, or stories packed with emotional appeal designed to wow the congregation and give them something to take home and remember throughout the week. A congregation can become so caught up in the momentum and energy of that kind of preaching that they encounter the sermon but miss God. Some contemporary sermons teeter close to the edge of the entertainment abyss—a baptized version of "Saturday Night Live." Preachers who preach this way would probably not recognize it if you brought it to their attention. Remember, no one is immune from the temptation of merely doing what works.

Please do not hear us saying that creativity in preaching must be avoided. To the contrary, sermons should be interesting, imaginative, and well-crafted in their composition and presentation.[6] Good preaching should hold a congregation's rapt attention. Creative, passionate preaching invites hearers to see and understand life differently. But preaching is not an end in itself. Preaching is a *means* to an end. The purpose remains an encounter with God. If my preaching allows such an experience, it can be understood as a rightful offering to God, a worship experience.

As a worship event, preaching recognizes the Bible's central role in nurturing the life and practice of the church in the world. Biblical proclamation ascribes worth to God by taking the Scriptures seriously. Biblical sermons must be more than just quoting a lot of Bible. Peppering a sermon with multitudes of Scripture quotations may please a congregation and may sound biblical, but if we take the texts out of context the sermon may be no more biblical than if we did not use the Bible at all. Effective biblical preaching transcends the use of proof texts selected to bolster our pet agendas, whether they are moral, political, or theological. When we take the Bible seriously through prayerful study, careful exegesis, and thorough exposition, we honor God. When a preacher stands before a congregation and preaches, the sermon points beyond itself—even beyond the Bible itself—to God. Through effective biblical preaching, a congregation encounters God's abiding care, creative power, and endless mercy as revealed and recorded in the pages of the Bible.

Fred Craddock, in *Preaching*, encourages preachers to see that at times they speak not merely *to* a congregation but on their behalf. This is an important concept for preaching as a worship event. The doctrine of the priesthood of believers reminds Christians that no human intermediary stands between us and God. However, your unique training as a practical theologian for a congregation enables you to articulate some things that they wish they had said, but you said for them. When this happens, your sermon voices the congregation's concerns to God, an opportunity to worship.

The entire task of preaching—studying the biblical passage; reflecting on a congregation's needs; praying for insights and imagination; presenting the composed sermon—should be viewed as part of your worship to God. Taking the preaching task seriously indicates that you attempt to "lead a life worthy of the calling to which you have been called" (Eph. 4:1, NRSVB), and in so doing, honors God.

SUMMING UP

We began this chapter with Jesus' words. There could be no more fitting conclusion to a chapter on worship than to close with his reminder concerning which commandment constituted the most important: "The first is, 'Hear, O Israel: the Lord our God, the Lord is one; you shall love the Lord your God with all your heart, and with all your soul, and with all your mind, and with all your strength.' The second is, 'You shall love your neighbor as yourself.' There is no other commandment greater than these" (Mark 12:29-31, NRSVB).

N O T E S

1. For a modification of Kierkegaard's model, see Raymond Bailey, "From Theory to Practice in Worship," *Review and Expositor* 58 (Winter 1983): 34.

2. Fred B. Craddock, *Preaching* (Nashville: Abingdon, 1985), 41.

3. Michael Perry, ed., *The Dramatized New Testament*, New International Version (Grand Rapids: Baker, 1993).

4. See Donald P. Hustad, "Baptist Worship Forms: Uniting Charleston and Sandy Creek Traditions," *Review and Expositor* 65 (Winter 1988): 31–42.

5. Thom S. Rainer, *Great Awakenings: Making the Most of 9 Surprising Trends That Can Benefit Your Church* (Nashville: Broadman & Holman, 1995).

6. See Warren W. Wiersbe, *Preaching and Teaching with Imagination: The Quest for Biblical Ministry* (Wheaton, Ill.: Victor, 1994).

FOR FURTHER READING

Doran, Carol, and Thomas H. Troeger. *Trouble at the Table: Gathering the Tribes for Worship.* Nashville: Abingdon, 1992.

Gaddy, C. Welton. *The Gift of Worship.* Nashville: Broadman, 1992.

————, and Don W. Nixon. *Worship Resources for Christian Congregations: A Symphony for the Senses.* Macon, Ga.: Smyth & Helwys, 1995.

Loscalzo, Craig A. *Evangelistic Preaching That Connects.* Downers Grove, Ill.: InterVarsity, 1995.

————. *Preaching Sermons That Connect: Effective Communication through Identification.* Downers Grove, Ill.: InterVarsity, 1992.

Lovette, Roger. *Come to Worship: Effective Approaches to Worship Planning.* Nashville: Broadman, 1990.

Stake, Donald W. *The ABCs of Worship: A Concise Dictionary.* Louisville: Westminster/John Knox, 1992.

Webber, Robert E. *Liturgical Evangelism.* Harrisburg, Pa.: Morehouse, 1986.

————. *Evangelicals on the Canterbury Trail: Why Evangelicals Are Attracted to the Liturgical Church.* Wilton, Conn.: Morehouse-Barlow, 1985.

————. *Signs of Wonder: The Phenomenon of Convergence in Modern Liturgical and Charismatic Churches.* Nashville: Abbott/Martyn, 1992.

Wren, Brian. *What Language Shall I Borrow? God-Talk in Worship: A Male Response to Feminist Theology.* New York: Crossroad, 1990.

13

THE MINISTRY OF SHEPHERDING

DAVID STANCIL

The Lord is my shepherd, I shall not be in want.
He makes me lie down in green pastures,
he leads me beside quiet waters, he restores my soul.
He guides me in paths of righteousness
for his name's sake.

PSALM 23:1-3

When was the last time you saw a shepherd? Although you probably have some idea of what shepherds are like and what they do, few of us in this postindustrial, postmodern culture have ever actually seen one.

Shepherds appear throughout the biblical narratives, beginning with Abel in Genesis 4. The best-known chapter in all the Bible, Psalm 23, is about shepherding. Jesus took the image of the shepherd as a primary metaphor to represent his relationship to us, and John promises that Jesus will be our shepherd throughout eternity (Rev. 7:17).

Jesus' most famous discourse on shepherding is found in John 10, where he said, "I am the good shepherd" (10:11). In that passage, Jesus described his relationship with his followers as personal, intimate, and mutually affectionate. He suggested that his shepherding offers protection, guidance, and friendship. Peter would later write that our calling is to imitate the example left for us by Jesus, following "in his steps" (1 Peter 2:21). Since

David Stancil is Associate Pastor of St. Matthews Baptist Church in Louisville, Kentucky.

Jesus is the Good Shepherd, persons in ministry sometimes refer to themselves as "undershepherds," as we offer care in his name.

The Greek word for "shepherd" is ποιμην *(poimén)*, and the study of shepherding skills for leadership in the church was once called "poimenics." Today it is much more common to talk about "pastoral care." A person who is a "pastor" (from L., *pastus*) is a "shepherd."

That dimension of Christian ministry which is known as "pastoral care" is not restricted to persons who hold or aspire to the office of "pastor." Whatever the nature of the call which has brought you to seminary, you will have daily opportunities to offer pastoral care to many Christians in your own local church, such as choir members, youth group members, missions study groups, and other seminary friends. It is this ministry to which this chapter will introduce you.

So what is pastoral care? My favorite definition of pastoral care is Rodney Hunter's affirmation that pastoral care "is concerned with discovering how to care for others in their concrete contingencies and problems so as to stimulate or enable their life of faith and their practical knowledge of God."[1] I like this focus on real-life issues and on "practical knowledge of God." The most famous definition, however, is the one Clebsch and Jaekle offered more than thirty years ago.

> The ministry of the cure of souls, or pastoral care, consists of helping acts, done by representative Christian persons, directed toward the healing, sustaining, guiding, and reconciling of troubled persons whose troubles arise in the context of ultimate meanings and concerns.[2]

We will return to this definition later, especially to "healing," "sustaining," "guiding," and "reconciling." For now, though, we need to think about the distinctions between "pastoral care," "pastoral counseling," and "pastoral psychotherapy," because these are often confused.

Airtight distinctions between these concepts are not possible, because they are similar in many ways, and oversimplifications are inevitable. For example, all three types of care may be either preventive or restorative in their focus. Preventive care helps folks to develop attitudes, skills, and character qualities that will assist them in moving through life in the direction of spiritual growth and maturity and which tend to reduce the likelihood of "shipwreck."

Restorative care focuses on assisting persons in moving through life crises successfully, whether these crises be developmental or eruptive in quality. Developmental crises include such things as the "identity" crises of adolescence, of moving away from home to establish one's own nuclear family (which may be either as a single person or as a married person), of beginning one's first job, of midlife revaluing, or of retirement. *Developmental crises* are fairly predictable parts of the human life cycle. *Eruptive crises*, while not "abnormal," don't fit a predictable schedule. These crises include such events as accidents, disease, divorce, being fired or laid off, and untimely death.

We could generally say that pastoral counseling tends to focus on eruptive crises, while pastoral psychotherapy tends to focus on developmental crises. Both counseling and psychotherapy are the work of ministers with specialized training (beyond what you will receive in an M.Div., though it will get you started), and these modes of care involve formal, scheduled sequences of conversations. Pastoral care, on the other hand, is the province of all ministers, tends to be informal, occurs in the context of daily relationships, and may respond to both eruptive and developmental crises.

WHAT'S "PASTORAL" ABOUT PASTORAL CARE?

To care for other persons is an intrinsic quality of being human. What makes some caring "pastoral"? *Pastoral* caring is distinguished by the *identity* of the caregiver, the *context* in which the care is given, the *ethic* by which the care is governed, and the *goal* toward which the care is directed. Let's look at these in detail.

The Person: Pastoral Identity
Clebsch and Jaekle's definition states that "pastoral" care is "representative" care. Ordination is one way in which congregations authorize particular persons to represent the community as a whole. Whether or not the caregiver is an ordained person, how-

ever, the representative dimension of the community is crucial for care to be pastoral. While it is often one-on-one, pastoral care is not "lone-ranger" care.

Whether you are a Sunday School teacher, a youth worker, a children's leader, or a choirmaster, such service involves being selected—and generally elected—as a representative of the community for leadership. As you consider your "flock," do you give evidence of a shepherd's sense of responsibility? Do you experience a deep affection for those under your care? Like the Good Shepherd, are you willing to go out into the wilderness searching for the ones who are lost? (Luke 15:1-7) Do you pray for them? Are you concerned about their spiritual growth? As Paul wrote to the Corinthians, "Besides everything else, I face daily the pressure of my concern for all the churches. Who is weak, and I do not feel weak? Who is led into sin, and I do not inwardly burn?" (2 Cor. 11:28-29)

The Context: Congregational Accountability

Because it is representative care, pastoral caregiving is an intensification of the ministry of the church, and is accountable to the church—most particularly the local congregation in whose name it is offered. The church, whether "universal" or local, is an imperfect and very human institution, full of persons like you and me who are still working out what it means to be "in Christ."

Your experience with the church may be positive or negative to this point—seminarians come from many backgrounds—but whatever your experience with it, *the church is not just another humanly created institution.* In the mystery of God's plan, "His intent was that now, *through the church,* the manifold wisdom of God should be made known to the rulers and authorities in the heavenly realms, according to his eternal purpose which he accomplished in Christ Jesus our Lord" (Eph. 3:10-11; italics mine).

For good or ill, then, pastoral caring stands within and represents the wisdom—and brokenness—of the church. Pastoral carers rejoice that the church is the bride of Christ, and commit themselves "to present her to [him] as a radiant church, without stain or wrinkle or any other blemish, but holy and blameless" (Eph. 5:27).

The Ethic: Biblical Values

The behavioral sciences, having attempted for decades to be "value-neutral," are beginning to realize that efforts to be value-free are ill-begotten and are really impossible. It is possible not to be aware of one's operative values, but it is impossible not to have any. Christian pastoral caring affirms that the anchor for our values and our commitments is the Bible, which is "God-breathed and . . . useful for teaching, rebuking, correcting and training in righteousness, so that the [person] of God may be thoroughly equipped for every good work" (2 Tim. 3:16-17).

As you begin your formal theological training, your understanding of yourself, of others, of God, and of life will be profoundly deepened. You will discover new ways to understand and to interpret God's Word. This is as it should be. While you are studying the Bible for class assignments, however, do not fail to be reading it devotionally for your own spiritual growth. The two approaches are rather different. As Helmut Thielicke noted:

> If . . . I move away from reading the Word of God as a document addressed to me personally, adopting instead an entirely detached, "professional" approach, then I have lost a precious treasure, and have taken "the first step towards the worst and most widespread ministers' disease." To move from "Lord Jesus, you have promised," to "the documents reveal this or that" is to have moved into the "far country" of the spirit.[3]

The Goal: Wholeness Centered in Christ

Finally, the central goal of pastoral caring is that "Christ be formed" in the lives of the persons with whom we work.[4] Pastoral caring involves asking questions which uncover the points at which persons have become broken and wounded in spirit, so that the good news of Christ may be conveyed appropriately to these points of pain. As Jacques Ellul exclaimed, we cannot keep silent

> when we know that there is a living hope in Christ, a power which can cause hope to be born. We do not have the right to hide this and cover it up under the pretext that we

are in danger of indulging in apologetics and that we have no right to influence people. When this person is in trouble, why should I not come to his aid? Why not bring him what he needs?[5]

We desire more than for folks to be "healthy." We want them to "grasp how wide and long and high and deep is the love of Christ, and to know this love that surpasses knowledge—that [they] may be filled to the measure of all the fullness of God" (Eph. 3:18-19).

WHAT DOES "CARING " LOOK LIKE?

Having said all this, what do we *do* when we offer pastoral caring? There are many skills involved in caregiving, but foremost among them is the ability to listen—to *really* listen. Active listening is intense, hard work, which is why we tend to do it so seldom. Still, listening is the key to all relationships—with ourselves, with others, and with God. Active listening exposes us to others' pain as well as to their hope. Active listening changes both of us. As Doug Manning has observed, "the ear is the most powerful part of the human body. People are healed by the laying on of ears."[6] And so it is that pastoral carers listen *before* forming opinions, making assumptions or statements about "right" and "wrong," giving advice, asking or answering questions, offering words of encouragement or forgiveness, sharing Scripture, or praying. The first task is *to hear the question.*

While listening is the primary mechanism of pastoral caring, it operates through the functions of: "healing," "sustaining," "guiding," "reconciling," and "nurturing."[7] Let's look briefly at these in turn.

Healing is that pastoral function in which a representative Christian person helps another person to be restored to a condition of wholeness, a restoration which also achieves a new level of spiritual insight and welfare. The wholeness which pastoral healing seeks to achieve is not simple restoration of prior circumstances, but an integration on a higher spiritual level than was previously experienced.

Sustaining consists of helping a hurting person to endure and to transcend a circumstance in which restoration to a former condition or recuperation from present illness is either impossible or is so remote as to seem improbable. Such sustaining goes beyond mere resignation, reaching toward spiritual growth through endurance and faithfulness in unwanted, harmful, or dangerous experiences.

Guiding consists in assisting persons in making choices between alternative courses of thought and action, especially when such choices are viewed as affecting the present and future state of the soul. Guidance commonly employs two complementary modes. *Eductive guidance* tends to draw out of the individual's own experiences and values the criteria and resources for life decisions, while *inductive guidance* tends to lead the individual to adopt an *a priori* set of values and criteria by which to make decisions. For Christian caregivers, both eductive and inductive guidance should ultimately be grounded in Scripture.[8]

Reconciling seeks to reestablish broken relationships between persons and between persons and God. Reconciliation is the antithesis of alienation and may be seen to be the ultimate purpose of God (Eph. 3:10-11). Both axes of reconciliation function together, that is, both horizontal and vertical dimensions need to be attended. The Christian disciplines of repentance, confession, and restitution work together with the grace of forgiveness to accomplish this task.

These four pastoral functions should be understood as working together, not in isolation. Rare indeed would be the occasion in which only one of them is brought to bear on a particular situation. They are *dimensions* of pastoral relationships. Taken together, I like to call healing, sustaining, guiding, and reconciling the ministry of "nurturing."[9]

Nurturing is centered on the birthing and development of persons who *witness* to the reality of the kingdom of God, who *embody* the life of the kingdom in daily experience, and who continually seek to *enlarge* the compass of the kingdom in the world. As such, it is caring which may be offered to families and to congregations as well as to individuals. It is God's desire that those who are given the gifts of pastoral leadership should "prepare God's people for works of service, so that the body of Christ may be built up until we all reach unity in the faith and in the knowledge of the Son of God and become mature, attaining to the whole measure of the fullness of Christ" (Eph. 4:11-13).

Individuals, families, and churches are always "on the journey" toward such maturity, and those who are undershepherds along the way have the responsibility and the joy of nurturing this growth, even as we continue to grow ourselves. Such nurturing requires considerable patience.

My favorite metaphor for such "pastoral patience" is the "story of the streetcar."[10] It happened one day that a man got on a streetcar in San Francisco—not the speediest of vehicles—and rather quickly began to berate the conductor, "Can't you go any faster? Can't you go any faster?" The conductor took it all in good humor, but after a while he felt constrained to make a response. The next time the passenger launched into noisy impatience, the conductor replied, "Yes, I could go faster, but my job is to stay on the streetcar." That's the task of pastoral nurture: to "stay on the streetcar" so long as God leaves us in that responsibility. The point, of course, is that the goal is not to get the conductor—or even the streetcar—to the end of the line, but to get the passengers there.

SIX PRINCIPLES FOR PASTORAL CARE

By now you may be wondering to yourself: "Who is equal to such a task?" It's a good question, to which the answer must be: none of us is by ourselves. The good news is that God has given us some principles by which to work. Let's examine six.[11]

The Principle of Love
The central principle for pastoral caring is rooted in the Great Commandment, where Jesus called on us to "love the Lord your God with all your heart and with all your soul and with all your mind . . . [and] love your neighbor as yourself" (Matt. 22:37-39). The "principle of love" means that we invest ourselves in an active, caring concern for the welfare of others, seeing past their brokenness and sin to see persons made in the image of God. I continue to be challenged by the realization that when we stand before the Lord for judgment, we will not be asked questions about theology so much as about behavior: Did you feed the hun-

gry, clothe the naked, and visit the sick? "Whatever you did for one of the least of these . . . you did for me" (Matt. 25:40).

The Principle of Sensitivity

How many times did Jesus say, "He who has ears to hear, let him hear" (Luke 8:8), and what did he mean by this enigmatic instruction? I think that he was talking about *listening* for the questions beneath the questions, for the meaning beneath the words, so that we might hear the deepest questions of the heart, and offer care at that core level. We can see at least four dimensions of such sensitivity in the ministry of Jesus.

Material seekers. The first sensitivity is to persons who seek "non-spiritual" help. The woman with the hemorrhage (Matt. 9:20-22) came to Jesus for physical healing. Sometimes folks want food, clothing, or help with the rent (see principle #1!), but their deeper need is a heart hunger. Our task—our opportunity—is to respond at both levels (James 2:15-16).

Hesitant seekers. Sometimes persons came to Jesus as "peripheral seekers." Zacchaeus was such a person, drawn to Jesus, but not knowing why. There is much about their luncheon conversation we would like to overhear, but it is clear that Jesus got to the "heart" of the matter and helped Zacchaeus see that his hunger was for redemption: for a clear spirit with God, with himself, and with those he had cheated (Luke 19:1-10).

Intense seekers. Occasionally, we are privileged to talk with persons who know that their questions are spiritual in nature. Nicodemus was such an "intense seeker," who earnestly pressed Jesus, asking, "How can this be?" (John 3:9) In such cases, we can head straight for the cross, as Jesus did (John 3:16).

Aimless seekers. Most of the time, though, our sensitivity is challenged by seekers who have no clue what they hunger for. The woman at the well of Sychar was "looking for love in all the wrong places" until she met Jesus (John 4:1-26). He told her, "Those who drink of the water that I will give them will never thirst" (v. 14).

The Principle of Presence

The "principle of love" and "principle of sensitivity" could feel a lot more like demand than like grace, were it not for the next four principles. The "principle of presence" is based on a promise God made to Moses (Ex. 3:11-12) and to Joshua (Josh. 1:5), and which then Jesus extended to us (Matt. 28:20). It is a principle of encouragement and of anchoring support: "I will be with you." *Never* do we enter the arena of care without the empowering presence of the Spirit. This principle is at work in the lives of those with whom we walk, as well. *Never* will we talk with someone in whose heart the Spirit of God is not at work (see 1 Cor. 2:14-15)!

One of the tasks of pastoral caring is to be *physically* present with persons on the journey. They may not remember what we said, but they will remember that we were there. Because God's Spirit acts through us to care for them, if we are able to be *emotionally* present with them through effective listening, they will also remember that God was there.

The Principle of Guidance

The "principle of guidance" builds on the first three principles to assure us that, as we are present with others, God will guide our hearts, even our very words. As Jesus said, "You will be given what to say, for it will not be you speaking, but the Spirit of your Father speaking through you" (Matt. 10:19-20).

You probably have a personal computer or will soon get one. If so, you are probably familiar with "hard drives." A hard drive is a storage device from which your computer gets its resources to follow your commands. A new hard drive will come with lots of free software on it, but not much of that is very useful. In order to be useful, hard drives have to be loaded with the programs and documents that we need for our work.

The "principle of guidance" is sort of like a computer hard drive. God will not "load your heart drive" for you. That is the reason for the psalmist's rhetorical question: "How can a young man keep his way pure? By living according to your word. . . . I have hidden your word in my heart that I might not sin against you" (Ps. 119:9, 11).

The study and memorization of Scripture is one of the many ways of "loading your heart drive" (seminary study is another). That is the work of obedience. Jesus' sure promise of divine guidance is that, once we have "loaded the drive," the Holy Spirit will "call to the screen" those words, verses, and principles we need in the moment of witness and ministry. That is the work of grace.

The Principle of Adequacy

Not only will God be with us, not only will the Spirit guide us, but what we offer in Jesus' name will be enough. It will be adequate. The miracle of the feeding of the 5,000 shows us that Jesus takes what we offer him and causes it to be *enough* (Matt. 14:13-21).

This is not to say that we always are in possession of all the skills and all the knowledge that are needed for the present situation. It is to say, though, that, however inadequate our effort in the scheme of things, if it is offered genuinely and in the name of Jesus, God will honor it. If we have "loaded our heart drive," and speak through the wisdom of the indwelling Spirit of God, then we live in the promise that "my word . . . will not return to me empty, but will accomplish what I desire and achieve the purpose for which I sent it" (Isa. 55:11). As Paul would later note, "neither the one who plants nor the one who waters is anything, but only God who gives the growth" (1 Cor. 3:7).

The Principle of Self-Care

The first five principles still have danger about them, though, without the "principle of self-care." Immediately after feeding the 5,000 Jesus "withdrew *again* to the hills by himself" (John 6:15, italics mine). The "principle of self-care" has two dimensions, that of *retreat*, of which this is an example, and that of *celebration*, of which the wedding at Cana is one example (John 2:1-11).

All ministry and no rest or celebration make Jack and Jill burned-out caregivers. Jesus spent time in retreat and prayer much more often than most of us are inclined to do, and he was also criticized for his much eating, drinking, hiking, camping, and fishing (Luke 7:33-34). The world knows how to be burned-out. What the world hungers for is to see persons who embody abundant life! One good measure of how you're doing with the sixth principle is to check your "joy meter." Is your life feeling "abundant" these days? Abundant life often takes a beating in seminary. Consider what steps you need to take to protect yourself.

JESUS, THE GOOD SHEPHERD, AT WORK

As we near the end of this overview, we need to point again to the example of Jesus Christ as a model for your own ministry.

Let's closely examine the healing of a blind man recorded in Mark 8:22-26.

After the man's friends brought him to Jesus, Jesus took him outside the village. This was unusual behavior for Jesus. Perhaps it was a way for him to connect with this man, to meet his particular needs, which are not apparent to us. In any event, when Jesus took the blind man's hand and led him outside the village, he established a *personal relationship* with him that was an important element in the man's confidence that Jesus could help him with his problem.

Pastoral caregiving is a coming apart from the group in ways very much like Jesus' taking of the blind man outside the village. The goal of pastoral caregiving is to focus the ministries of healing, guiding, sustaining, reconciling, forgiving, and nurturing in such a way that *crises and other life events become instruments of God's grace* in the lives of the hurting.

After they got to a more isolated spot, Jesus spit on the man's eyes, and then asked whether the treatment had been effective. This part of the story has always seemed both strange and unpleasant to me. Part of the message of the spit, I think, is that soul healing can be a pretty messy endeavor. By the time persons have realized that they are broken and wounded in spirit, their wounds are quite often "infected." The process of healing requires that the pastoral caregiver be willing to help "lance the wound" and that the wounded person be willing to endure the pain of healing.[12]

After spitting on the man's eyes, Jesus asked him a question: "Do you see anything?" The man responded that he saw people who looked like "trees walking around." The man participated in the process of his own healing by responding to Jesus out of his own inner experience—as is true in contemporary caring as well.

After the man's response, Jesus touched his eyes again, and this "second touch" brought full healing and restoration. Perhaps this can represent the fact that *spiritual* healing is not so much instantaneous as it is a *process*. Persons usually do not become broken and wounded in a single moment. The process of soul healing, like the process of physical healing, usually requires time, as old patterns of behavior are discarded and new ways of being in relationships are learned.

CONCLUSION

The task of the pastoral caregiver is much like the work of a gardener. By careful listening and by gentle probing into the soil of the spirit, pastoral caregivers discover seeds that need planting, that are germinating, that need watering, or that have died. The caregiver, with the help of the person desiring wholeness, may sow a little, water a little, cultivate a little, and prune a little, so that God may have greater freedom to cause the fruit of the Spirit to ripen and to bear more fruit.

Pastoral caregiving, then, is one way in which the body of Christ is strengthened and the presence of Jesus is felt. Jesus met people where they were, mired in the muck of their own attempts at living, and gave them permission to begin again. Pastoral caregivers are midwives of eternity, seeing in persons more than they are able to see in themselves, as Jesus did. Pastoral caregivers listen for the point or the points at which the gospel fits the pain, and attempt to make that good news hearable through personal caring ministry. When this takes place, life begins to reveal the extraordinary possibilities God has promised.

N O T E S

1. Rodney J. Hunter, "The Future of Pastoral Theology," *Pastoral Psychology* 29 (1980): 69.

2. William A. Clebsch and Charles R. Jaekle, *Pastoral Care in Historical Perspective: An Essay with Exhibits* (Englewood Cliffs, N.J.: Prentice Hall, 1964), 4.

3. Helmut Thielicke, *A Little Exercise for Young Theologians* (Grand Rapids: Eerdmans, 1962), 32–33.

4. Wayne E. Oates, *The Christian Pastor* (Philadelphia: Westminster, 1964), 77.

5. Jacques Ellul, *Hope in Time of Abandonment*, trans. C.E. Hopkin (New York: Seabury, 1973), 162.

6. Doug Manning, *Don't Take My Grief Away* (Hereford, Texas: Insight, 1979), 99.

7. Seward Hiltner was the first to identify the functions of "healing," "sustaining," and "guiding." Clebsch and Jaekle added "reconciling" to the list. See Seward Hiltner, *Preface to Pastoral Theology* (Nashville: Abingdon, 1958), 89–174; and Clebsch and Jaekle, *Pastoral Care in Historical Perspective*, 32–66.

8. Don S. Browning, *The Moral Context of Pastoral Care* (Philadelphia: Westminster, 1976), 68.

9. See Howard Clinebell, *Basic Types of Pastoral Counseling: Resources for the Ministry of Healing and Growth*, rev. and enlarged (Nashville: Abingdon, 1984), 42–43.

10. I am indebted to Scott Tatum, one of my preaching professors at Southwestern Baptist Theological Seminary, for this story.

11. These principles are adapted from Homer Carter, *Equipping Deacons in Caring Skills* (Nashville: Convention, 1980), 10–12; and from James Hightower, *Called to Care: Helping People through Pastoral Care* (Nashville: Convention, 1990), 19–20.

12. The pastoral function of sustaining reminds us that not all problems can be removed. Eliminating the "problem" may not be as important as *establishing faithful relationships* which can be for you the signs of God's steadfastness and grace.

FOR FURTHER READING

Anderson, Ray S. *Self-Care: A Theology of Personal Empowerment and Spiritual Healing*. Wheaton, Ill.: Victor/BridgePoint, 1995.

Browning, Don S. *The Moral Context of Pastoral Care*. Philadelphia: Westminster, 1976.

Capps, Donald. *Life Cycle Theory and Pastoral Care*. Philadelphia: Westminster, 1983.

Fowler, James W. *Stages of Faith: The Psychology of Human Development and the Quest for Meaning*. San Francisco: Harper & Row, 1981.

Gerkin, Charles V. *Crisis Experience in Modern Life: Theory and Theology for Pastoral Care*. Nashville: Abingdon, 1979.

Nouwen, Henri J.M. *The Wounded Healer*. Garden City, N.Y.: Doubleday Image, 1979.

Oates, Wayne E. *The Christian Pastor*. 3d ed. Revised. Philadelphia: Westminster, 1982.

Pruyser, Paul W. *The Minister as Diagnostician: Personal Problems in Pastoral Perspective*. Philadelphia: Westminster, 1976.

Wimberly, Edward P. *African-American Pastoral Care*. Nashville: Abingdon, 1991.

14

TEACHING: A LITTLE PIECE OF HOLY GROUND

JOHN D. HENDRIX

Buddy Glass, age forty, considers his career of teaching and compares it to a spiritual calling. "I have a nine o'clock class," he concludes. "I know—not always, but I know—there is no single thing I do that is more important than going into that awful Room 307 . . . (The students) may shine with the misinformation of the ages, but they shine." This thought manages to stun me: There's no place I'd really rather go right now than into Room 307. Seymour once said that all we do our whole lives is go from one little piece of holy ground to the next.[1]

What happens in Room 307 at 9 A.M. and other such times and places will do much to shape the way we see educational ministry in the church. Most of us teach the way we have been taught. So it's important to examine what goes on in Room 307. Let's shape our discussion around the teachers, learners, and events in this "little piece of holy ground."

John D. Hendrix is the former Basil Manly, Jr. Professor of Christian Education at the Southern Baptist Theological Seminary, and is currently Pastor of the Northside Baptist Church in Clinton, Mississippi.

TEACHERS ON HOLY GROUND

For some teachers walking into Room 307 is like a performer entering a stage. They see their work as a solo performance. The performance arena is the classroom, and the performance literature is the course content adapted to particular skills. The stage is an area at the front of the room and there is an audience sitting in such a way as to observe the performance. Teachers perform with script on lectern, command of language, stage presence, gestures, facial language, body movement, and voice modulation. Sometimes they use improvisation through the spontaneous creation of performance materials.

Other teachers enter Room 307 with a different agenda. Theirs is not a solo performance. Rather, they are conductors of a performance. The whole room becomes a stage and the audience becomes the actors. The stage is filled with imaginative sets. Here teachers stand in front of a strange array of expectant students. These students play complicated and diverse instruments, a combination of learned skills and personal styles. On the music stand lies a complex score. The score does have some familiarity and the music has been performed before with some success. But past successes hold no guarantees. Day in and day out all those diverse sounds come together again with focused concentration, a playful spirit, a nudge toward spontaneity, an overwhelming love for the score, and an unfaltering faith in the players.

A teaching style is a teacher's preferred pattern of providing learning opportunities which distinguishes him or her from other teachers. Every teacher has a different style. Is the teacher the director, the actor, or the stage manager? Does the teacher originate the work, interpret the work, or carry out the interpretations?

What makes for good teaching? Is it the subject? Recall the best teachers you ever had. What did they teach? What led them to become teachers? Are they coaches, friends, tyrants, experts, or counselors? Without having particular teachers in mind, good teaching is a fictional ideal. The ideal says teachers never lose their cool, have no biases, hide their feelings, never play favorites, provide perfect learning situations, are consistent, know all the issues, and answer all the questions. In other words, they deny their humanity. The truth is teachers may contradict all those characteristics and still be good teachers.

What teachers do speaks volumes about who teachers are. Teachers cannot hide in the classroom. Mood, temperament, and attitude are communicated unconsciously. Teachers are part of the "hidden curriculum," the message that is conveyed beyond the content. If teachers are enthusiastic, bored, happy, or sad, learners probably will be the same. Regardless of what or who teachers report themselves to be, their behaviors reveal who they really are.

Honest teachers know that they are vulnerable. One teacher had a dream that dramatized the deepest fears of most of us. In the middle of a lecture a student stood up and spoke in a clear, controlled voice. "This class is so boring! Some of us have been talking and we've decided that we don't have to put up with it. We're walking out and we hope all the rest of you will come with us." And they did.

A dream like that would make any teacher wake up in a cold sweat. But it is that kind of fear that makes us more controlling and less willing to take risks for a more energetic classroom. We try to stay in control of the teaching situation and hold on to the lectern for dear life. As long as we are playing it safe we can be sure that students will do the same. Safe, predictable learning is often a mirror of a safe predictable teaching style. The spirit of excitement and adventure, a hallmark of the educational enterprise, is lost in controlled predictability. The holy ground needs an atmosphere and climate that energy, excitement, adventure, and high spirits provide.

I have a framed picture that sits behind my office desk. It is a picture of "Missions Day" at Midwestern Baptist Theological Seminary in Kansas City, Missouri in the fall of 1958, the first semester of the school's existence. It pictures the student body (115 students), four faculty members, a business manager, and a librarian.

Let me tell you about this student body. There was one woman, one African American student, and one Hispanic student. All the rest were white "anglos." We were young—mid twenties to early thirties in age. It would be difficult to picture a more homogeneous group. If someone were to have asked, "What kind of ministry do you plan to do?" most would have said, "I plan to pastor," and most of them have. A few might have mentioned missions. Still others were not sure. I was one of those.

This story illustrates the dramatic changes which have taken place in student bodies at most theological seminaries. Most likely our classes have a good number of women students, a mixture of races, and a healthy sprinkling of second and third career students. Many of today's professors have been trained in a teaching style that was and still is well fitted for young adult white males. Behind these issues are significant but unexamined factors of young men in relation to older male authority figures. Although these kinds of transactions still occur, they would seem strange and foreign to many. Given the diversity of student bodies, it is hard to imagine one kind of teaching style that would be beneficial to all students today.

LEARNERS ON HOLY GROUND

How do people experience learning? The obvious and simple answer is to ask them. What learning experiences are remembered as most significant? Instead of focusing on what the teacher hopes and plans to happen, attention is given to what actually happens in the learner's experience. Stephen Brookfield calls this "grounded teaching," admitting that what actually occurs in a learning setting differs sharply with what was planned because it gives attention to the learner's experience of learning.[2] The learning process is continually dealing with the feelings generated, the peaks and valleys of a learning episode, the excitement, boredom, fears, and frustrations of learning, and what is remembered as being most significant. The most precious trait of the learner, which usually slumbers fitfully during safe and predictable learning methods, is curiosity, the golden nugget of learning excellence. Whatever else the teacher tries to reach in the classroom, whatever other targets the instructional process seeks to hit, learner curiosity is the bull's eye. It is the major process in creative learning. But, you say, how do you do that?

This process is deceptively simple. Learners are asked to reflect on their most recent learning experiences and to describe in a simple, concrete, and narrative form how these experiences were growth enhancing or hindering:

1. The incident, or incidents that were most exciting and rewarding, a learning "high," where you felt something important and significant was happening to you.

2. The incident or incidents that were distressing, disappointing, or demeaning, in that they represented learning "lows."

3. The characteristics and behaviors of teachers and leaders that were helpful and hindering to learning.

4. Times when you felt valued and affirmed or demeaned and infantilized.

5. The most important insights about you as a learner.

6. The most pleasurable and distressing aspects of learning you experienced.

7. The changes and developments noticed in personal processes and responses.

In responding to these issues we begin to see the various aspects of learning. Learning style is the complex way we concentrate on, process, and retain information. Once a learner has that information safely locked within memory, it can be engaged in challenging activities. The process seems to be different and unique in each person. Learning style has to do with the process of triggering concentration and retrieving information. Some learn more easily in step by step sequential patterns. Others need to see the whole picture first through stories, examples, and graphics. Some can work long periods of time without distraction. Others need a background of distraction with frequent breaks. Some are driven self-starters while others need frequent feedback and constant supervision. Some prefer working alone while others prefer teams, mentors, and a variety of groupings. Perceptual preferences refer to the different paths through which we absorb information (auditory, visual, tactual, or kinesthetic). No learning style is better or worse than the others. Each style encompasses similar intelligence ranges.

There is one other issue that is critical to learning style—the role of life experiences. The naming of experience has often been dismissed, ignored, or never mentioned in the traditional classroom of theological education. It is a part of the null curriculum, that vast reservoir of rich learning potential that lies hidden in the void and darkness that never comes to light.

Our experience is who we are. We are a unique series of experiences, and we all have a deep investment in the value of those experiences. When we find ourselves in situations where our experiences are ignored or minimized, it is not just our experience that is being rejected. Our whole beings feel that rejection. At some deep level, if not consciously, we feel abandoned because we are unable to project our own experiences to arrive at the conclusions dictated by some authority outside ourselves. There is the feeling that who we are and what we know doesn't count.

On the other hand, all life experience provides the capacity to engage in meaningful dialogue. Knowledge is inseparable from life experience and should be linked or integrated with the experience of the learner. It is seen most clearly in group interaction, participation, experimentation, and discovery. Our experience comes into focus when we ask some of the following questions.

1. What is the role of my life experience in the subject matter?
2. Does this course place value upon my experience as a source of knowledge?
3. What type of student learning experiences are reflected upon?
4. What really counts as knowledge?
5. How does this setting think people learn the best?
6. How would an educated person be described from taking this course?

A part of our learning is the ability to make sense of the raw and sometimes chaotic data of firsthand experience rather than from the orderly, neat structure of a textbook or lecture.

WHAT HAPPENS ON HOLY GROUND

Biblical Model #1

Let's examine two biblical models of teaching. The first model comes from 1 Thessalonians 2:7-11 where Paul gives us a picture of a mother feeding (nursing) her children. The mother caresses her children, comes down to their level, uses their language, and plays their games. Paul likened himself to a mother feeding children. The same word is used in Deuteronomy 22:6 of a mother bird sitting over the young in a nest.

The mother-and-child model of interpersonal relationships has much to say about Christian teaching. All religious experience of significance must recognize otherness. Experiences may shake us or arouse us to new insights, but they have no powerful spiritual significance unless they hold an unmistakable presence of something other than ourselves.

In the mother-child relationship there is someone who is close to the mother who is not the mother. A mother may fail to recognize this otherness of her child. She may only see the child as an extension of herself. She may be caught only in her experience of the child. She may be concerned with what the child makes her feel more than she is struck by what the child is feeling apart from her. The denial of otherness blocks human communication. The block may occur in two ways. We may see others as extensions of ourselves. Or we may experience others as threatening. Teaching is that intimate encounter that recognizes and affirms difference and distance.

Paul's life was intermingled with the Thessalonians. He spoke of being "among you" (2:7). There seems to be the taking of a place of equality. Jesus used the same expression in Luke 22:27, "But I am among you as one who serves." All good communication brings us to similar levels with others, which is the essence of empathy and compassion. Paul, who could at times be quite stern, confronting, even abrasive, was frequently very gentle in the midst of the people, as one of them and not as one apart from them.

In 1 Thessalonians 2:8, Paul used some of his most intimate conversation. With the affection of a wet nurse (or mother), he was eager "to share not only the gospel of God but our lives as well" because the people had become very dear to him. Paul said that he "yearned" after them. He was no detached communicator of truth. His life's blood was mixed with this teaching. It has been said that the medieval painters mixed their own blood with their paints in order to get "their own selves" into the canvas. The thought of giving oneself is the very essence of all genuine Christian teaching. In the most profound kinds of communication, we are not allowed to keep our innermost selves to ourselves. A cool, detached verbalization of content without mixing it with one's own life story is at the root of much ineffective communication. Paul was a two-handed teacher—in one hand, good news (content); in the other hand, his own life (experience).

The other picture of communication that Paul used was that

of a father with his children (2:11). Again, note the very personal dealing that Paul had with the people. "Each one of you" implies attention to individuals. Each one was cared for personally. Paul was both mother and father to them. They received both a mother's affection and tenderness (2:7) and a father's thought and counsel (2:1).

Paul used three words in 2:11 that describe this kind of fatherly communication. First, he speaks of exhorting. Exhorting is a powerful summons or appeal. It is a process that penetrates with warnings, consolations, and encouragement. The purpose of exhortation is to arouse out of indifference and to overcome the resistance of the will. Here it carries with it a direct and personal force toward quality spiritual living.

Paul then speaks of encouragement or comfort. Encouragement is needed to help people to be sustained in trouble and to assist them to overcome difficulties. The same word is found elsewhere in the New Testament in 1 Thessalonians 5:14 and John 11:19, 31. In 1 Thessalonians 5:14, it expresses encouragement for the fainthearted. In John, it expresses comfort for the bereaved. It implies consolation. The word of encouragement is spoken specifically to those who find difficulty in living in the face of opposition.

Finally, Paul speaks of urging or charging. The Greek word used here is difficult to translate. It is much like the legal process in which a witness was brought forth with a strong testimony. It is used this way in Acts 20:26 and in Galatians 5:3. Charging is a solid declaration of truth. It may refer to those serious words addressed to those who have lost a sense of discipline. It includes the expectation that the hearer will respond. It promises observation in order to guarantee accountability. The father is the one who is ready to testify about performance. He watches over with both a loving and critical eye.

A firm sense of identity comes from finding a work to do and being loved for doing it. This sense of identity is helped along by fathering—a mixture of warmth, instruction, and expectation. The message that comes from fathering is the strong challenge to "do it!" Without this toughness in relationships, the soft side often remains the only side, and we remain childlike and insecure without any kind of direct confrontation. Because we are aware of this vulnerability, of this soft and fragile side, we often fail to deal with people with directness and candor.

In summary, teaching provides both comfort and challenge. The two always seem to go together. Love is the binding force. Love requires us to respond to the same person tenderly at one time and toughly at another time. There is always a place for the warm, tender response. More frequently than we wish, there is a place for a tough and confronting word. In teaching, we must learn how and when to give both.

Biblical Model #2

First Thessalonians 2 gives us an adequate model for basic teaching skills. *Attending* is the first skill—learning to listen; paying close attention to the full context of the conversation; listening to both words and silences, to emotions and ideas, and to the full situation in which the conversation takes place. Attending is the first act of communication. If I really care, I pay full attention. If I cannot pay full attention, or more accurately if I choose not to pay full attention, it will be difficult if not impossible for me to understand accurately and effectively.

Asserting is the other skill. This means presenting our own insights and beliefs forcefully, but without manipulation. Asserting is based on a search of my own self to verify where I stand on whatever is of importance in this conversation and includes a message of challenge. It calls for an appreciation of my own experiences, needs, and purposes in such a way that I can state them clearly. It calls forth from me an expression of what I really believe. It demands a skill of concreteness—my ability to be clear and specific in what I want to say. It also implies respect for the person to whom I speak. They are worthy of my best, not some concocted half-truth that falls short of authentic assertion.

The second model is found in Ephesians 4:11-16, a long complicated sentence of mixed metaphors that no students in their right minds would attempt to exegete in a term paper. For a period of time, usually referred to as a semester, we are called to a piece of holy ground, Room 307. The "called out ones" are taken out of one sphere of life and placed in a different order of relationship. We are no longer just individuals but a body, a community of believers. In this new setting, we are fitted together. All the parts of the body that have been dislocated are now in an environment where the major goals are repair, mending, and proper fitting together.

The Apostle Paul's imagination knows no bounds in Ephesians 4:11-16. Let us use that imagination in seeing the possibilities in Room 307. No metaphor is able to say it all. Paul begins with a building and ends with a body. When the body is working properly it is fitly joined together and compacted. The supply is an abundant supply. The supply of energy is not merely sufficient. There is an overabundance of supply, plenty for all that is needed. The supply is an "effectual working energy," an operative energy that does something and accomplishes results. Every single part is absolutely full. Every part has all it needs and more according to capacity. Every part is in the process of becoming fully grown.

The members are not identical, nor do they conform to a pattern. The glory of the body is in its extraordinary variety that communicates unity through the working together of every part. No part is missing and no part will be lacking. The secret of it all is that it will not be complete without each one of us.

Several images are presented in its building "itself up in love." There is the image of the musical score where instruments, score, players, and conductor are fitted together. When the baton of the conductor comes down on the first beat, all instruments play in perfect harmony. There is the image of the living plant, rooted and planted, a living evidence of God's "holy ground" in the world. There is the image of a house in the process of being built, a construction lot of God on earth. There is the image of a new adult being created out of those who were formerly enemies. Finally, there is the image of a human body, where all parts come to the rescue of any wounded and damaged part.

There is one image that can cover and carry the complexity of Ephesians 4:11-16. That is the image of the learning organism. The pictures presented are all about learning. Learning organisms are possible because we are all learners. It is our nature to learn and to learn in concert with others. Most of us, at one time or another, have been part of a learning organism, a team that took on the characteristics of a house, a plant, a building, an orchestra, or a body. This group of people functioned in an extraordinary, almost mystical way. We made commitments to one another in childlike trust, complemented each others' strengths, compensated for each others' weaknesses, and came to a consensus of goal definitions that were larger and more meaningful than personal goals. Many of us have spent our lives looking for that experience again or trying to reproduce it in every imaginable kind of setting. What we were experiencing were many of the dynamics found in Ephesians 4:11-16. And the common characteristic in all those experiences was learning how to do it in the process of being it. There are times when we get a taste of Ephesians 4:11-16 in Room 307.

GROUNDED IN HOLY GROUND

When we leave Room 307 we should have our imagination stirred and our awareness charged. We find ourselves entertained, prodded, and illuminated. We have had our intellects challenged, our faith stretched, and enough clarity revealed that we are not disoriented and confused. We have had our emotions engaged and intensified. We have had our curiosities nurtured back to life and health. We have even laughed some. It leaves us with the reassurance that this little piece of holy ground provides some order in an otherwise chaotic world. All of those elements taken together create a series of inner tensions that resulted in newly created life. We understand a process difficult to define but recognized anyway. Learning has become *the* thing for us.

N O T E S

1. J.D. Salinger, *Seymour: An Introduction* (Boston: Little, Brown, 1956), 247–48.
2. Stephen D. Brookfield, *The Skillful Teacher* (San Francisco: Jossey-Bass, 1990), 32–33.

F O R   F U R T H E R   R E A D I N G

Allport, Gordon. *Becoming.* New Haven: Yale Univ. Press, 1995.

DeJong, Norman, ed. *Christian Approach to Learning Theory: The Nature of the Learner.* Lanham, Md.: Univ. Press of America, 1985.

Knowles, Malcolm S. *The Modern Practice of Adult Education.* Revised and Updated. New York: Adult Education Co., 1980.

Lines, Arthur Timothy. *Functional Images of the Religious Education.* Birmingham, Ala.: Religious Education Press, 1992.

Havighurst, Robert. *Developmental Tasks and Education.* New York: David McKay, 1961.

McKenzie, Leon. *The Religious Education of Adults.* Birmingham, Ala.: Religious Education Press, 1982 (esp. chapters 7 and 8).

15

SOCIAL MINISTRY IN THE COMMUNITY

JOHN DEVER
AND
JANET FURNESS SPRESSART

In the halls of evangelical schools across the country one can occasionally hear rather heated discussions between two groups of students concerning the major task of the church as it prepares to move into the twenty-first century. One side quotes verse after verse of Scripture undergirding the claim that the saving of individual souls through evangelism is the central task. After all, the argument goes, if we get people saved, then their lives will be changed and they will change society. Sin will be attacked from two sides, within individuals and within society. The second group counters with an equal number of Scriptures that justify its stance that the primary task of the church is to challenge the evil structures of society and to bind up the wounds of those who are victims of the social system. The root of sin lies in society and its institutions. Destroy collective evil and personal sin will be controlled.

John Dever is William Walker Brookes Professor of Church and Community at the Southern Baptist Theological Seminary. **Janet Furness Spressart** is Associate Professor of Social Work at Roberts-Wesleyan College in Rochester, New York.

Such discussions are nothing new; our evangelical ancestors wrestled with the same arguments. The same debate is played out at evangelical theological seminaries across the land. Since the turn of the century there has existed a destructive dualism of "revivalistic conversionism" versus "modernistic social gospel" within American Christianity. Individual sin versus social evil, or evangelism versus social concern, or personal piety versus social compassion, whichever form it took, the lines between the two Christian camps were drawn. David Moberg attributes this conflict to what he calls the "Great Reversal" of the early twentieth century.[1] Prior to that point in history, evangelicals had been strong advocates of both social action and social ministry. John Wesley, George Whitefield, and Charles G. Finney were just a few that were personally involved in social reform. Finney wrote, "Revivals are hindered when ministers and churches take wrong ground in regard to any question involving human rights."[2] Social action marked his entire ministry.

In the "Great Reversal" many evangelical Christians retreated from this earlier involvement in social action and placed an almost exclusive emphasis on personal evangelism. They did give some attention to the victims of social injustice, but they withdrew from social reform. Whether this was a reaction to the modernist "social gospel," or due to rapid social change and urbanization, or attributable to the rise of dispensational premillennialism, the result was the same. A division occurred in American evangelicalism.

It will be our contention in this chapter that this evangelism/social action split is a false dichotomy. We believe that the Bible supports the goals and the ideological values of groups embracing either evangelism or social action. As Moberg puts it, "It is the reductionistic emphasis by members of each party that is in error. Evangelism to win souls to Christ, social action to promote justice in society, and social ministries to aid the victims of sin and structural evil are all important aspects of God's will for the Christian family."[3] When people are hungry, living in substandard housing, jobless, receiving inadequate health care, and constantly on the edge of their emotional endurance, offering Jesus as the answer is only an abstraction. The Christian church must address the social forces that dehumanize God's children, as well as evangelize persons for the kingdom of God. Only then will the church truly reflect the holistic teaching and ministry of Jesus Christ in its work and witness.

When one studies the life of Jesus, exegetes the Scriptures thoroughly, and observes the work of the Holy Spirit within the history of Christianity, the only valid conclusion is that evangelism and social ministry (including social action) are simply the reverse sides of the same coin. Within the theological framework of the Bible they are not separate categories. They are integral parts of the gospel. The Scriptures know and proclaim nothing less than a "wholistic gospel" concerned with the "spiritual, physical, emotional, mental, and relational well-being of persons, families, groups, and communities both inside and outside the community of faith."[4]

Since the middle of the century, many leading American evangelicals have adopted this same perspective. They have said in very strong terms that both evangelism and social action are important and that the exclusion of one or the other is unbiblical and a failure to submit to the Bible as the authoritative guide for life.

Robert Kysar writes:

> The human being in his or her total existence was the object of Jesus' love. Physical, emotional, economic, social, political, as well as intellectual and spiritual needs were all objects of the words and actions of Jesus. Consequently, one must conclude that the God revealed in that human life is a God who is concerned for the whole life of the divine creation. In view of the life and ministry of Jesus, the claim that God cares only for the soul of humans and acts only for the spiritual welfare of people cannot be justified.... More truthful is the proposal that the Jesus image of God is of one passionately devoted to human welfare in all of its various dimensions and components.[5]

Having strenuously stated the case for the integration of evangelism and social ministry, we dedicate the remainder of this article to an introduction to social ministry. We do this knowing that the equally important topic of evangelism is presented in a holistic manner in another chapter in this volume.

DEFINITIONS

Defining social ministry is not quite as easy as it may first appear. Everyone seems to have a preconceived notion of what is involved in Christian social ministry, so definitions seem to be filtered through this predetermined bias. Rather than giving a definition, David Claerbaut offers three types of social concerns that need to be addressed: social reconciliation, social relief, and social reform. The first, social reconciliation, involves peacemaking—an attempt "to reach across the barriers of economics, race, and community to love and care for people regardless of social category." The second, social relief, is directed toward the giving of a "cup of cold water"; that is, meeting immediate physical needs. The third, social reform, seeks to change "the basic unjust conditions and systems that oppress and dehumanize people."[6] These types of concerns certainly assist us in grasping the breadth of social ministry, but we still lack a precise definition.

The definition offered by Derrel Watkins seems to be comprehensive. For him, social ministry is

> an organized process used by redeemed individuals who are called by God to proclaim the good news, demonstrating Christ's concern for the spiritual, physical, emotional, mental, and relational well-being of persons, families, groups, and communities both inside and outside the community of faith.[7]

Anne Davis defines social ministry as "the activities carried out by redeemed individuals, called by God to proclaim the good news, to minister to the needy, and to seek justice for all."[8] But once again, preconceived ideas may tend to erase much of the comprehensiveness of these definitions. We prefer to combine the efforts of Watkins, Davis, and Claerbaut by dividing Christian social ministry into two rather distinct endeavors: social ministry and social action. Social ministry will refer to *any direct intervention by Christians to minister to individuals or groups who are victims of personal or social problems.* The alleviation of suffering is the ultimate goal of social ministry, but as we define it, it deals with individuals or groups and not social structures.

In his book, *A Social Action Primer*, Dieter Hessel defines social action as "a process of deliberate group effort to alter community or societal structures for the common good."[9] Here there is a deliberate effort to address and alleviate institutional injustice. Note that it is a group effort. Individuals working alone will seldom accomplish political and governmental policy change; it usually takes the efforts of a social action group. This becomes a *Christian* social action when the local church, or a coalition of churches, or a group of dedicated Christians, form such a social action group for the express purpose of bringing God's mercy, grace, and justice to bear on the situation.

BIBLICAL BASIS

Social ministry and social action are grounded in both Old and New Testament images of God. The God of the Exodus is a liberator God. The Bible makes it quite clear that God is involved in human history. Kysar notes, "The primary revelatory event for the Old Testament is found in divine action that changed the social and economic condition of a people."[10] God sides with the oppressed against their oppressor. God is involved in social action.

The Old Testament also reveals a God who is an advocate of the poor. Exodus 22:25-27 indicates that human beings have a right to personal dignity and that this dignity must be honored by those who are more fortunate. No interest should be charged on loans; if a person's cloak is taken as collateral, it must be returned before sunset. Persons should never be stripped of their basic human rights to food and shelter. The prophets Amos, Micah, and Jeremiah preach of a God who is an advocate for justice. God demands just relationships within society (cf. Jer. 5:26-29; Amos 2:6b-7a; 5:24; Micah 3:1-4). Amos makes it quite clear that the calamities experienced by both the northern and southern kingdoms result from their lack of social justice (Amos 3:1-2).

For Christians, the establishment of a New Testament foundation for social ministry and social action is crucial. The New Testament's images of God are just as convincing. Penetrating nearly every chapter of the gospels is the image of God as love. This image, perfectly manifested in Jesus and actualized by the Holy Spirit in Christians, depicts a God who wills the welfare of others. As Watkins puts it, "Any action, attitude, ideology, or system that hurts people and hinders them from reaching a state of well-being stands under the judgment of love."[11]

God, as revealed in Jesus, is concerned for the physical, emotional, economic, social, and political welfare of all human beings (Mark 1:21–2:12; 7:1-8; Luke 4:16-21; 7:36-50; 12:13-21).[12] This, coupled with Jesus' emphasis on the spiritual and intellectual aspects of human life, constitutes a holistic concern. The healing stories, the exorcisms, the concern for the poor, the challenge to the class system, and the refusal to be intimidated by authorities, all portray Jesus' social concern for individuals and the community. The Incarnation is God's identification with persons and their needs, and Jesus' radical inclusiveness (the lame, the blind, the deaf, the leper, women and children, elderly, sinners, tax collectors) in his ministry gives evidence of the extension of God's concern to all persons.

The church is "the body of Christ." If it is the "body of Christ," then it should be involved in the same ministries and tasks that occupied Jesus. In applying Isaiah 61:1-2 to himself (Luke 4:16-21), Jesus made it quite clear that he was concerned about the social plight of people. The captives are released and the oppressed set free. G. Willis Bennett argues that this means that the church should function to help "fashion a personal and social environment wherein its members and other human beings shall be able to realize the potential which God intends for his children."[13] Social ministry and social action are functions of the church.

The early church recognized the importance of caring for its community when it appointed deacons to care for the widows and the poor. Acts records the deliberate selection of seven members who were "known to be full of the Spirit and wisdom" (Acts 6:3) for the express purpose of taking responsibility for these physical needs. In this way apostles were able to pay attention to prayer and the ministry of the word while knowing that equally important tasks were being handled by skilled leaders who were also called to ministry.

Apostles returned from missionary travels carrying offerings from believers for the poor in Jerusalem. If under Old Testament law it was obligatory to help all who were in need, certainly the covenant of grace obligated the Christian to do at least as much. James' epistle notes that care of orphans and widows is part of acceptable religion before God, coupled with keeping oneself from being "polluted by the world" (James 1:26-27). In the early years of the church, attention to the needs of these orphans and widows marked the followers of Christ as distinctive, for such persons were outcasts and the most rejected in society. They had no property or status. Response to their needs and their suffering involved innovative rescue efforts among Christians. Children were welcomed into homes. Widows received aid without expectation of payment for services rendered. Here were examples both of social ministry and social action.

It is true that the human needs we confront today are complex. Perhaps we know social concern is biblical, but we are inclined to create categories, to draw lines separating those worthy of our efforts and those not worthy. Alan Keith-Lucas offers a compelling perspective on this tendency.

> Who, then, are these people on relief [welfare]? We can search in vain for a common factor. What are they like? They are all sorts. Some are lazy, some industrious. So are we. Some are dependent; so are some of us, on our parents, perhaps, or on money we did not make ourselves. Some are moral, and some immoral. So, if I may say so, are we. Some cheat. So do some successful business men. They cheat the same government on income tax, not on an assistance grant. . . . Some are fortunate. Some are sick, and in ways that are not always apparent, particularly since the most prevalent sickness in the country today is mental rather than physical illness. Some are confused, some ambivalent, some discouraged, some without skills that the world can use, some victims of circumstance, and probably most a bewildered mixture of weakness, sin and plain bad luck that it would take more than a Solomon to know how much there was of each. The point is that they are people and in no way a class. Their only real common factor is that they do not fit in. They are outside. They have committed the world's most unpopular social sin—the failure to support themselves. And we, in our indignation, ascribe to them all the other sins, too.[14]

The Apostle Paul wrote with similar intent to the Galatians. "As we have opportunity, let us do good to all people, especially to those who belong to the family of believers" (Gal. 6:10). The family of believers may be those who attend one's local church or may be Christians in the church universal who suffer as a result of sin's destruction in this world. God's people spurred on to active social ministry never realize the full impact their endeavors may have on members of the family of faith, nor, for that matter, on the human family in general. This truth characterizes all ministry efforts, reminding each Christian that, just as with the gifts of preaching and teaching, the power of the Holy Spirit compels and administers helping ministries where individuals are dedicated to faithful service.

FORMS OF SOCIAL MINISTRY TODAY

To be effective, contemporary Christian social ministry must combine vision and passion with strategic planning, much like that evidenced by early Christian leaders. The urban crises our nation experienced in the sixties revealed the absence of interventions, Christian or otherwise. Since then American cities have been a focal point of revived social action efforts. Unfortunately, during the sixties, many churches left the crumbling cities rather than redesign their identity and ministry to reflect changing contexts. Churches which remained were often confronted by their own entrenched attitudes concerning the people and the problems in the cities. Cold, stone edifices became monuments to religious influences of the past while storefront churches embodied the new dynamic of the city at worship.[15]

Where churches did not or could not respond to human suffering, parachurch organizations linked their unique visions for social ministry with the mission of the local church. Some of today's parachurch ministries have become household words, and Christians generate great energy around opportunities to serve in programs such as Habitat for Humanity, SHARE, and Prison Fellowship. Such organizations are unique in bringing local church volunteers into one-to-one contact with suffering people in a well-organized manner so that ministry and assistance are truly redemptive.

Many cities are served by rescue missions, some of which are based in denominational ministries while others are freestanding and led by boards of volunteers from local churches. Historically, these organizations have served on behalf of local church bodies who were unable to be present in the most difficult sections of cities or to serve the neediest persons day after day. For more than a century, rescue missions have provided housing and food for transient men and women whose lives have been profoundly disrupted by economic and emotional upheavals. Contemporary missions frequently operate thriving social service centers and take leadership in social action efforts which call for the improvement of conditions for the homeless, provision of medical care for the indigent, and other necessary reforms needed to help distressed members of the community.

Some local churches operate thriving social ministry programs in their communities. The ideal social concern programs use church members as valued resources in various helping ministries within their own fellowship. Getting to the point of providing a thriving program requires substantial effort. For many churches, the options simply seem overwhelming. Where to begin? How to know which need most merits their attention? William Pinson suggests a few test questions by which a church might determine its priorities for social ministry:

1. Which social problems affect the most people in our community?
2. Which problems are the most seriously damaging to human life?
3. Which needs are being dealt with in the least adequate way by other groups?
4. Which problems are we best equipped to handle in light of our resources?
5. Which needs do we feel God is leading us to deal with?[16]

Christians should be involved in real and urgent situations about which it is clearly the business of the church and its members to do something, provided they have the ability and personnel to do the work. The temptation to dabble in other issues which are not in the nature of clear need and do not call for immediate action should be avoided. "There are enough chronic social ills present and continuing, like poverty and the harm it does to the many poor, to give reason for ongoing action ministries between emergencies."[17]

Often, ongoing programmatic efforts in local church ministries follow on the heels of crises which serve to mobilize church activity on behalf of persons previously unknown to the church, but whose circumstances point to an opportunity for service over the long term. For instance, a fire in one urban community left hundreds homeless. Businesses were destroyed and families already at their limit now were without shelter, clothing, work, or food. Basic struggles associated with devastating loss immobilized families. Emergency supplies of food and clothing collected by church groups throughout the region mitigated the urgent needs, but ongoing relationships between those suffering and the church volunteers truly ministered grace.

Volunteers helped families wade through the paperwork required to claim emergency relief. Contacts with church members helped some locate jobs. An after-school program was identified as a long-standing need in the community, and the church launched a program to that end. Other real needs were discovered which one church took to its church-wide planning process so that as a body it might determine the potential for future intervention. This relationship, generated through emergency, became the context for a response when future matters of urgency surfaced. These included issues related to pending public policy debates, including discussion of financial services to senior citizens, many of whom had become involved in the local church ministries as a result of the outreach of the church during the crisis. The social ministry of these churches changed the image the community had of them and gave credibility to everything else they did.

Social ministry projects can be administered from a central source, such as ecumenical community ministries, or under the auspices of individual programs, including churches or voluntary agencies which may serve as representatives of a specific denomination. The term "ecumenical community ministries" describes a group of two or more churches of more than one denomination which come together for the purpose of providing ministry within a specific community. They organize themselves legally as nonprofit agencies and are funded by donations from neighborhood congregations and public and private sources. Professional social workers lead these programs and rely heavily on volunteers from supportive churches.[18] Each center addresses basic life issues and needs that are unique to a particular location. One potential drawback of this centralized approach is that the service location is often geographically distant from the local church that sponsors it. Members of the church can then view social ministry merely as a line item on a budget, an obligation to be satisfied by dropping money into an offering basket, rather than a place of firsthand encounter with brothers and sisters in need. On the other hand, community ministries can unify the noblest of energies as outlets of social concern.

One remarkable example of a thriving Christian social ministry program is found in First Baptist Church, Montgomery, Alabama. An array of programs has been cultivated there under the leadership of Jane Ferguson. Ferguson believes that any church which operates its own Christian social ministry program must have as a goal "always to complement other ministries in town, never oppose and never compete with services offered in other places."[19] In fact, First Baptist has taken leadership in organizing the city on the basis of housing developments so that resources of local churches can be best put to use. One white and one black church work together in one community focused on the neighborhood housing development. Some activities include: work with the homeless shelters to provide personal care items on a regular basis; ministry to victims of urban crimes such as drive-by shootings; a Christmas shop for children to buy gifts for their parents and siblings; cultural introductions to new members of the community—a new kind of hospitality evangelism; GED tutoring and classes in English as a Second Language (ESL); citizenship classes; drug education; care teams for persons with AIDS; and 12-step support groups.

CONCLUSION

Relationship goes to the heart of ministry. Following the example of Jesus requires moving from an isolated "checkbook ministry" to involvement with people whose lives may have taken a different turn, but whose spirits often minister equally to the one who sees himself or herself as the helper. Much of community ministry consists of educating church members to do the work of social ministry. In a time when public funding is continually in jeopardy and human need increases, when the church is confronted with more needs and more people in need than ever before, the church is also blessed with many creative people poised to respond in a Christlike way. As you prepare for Christian ministry, you are challenged to become one such person—and to train many others as you undertake your ministry in the years ahead.

N O T E S

1. David O. Moberg, *Wholistic Christianity: An Appeal for a Dynamic, Balanced Faith* (Elgin, Ill.: Brethren, 1985), 103.

2. Charles G. Finney, *Lectures on Revivals of Religion*, quoted in Donald W. Dayton, *Discovering an Evangelical Heritage* (New York: Harper and Row, 1976), 18.

3. Moberg, *Wholistic Christianity*, 112.

4. Derrel R. Watkins, *Christian Social Ministry: An Introduction* (Nashville: Broadman, 1994), x.

5. Robert Kysar, *Called to Care: Biblical Images for Social Ministry* (Minneapolis: Fortress, 1991), 44.

6. David Claerbaut, *Urban Ministry* (Grand Rapids: Zondervan, 1983), 25–26.

7. Watkins, *Christian Social Ministry*.

8. C. Anne Davis, "The Practice of Urban Ministry: Christian Social Ministries," *Review and Expositor* 80 (1983): 523.

9. Dieter T. Hessel, *A Social Action Primer* (Philadelphia: Westminster, 1972), 29.

10. Kysar, *Called to Care*, 11.

11. Watkins, *Christian Social Ministry*, 54.

12. Ibid., 32–44.

13. G. Willis Bennett, *Effective Urban Church Ministry* (Nashville: Broadman, 1983), 33.

14. Alan Keith-Lucas, "Christian Maturity and the Helping Process," from a series of three talks given to the Southern Baptist Counseling Guidance, Nashville, Tenn., 1963.

15. Janet Furness Spressart, "Social Action and the Church," in *Church Social Work*, ed. Diana R. Garland (St. Davids, Pa.: North American Association of Christians in Social Work, 1992), 110.

16. William M. Pinson, Jr., *Applying the Gospel* (Nashville: Broadman, 1975), 82.

17. Charles Y. Furness, "Helping Ministries Handbook: A Handbook for Guidance to Local Churches in Helping Ministries" (Ph.D. diss., Western

Conservative Baptist Seminary, Portland, Ore., 1978), 241–42.

18. Patricia L. Bailey, "Social Work Practice in Community Ministries," in *Church Social Work*, ed. Diana R. Garland (St. Davids, Pa.: North American Association of Christians in Social Work, 1992), 60.

19. Personal communication with Jane Ferguson, 1995.

For Further Reading

Bennett, G. Willis. *Effective Urban Church Ministry*. Nashville: Broadman, 1983.

Claerbaut, David. *Urban Ministry*. Grand Rapids: Zondervan, 1983.

Furness, Charles Y. "Helping Ministries Handbook: A Handbook for Guidance to Local Churches in Helping Ministries." Ph.D. diss., Western Conservative Baptist Seminary, Portland, Ore., 1978.

Garland, Diana R., ed. *Church Social Work*. St. Davids, Pa.: North American Association of Christians in Social Work, 1992.

Hessel, Dieter T. *A Social Action Primer*. Philadelphia: Westminster, 1972.

Kysar, Robert. *Called to Care: Biblical Images for Social Ministry*. Minneapolis: Fortress, 1991.

Moberg, David O. *Wholistic Christianity: An Appeal for a Dynamic, Balanced Faith*. Elgin, Ill.: Brethren, 1985.

Pinson, William M., Jr. *Applying the Gospel*. Nashville: Broadman, 1975.

Watkins, Derrel R. *Christian Social Ministry: An Introduction*. Nashville: Broadman, 1994.

16

EVANGELISM THROUGH CHURCH PLANTING

THOM S. RAINER

Church planting is "the single most effective evangelistic methodology under heaven,"[1] reports C. Peter Wagner, one of the foremost authorities in church planting. The Christian denominations experiencing the most rapid evangelistic growth have been those that give a high priority to church planting. The Church of the Nazarene, the Assemblies of God, and the Southern Baptist Convention are among the leading denominations in conversion growth, with a significant portion of that growth coming from newly started churches.

A study of churches of all denominations in California's Santa Clarita Valley concluded that newer churches are much more likely to reach people for Christ than older churches. The older churches in this region were baptizing 4 persons for every 100 members, while newer churches were baptizing 16 persons per 100 members![2]

As you consider God's call in your life, you may find yourself

Thom S. Rainer is Associate Professor of Church Growth and Evangelism and Dean of the Billy Graham School of Missions, Evangelism, and Church Growth at the Southern Baptist Theological Seminary, Louisville, Kentucky.

leading or participating in the starting of a new church. In the Billy Graham School of Evangelism, Church Growth, and Missions at the Southern Baptist Theological Seminary, one of the fastest-growing vocational objectives for students is church planting. This chapter will seek to impress upon you the great need for new churches, some of the compelling challenges of planting churches in your generation, and a brief introduction to the proven effective approaches to starting new churches. In the process, I hope you may be able to discover some of the excitement others have experienced as you open yourself to the leading of the Holy Spirit to the possibility of being called to the vocation of church planting as your focused task in ministry.

DO WE REALLY NEED MORE CHURCHES?[3]

"I drive four miles to attend this church," the member protested. "And I must pass at least ten or more other churches to get here. I know for a fact that many of these churches are struggling. The last thing we need is another church. We need to build up these other churches first—including our own!"

That voice of protest was registered at a church business meeting where a proposal was made to start a new church. It is perhaps the most common objection raised by Christians who are concerned about church planting. Do we really need new churches? Are such objections valid? Could we be better stewards of people, time, and money by stimulating growth in existing churches rather than starting new ones?

In 1820 our nation's population was 9.6 million. With nearly 11,000 congregations, the new nation had one church for 875 residents. By 1860, an aggressive four decades of church planting resulted in a fivefold increase in churches to 54,000. With the population increased to 31.6 million, a church was available for every 600 residents. Unfortunately the trend toward more churches per capita stopped in 1860. By 1990 the ratio of churches to the population remained about the same, despite the passage of 130 years.[4]

The Growing Unchurched Population

A more important consideration than the ratios of churches to the population is the number of people who do not attend church at all. In the last quarter of a century our nation has become a true mission field. A growing percentage of the population of the United States has dropped out of church involvement. One of the consequences of this trend is that as many as 85 percent of all churches have either plateaued or are declining.[5]

The baby boomer generation accounts for the greatest number of unchurched Americans. The reasons for this phenomenon are twofold and straightforward. First, the boomers are the largest generation in America's history. Those persons born between 1946 and 1964 number over 76 million and represent one-third of the total population.[6] Second, the boomers were the first American generation to abandon the church in such extraordinary numbers. Enough has been written about this over-studied generation to fill a library. Many boomers say that the church is irrelevant to them, so the average boomer attends church only six times a year.[7] Of course, included in that number are boomers who do not attend church at all as well as some who are very faithful attenders.

The baby busters and their children represent another significant portion of the unchurched population. What is perhaps most significant about the busters is that they are a second generation of unchurched people. For many of the busters and their children, the experience of attending church is unknown.

An article in the *Dallas Morning News* speaks of this religious gap when telling the story of boomer parents who decided to return to church. Their pilgrimage was a return based upon their young son's confusion. Blake, four years old at the time, had spent the night with his grandparents. The next morning the grandparents were preparing to attend worship services when the parents came to get their son. Blake, however, insisted on staying longer, saying his grandparents were "going to Church's and I want to stay for fried chicken."[8] The child's concept of church was a fried chicken fast-food chain!

We must see that our present and future generations in America are true mission fields. Today a new zeal is evident. Many Christian leaders desire to reach the unchurched with the same enthusiasm that was evident for international missions in the nineteenth and early twentieth centuries. This zeal will manifest itself in thousands of new churches. And God may call you to be a part of this exciting ministry in missions.

A Need to Reach New Cultures

A proponent of cross-cultural church planting notes that the Southern Baptist Convention will soon have 10,000 ethnic congregations and 4,000 congregations in predominantly black communities.[9] This is an amazing development for a denomination whose origins include issues of race. In fact, Southern Baptists probably would not be growing numerically without the non-white congregations.

The American church is waking up to the fact that the congregations in their existing structures can not reach the wide variety of cultural and ethnic groups in our nation. New churches must be started for such evangelistic endeavors. Some churches and denominations are admittedly responding only to precipitous and long-term declines. But even the motive of survival can be used of God to reach people groups for Christ.

One particularly exciting trend in this type of church planting is a positive response to changing communities. For many years the response of churches located in neighborhoods that have changed from a single race of residents to a mixed racial population, has been to die a slow death or to close its doors and relocate again in a homogeneous suburb. The net result has been the loss of a Christian witness in the community. Sad to say, many of these perfectly usable church buildings have been sold to small business owners who have used them for restaurants, furniture stores, or warehouses.

Today many churches are responding two different ways to keep the witness for the gospel alive in such a situation. A small number of congregations are reaching out to witness to the new residents, regardless of their race, leading them to faith in Christ, and discipling them to assume the leadership responsibilities of the church. I consulted with a church in Florida whose attendance had dropped dramatically when African Americans moved into the neighborhood and whites exited in large numbers. Though most of the whites left the area surrounding the church, slightly over 100 decided that they would not let their church die. When a pastoral vacancy occurred, the all-white church called an African-American pastor. Eventually, the black community began to sense that the church was "theirs." Within two years the church was growing again, but this time with a majority of the church comprised of African Americans. In essence a new church was planted in anticipation of the death of another church.

A more common occurrence today is the sale or gift of a church in a transitional neighborhood. In Birmingham, Alabama, Hunter Street Baptist Church's attendance had declined to the point where almost everyone realized that the church's death was imminent. Hunter Street was an all-white church in what had evolved into a mostly black community. Nearby, Sardis Baptist Church, an African-American church, was bursting at the seams as it reached the residents in the area. Had nothing taken place, Hunter Street would have closed and Sardis would have been limited because of its small facilities.

In an arrangement beneficial to both groups, the Hunter Street congregation sold its facilities to the Sardis congregation. Hunter Street then moved to the Birmingham suburb of Hoover. In less than ten years Sardis had grown a strong congregation to an average attendance approaching 1,000 while Hunter Street's former congregation grew in its new location and surpassed 2,000 in attendance. In essence, two new churches were planted though both existed prior to their relocation. Hunter Street Baptist Church particularly was a church plant because it was just a few short years from death.

The Growing Diversity in Worship Styles

Shortly after his departure from Keith Baptist Church, pastor Phillip Lewis shared with me his frustrations that ultimately led to his resignation. (The names of the pastor and the church have been changed; the story is true.) A significant number of the younger adults had complained about the "slow and boring" worship services. They wanted to invite their friends to church, but they were afraid their friends would feel the same way about the worship services.

As the church leadership began discussing a more contemporary worship service, the fights began. Never had such heated emotions emerged in the church's history. James Emery White says, "Growing churches which have transitioned . . . to non-traditional forms of music have often, as a result, received enormous criticism."[10] Elmer Towns agrees that worship styles are the greatest source of controversy in churches today.[11] And Russell Chandler sees the debate continuing: "Nowhere is the dissonance greater than in discussion about what's 'proper' in 'Christian' music."[12]

Phillip Lewis decided to try to please everyone. He proposed moving the traditional service to 8:30 A.M. The 10:45 A.M. service would be a contemporary worship service. The later time would benefit the young adults who had to get children ready on Sunday mornings. With some acrimony still remaining, Keith Baptist Church made the transition to two worship services.

For two months there was peace in the church family. The younger adults were particularly happy with the new contemporary format. They invited their friends and growth was obvious. Then the murmuring began again.

Those in the early service missed the later worship time they had enjoyed for years. "Why were we the ones who had to move?" they complained. Furthermore, the multiple worship services left many vacant pews. And their service was not experiencing growth.

The murmur became a roar as the traditionalists threatened to withdraw their financial support. Phillip Lewis decided that the fight was not worth it, so the single worship service returned. But this time no one was happy with him, so his resignation became inevitable.

Another trend that is accentuating the growth of church planting is the realization that America's wide cultural diversity often manifests itself in worship-style preferences. Sometimes it is simply not possible to please everyone in a single location, so a new church is started.

When I was a pastor in Birmingham, one of the reasons we started a new church was to offer a contemporary worship service. One location had hymnals; the other did not. One location had a choir, the other did not. One location had an organ and piano, the other had a variety of instruments. One location had padded pews, the other had padded folding chairs.

American missionaries in foreign mission fields have long recognized the need to contextualize or to adapt culturally to their mission field. American churchgoers must realize that our nation is culturally diverse, and new churches are needed to offer worship services in the culture that is being reached.

Several of my former students have served churches with a

variety of worship styles: liturgical, traditional, blended, and contemporary. One of them actually started an innovative church in Indiana where the service and the music are designed for country and country-gospel music lovers to the joy and satisfaction of its new members! These are just a few examples of the many changes taking place across our nation. It appears that there will be an increase in new churches in the twenty-first century and that will be in part a response to our nation's cultural diversity. Meeting the challenge to win people to Jesus Christ and to establish discipling churches in this kind of environment will take courageous, faithful, and persevering ministers of the gospel for generations to come.

THE CHALLENGES OF PLANTING CHURCHES

As the dean of a school whose focus is Great Commission ministries, I tell our students interested in church planting to prepare for the most exciting *and* the most challenging days of their lives. Typically the challenges in church planting will come from one of five areas.

Giving Up Members
Change rarely happens without some kind of grief. This is certainly true when a church has long established customs and multiple generation families. Consequently, there is pain in seeing members of a church family move to a new church start even if the congregation has felt led to establish it. In some instances, the grief is handled in open and supportive ways, but sometimes the grief is unresolved and hardens into bitterness. The members who decide to plant the new church are usually among the best stewards of the older church. The sponsoring church is really giving its best. Much of the resistance to starting new churches results from the pain of anticipated separation and loss, both in persons and finances.

There are many reasons for the intensity of this grief process, especially the situations where bitterness is a major result. One of the primary and often hidden reasons comes from a misapplication of loyalty to a single local church. Unfortunately, Christians often commit themselves in loyalty to their own congregations much as they do to their favorite college or university sports teams. That makes other churches, especially new ones, the "competitors," even "enemies," in the struggle for institutional life. How much closer to New Testament teaching that other Christians and other churches are friends and allies in the task to reach each new generation to Christ and together to do battle against every force of evil. We need a generation of pastors and other ministers to lead members of their churches to catch the vision of a Great Commission mission mind-set. The focus must be on eternal kingdom growth rather than short-term losses the church may experience.

Loss of Funds

When a sponsoring church has enough vision to send some of its people to start a new church, it is aware that it is giving away tithers and above-tithers. This impacts the sponsoring church, lowering both their budget and cash flow. God, however, honors the commitment of the parent church. Wagner noted a study showing that a sponsoring church usually replaced its people sent to the new church within six months. The same holds true for finances. He also discovered that the pattern depends significantly on the attitude of the parent church, particularly the pastor. "If the pastor has a negative attitude toward the church planting process it might negatively affect the parent church's subsequent growth."[13]

Start-up Cost

Some denominations may spend as much as $500,000 to start a new church.[14] If such expenditures were the norm, the argument that high start-up costs make church planting prohibitive might have validity. In a new church in which I was involved we were able to start the church for $9,000. Since we had received a gift for new church work for about that same amount, the sponsoring church did not have to take any money out of the budget. Wagner discovered that an Assemblies of God district in North Carolina had planted eighty-five churches in the 1970s at a cost of about $2,500 each! Church consultant Lyle Schaller has long maintained that financial subsidies hinder new churches. This suggests that careful attention should be given to discern whether the money needed to pay for staff, land, buildings, and general operating expenses in a church plant situation should come from the growth and income of the church rather than an up-front allocation for these costs.

Hurting Other Churches

Many fear that established churches will be hurt if a new church is started in an area of existing churches. Since we are to love other brothers and sisters in Christ, perhaps church planting in an area of existing churches should not take place. Such an approach presents a problem since almost every place in the metropolitan areas of the United States has several churches. Most studies, however, have identified improvements in the entire Christian community when new churches are planted.[15]

Wagner is right when he says that, regardless of other churches' approval, the task of church planting must not be hindered. I am well aware, from my church's experience in planting a new church, that the whims of all churches in the area will never be satisfied. How then should we respond? Wagner says to love them and plant churches anyway.

I believe it is important and beneficial to enjoy the approval of existing churches when a new church is planted. But while such an approval is a plus, it should not be regarded as a prerequisite. As the parable of the shepherd indicates, the needs of the lost are a higher consideration than the needs of those who are safe and sound in the churches. As we learn from the modern shopping mall theory of merchandising, two churches even in close proximity to each other will reach many more unchurched than either one could hope to do alone.[16]

Harder Work

An unspoken but very real concern of some people in existing churches is that continuing growth (or even maintenance) of their churches will be more difficult with a new church in the area. I believe that a new church can raise the outreach consciousness for an area. Greater effort may need to be expended in the area by old and new churches alike but, after all, such *is* Great Commission obedience.

OPTIONS FOR PLANTING CHURCHES

Church planting will indeed be a method for church growth that will take many believers from their comfort zones, but Christianity was never meant to be a business-as-usual faith. The early church was always on the cutting edge of reaching people for Christ. Even when persecution broke out against the church, Christians scattered throughout Judea and Samaria. They shared their faith and started churches as they fled (Acts 8:1-4).

How then do we start churches? As a Southern Baptist, I was not familiar with the many options available to plant a church. My background had exposed me only to the traditional methods of church planting. Now, in my denomination and others, may new options for church planting abound. In fact, Russell Chandler, former religion writer for the *Los Angeles Times*, wrote that Southern Baptists and others are now on the cutting edge of new forms of church planting: "Southern Baptists talk about 'satellite' churches. Elmer Towns, head of the Church Growth Institute in Lynchburg, Virginia, calls the concept 'the geographical expanded parish church.' Others refer to it as the 'perimeter' church. Whatever we call the idea, churches practicing it are certainly among the pacesetting ministries on the leading edge of the coming millennium."[17] Let us examine some of these options open to starting new churches as we approach the twenty-first century.

Traditional

In the traditional model of church planting, a sponsoring church sends a nucleus of members to start a new church in a geographical area. The new church is usually located within driving distance of the sponsoring church. The goal is for the new church to become totally autonomous as soon as possible. The success rate of these new churches is very high. Members of the nucleus are typically dedicated givers and workers. Because of the good base, the chances of survival are excellent. The disadvantage, especially in congregationally governed churches, is that this system does not have any mechanism of accountability for the new church to become a parent church. For example, my former church, Green Valley Baptist, was started by Philadelphia Baptist Church in Birmingham, Alabama. Twenty-seven years elapsed before Green

Valley started a church! Why? One of the primary reasons is that Green Valley as a church was accountable to no one or no group. An autonomous church has its advantages, but lack of account-ability is a definite disadvantage. One of the valuable improve-ments needed as new churches are planted would be the devel-opment of a local congregationally based satisfactory system of church-starting accountability.

Colonization

Colonization is identical to the traditional model with one major exception. The nucleus of members sent by the parent church move to a different geographical area. Those members must sell their homes, find new jobs, and send their children to new schools. A radical level of commitment to the Great Commission is a requi-site for the success of the Colonization Model of church planting.

Adoption

A Southern Baptist church in Texas heard of three churches in the area that had made a decision to close their doors. The pastor of the thriving church made a commitment of providing the people, the funds, and the leadership to keep the churches open. Though new churches were not planted, three churches were kept alive and the impact was similar. While it is easier to have babies than to raise the dead, God needs mission-minded leaders to turn around dying churches.

Church Splits

When churches split, the result is usually pain and dissension on both sides. God definitely does not approve of divisiveness in the body of Christ. Yet God can use a bad situation for good. Wagner addresses the predicament positively.

> What can we say to this phenomenon? I'm sure that God does not approve of church splits or the causes of them listed by McGavran and Hunter. Nor would I go on record as advocating church splitting as a church planting method-ology. It is much better to pray and plan and minister in harmony. Nevertheless, when the dust settles, I have to believe that God loves both of the resulting churches and

accepts them as the bride of Christ. . . . He can be glorified through the offspring of accidental parenthood.[18]

Satellite

For many the satellite model is the most exciting development in church planting. John Vaughn describes this method in *The Large Church*: "Large churches with satellite groups combine the best of two growth strategies. . . . Although many of these churches are committed to building a large central church, most are just as committed to penetrating and reaching the city through the use of small groups coordinated fully, in most instances, by the parent congregation."[19] The satellite model is similar to the secular model of branch banking. Each new location has a high degree of autonomy, but it is still a part of the same church. In other words, there is one church with many locations. This method may be the way of the future in American churches. The new church satellite can reach a new geographic area but still have all the combined resources of the parent and other satellite churches. This model also engenders accountability. Each of the locations look to one another to start new churches. This model usually includes a plan for mutual accountability in a variety of areas and is probably the single greatest strength of the satellite model.

Multicongregational

The multicongregational model of church planting allows for the planting of a new church in the facility of an existing church. This method works best in a multiethnic area. An English-speaking church, for example, shares its facilities with Korean, Hispanic, and Chinese churches. Each church uses the building at different hours. The different groups may choose to be autonomous, or they may decide to be subgroups of a larger, single church.

Multicampus

This model is slightly different from the satellite approach. Multicampus refers to one church in more than one location. Unlike the satellite model, the multicampus church has one membership roll, one budget, and one staff. The two more well-known examples of this model are Mt. Paran Church of God in Atlanta, Paul Walker, pastor; and The Church on the Way in Van Nuys,

California, Jack Hayford, pastor.

Sodality Models
In the church-planting models previously described, the institution planting new churches was the local church. In the sodality model of church planting some agency other than a local church starts the new church. That agency can be a denominational agency, a parachurch organization, or it could refer to the starting of churches by individuals not specifically sponsored or connected with a local church.

CHURCH PLANTING: A MOST EFFECTIVE EVANGELISTIC METHODOLOGY

Our Lord commanded us to make disciples of all nations. Those of us who study churches have found with consistency that church planting truly leads to disciple-making. Not only are individuals confronted with the claims of Jesus Christ as the new church grows, they are also incorporated into the body to become fruit-bearing disciples themselves. Church planting may very well be one of the most effective evangelistic and disciple-making methodologies under heaven.

You may have the opportunity to be involved in church planting while you are at seminary or after you graduate. If so, you may well discover such ministry to be among the most challenging ventures of your life. But you will also find that it can be the most exciting and rewarding as well. If indeed you become a church-planting minister, you will have no doubt that you have answered God's call to make disciples of all nations.

N O T E S
1. C. Peter Wagner, *Church Planting for a Greater Harvest* (Ventura, Calif.: Regal, 1990), 11. One of the most practical books on church planting in print.
2. Thom S. Rainer, *The Book of Church Growth: History, Theology, and Principles* (Nashville: Broadman and Holman, 1993), 206.
3. Portions of this section adapted from Thom S. Rainer, *Giant Awakenings* (Nashville: Broadman and Holman, 1995). See chapter 8, "Therefore Go . . . :

The Explosion of Church Planting."

4. Lyle E. Schaller, *44 Questions for Church Planters* (Nashville: Abingdon, 1991), 15. Schaller's book has a wealth of information about the American historical data on church planting.

5. Aubrey Malphurs, *Planting Growing Churches for the 21st Century* (Grand Rapids: Baker, 1992), 13.

6. Ibid., 14.

7. Ibid., 36.

8. Cited in Malphurs, *Planting Growing Churches*, 36–37.

9. Charles L. Chaney, *Church Planting at the End of the Twentieth Century*, rev. ed. (Wheaton, Ill.: Tyndale, 1991), xi.

10. James Emery White, *Opening the Front Door: Worship and Church Growth* (Nashville: Convention, 1992), 82.

11. Elmer Towns, *Ten of Today's Most Innovative Churches* (Ventura, Calif.: Regal, 1990), 15.

12. Russell Chandler, *Racing toward 2001: The Forces Shaping America's Religious Future* (Grand Rapids: Zondervan/HarperCollins, 1992), 299.

13. Wagner, *Church Planting*, 38.

14. Ibid., 39.

15. See specifically the citing of a study of churches on the Oahu island of Hawaii in Wagner, *Church Planting*, 40. All churches on the island experienced a growth in attendance after a Southern Baptist church was planted there.

16. Ibid., 40–41.

17. Chandler, *Racing toward 2001*, 240. Chandler's book is an excellent study of trends in religion as we approach the twenty-first century.

18. Wagner, *Church Planting*, 65.

19. John N. Vaughn, *The Large Church* (Grand Rapids: Baker, 1985), 23.

F O R   F U R T H E R   R E A D I N G

Faircloth, Samuel D. *Church Planting for Reproduction*. Grand Rapids: Baker, 1991.

Green, Michael. *Evangelism through the Local Church*. Nashville: Oliver Nelson, 1992.

Hadaway, C. Kirk. *Church Growth Principles*. Nashville: Broadman, 1991.

Petersen, Jim. *Evangelism as a Lifestyle*. Colorado Springs: NavPress, 1980.

Rainer, Thom S. *Great Awakenings*. Nashville: Broadman, 1991.

Schaller, Lyle E. *Forty-four Questions for Church Planters*. Nashville: Abingdon, 1991.

Wagner, C. Peter. *Spiritual Power and Church Growth*. Altamonte Springs, Fla.: Creation House, 1986.

Warren, Rick. *The Purpose Driven Church*. Grand Rapids: Zondervan, 1995.

17

CHURCH STAFF RELATIONS

DENNIS E. WILLIAMS

At the turn of the century in American churches, pastors with occasional assistance from part-time ministry helpers, managed the ministry and leadership needs of most Christian congregations. Some of these pastors developed their assistants into coordinated ministry teams and provided their congregations with well-organized ministries. Many of them operated their churches and their ministry helpers with permissive supervision, or no supervision at all, which yielded a wide degree of independence between ministers and little if any coordinated activity. Both of these, the coordinated and the uncoordinated traditions, live on in the present.

During that same period of time, the churches grew rapidly. Many church members have had excellent experiences in their everyday secular vocations and have experienced the high productivity of coordinated leadership teams. They continue to expect, even demand, good if not professional teamwork from the multiple ministers serving their congregations. Many church-

Dennis E. Williams is Professor and Dean of the School of Christian Education at the Southern Baptist Theological Seminary, Louisville, Kentucky.

es have developed some of the finest staff ministry teams the church has ever known. It is also unfortunately true that many church staff groups seem infected with the twin virus of continuous conflict and dysfunctionality.

Today, thousands of well-trained and seasoned ministry specialists are available to be called and employed to serve a congregation's needs for ministry leadership. Because all of these called and competent ministers possess differing gifts, have been well trained to offer specialized leadership programs, and actually work with different groups of members within their congregations, one would think some sort of successful plan to coordinate their goals and activities would have been developed routinely. Of course, many different ones have been developed. Some of the better plans, however, prove to be the most ineffective.

The most popular staff supervision method is the pastor-directed ministry staff. In this arrangement, the various ministers of the congregation serve under the supervision of the "preaching pastor," or the pastor designated as the senior minister. This is the kind of solution most Baptist and evangelical congregations seem to understand best. However, completely harmonious teams of ministers in this plan are often the exception in many of these churches. Some problems related to differing priorities, differing ministry styles, conflicting personality types, or inept or absent supervisory skills frequently cause major difficulties as church staff groups work out their ministries together. Only when an agreed-upon plan to assign areas of responsibility, accountability, equitable allocation of available resources for each staff ministry, and a regularized method of staff coordination is in place, does the local church have any hope to enjoy the benefits of a nurturing and productive staff. Then, the staff members become committed to the accomplishment of holistic church mission goals in a balanced and harmonious manner.

Of course, there is no one plan suitable for every, or even most, congregations. However, the main thrust of this chapter is to speak about some of the ingredients of a biblically based and successfully functional church-staff organization process. To do so, I will share somewhat of my experience of current ministry teams now serving in local evangelical churches. Some patterns of leadership which have emerged from our American culture

and some scriptural principles to inform your thoughts and discussions about a church staff and its working relations have also
been included.

WHAT IS A CHURCH STAFF?

For the purposes of this essay, a church staff consists of a group of
ministers assembled by a single congregation to meet its own
ministry needs. Ideally, the ministers on a church staff serve
under the supervision of a lead minister or senior pastor and
have been "called to" and "employed by" their local churches to
serve in either full- or part-time ministerial roles.

WHAT IS THE CHURCH STAFF'S MISSION?

The church staff's overall goal is to minister to the members and
to assist the church in the accomplishment of its mission: that
mission being at least to lead the congregation in worship, evangelism and outreach, local and worldwide missions, Christian
education including discipleship training, age-group ministries,
prayer, mutual caring, fellowship, and much more. While each
individual minister has specialized preparation for ministry with
a specific set of programs to administer, each staff member is
expected to be committed to the smooth flowing function of the
local church as a unity, that is, as a "body of Christ."

WHY HAVE A CHURCH STAFF?

Many local churches in twentieth-century America have experienced unprecedented growth in numbers of members. This
growth has produced demands for a variety of ministries and a
requirement for "excellence" in their performance. A "consumer
mentality" in the nation at large has also invaded the churches.
Most subgroups within larger congregations have had their own
full-time minister on their church staff for years, each with a specialized presentation such as Christian education, youth, children, music, evangelism, and pastoral care. In this transitional
age, swelling populations of midlife members and the ever
enlarging group of post-sixty-five-year-old members are now

clamoring for their own ministry specialist as well. As congregations have continued their mushroom-like growth, the pastor's time for preaching, pastoral care, leadership, and institutional management concerns, not to mention community and denominational ministries, have taken more than the time one has to offer. Now, some sort of administrative arrangement to concertize mission statements, prioritize programs, allocate resources, and coordinate and "calendar" activities is quite necessary.

THE CONCEPT OF THE STAFF IS BIBLICAL

The idea of a church staff is quite biblical. Jesus, in a sense, had a multiple staff with the twelve disciples. The division of labor in Acts 6 sees "seven men of good reputation" (v. 3, NASB) set aside to govern the distribution of food at the church's tables. The diversity of functions as found in Romans 12, 1 Corinthians 12 and 14, and Ephesians 4 illustrate multiple and differing gifts for ministry. It takes little imagination to visualize the usefulness of Paul's companions as we trace his missionary journeys across the first-century Roman world. While the term "church staff" is not found in the Scriptures, the idea of people working together in ministry with each assisting others is certainly quite biblical.

Westing states that it is rare to find a church where a large segment of the congregation sees the hiring of staff as a means of training and mobilizing the laity for ministry.[1] We, however, must follow the outline given in Ephesians 4 where the called leaders are to equip God's people for ministry. Churches which add staff members to do what should be the congregation's work are missing the biblical model. Sometimes affluent churches will pay to have all of the work done rather than having the laypeople of the church involved in the ministry. When this happens laypeople are kept from exercising their gifts and the church is left with serious vacancies. In addition, if finances ever become limited, these extra staff positions are the first to go.

The biblical rationale for the position of staff member is that he or she is added in order to lead the people of the church to do the work of the ministry by equipping and training them. This can be in many different areas, but it is all ministry. The greatest compliment to a staff member, when he or she leaves a church, is that the ministry is carried on effectively by those who remained and were trained.

The key to successful ministry in the church is a team approach using the gifts and abilities of the congregation to fulfill the church's mission as stated. Notice again, not just the gifts of the "professional" staff members, but those of the entire congregation. The church staff is called to train and equip the congregation for this task.

HOW CAN A CHURCH STAFF WORK TOGETHER IN HARMONY?

Many crucial work issues arise in a multiple staff situation; these must be addressed. Expectations of a team ministry, accountability structures, interpersonal relationships, personal traits such as loyalty and respect, and the understanding of the church's ministries, its theology, and leadership patterns will be discussed in this section.

Expectations

Each staff member is to have a clearly assigned role and specific tasks of ministry to perform. There is no substitute for a clearly written job description for each position of staff ministry. While it is difficult to write a job description for the pastor, at least a broadly written document indicating areas of responsibility should be developed. It is especially important for staff team relations that the supervision responsibilities of the pastor in relation to the staff be forthrightly stated. If other more senior members of staff besides the pastor will supervise some other staff members, that should also be clearly written. If the pastor is to provide supervision for the staff member who is also giving supervision to a more junior staff member, that too should be clearly written.

Usually, when a church calls individuals to specialized ministry, the expectation of the church is that the work of that ministry would improve with the passing of time. Improvement will at least include additional accomplishments in the area of the mission statement of the church directly related to the particular area of service provided by the new staff member. These expectations should be clearly communicated in the job description or at least a letter of employment with a description of the way in which the new staff member will be evaluated also included.

The congregation's clear understanding of the role of each staff member is vital to the staffer's relationship with church members and the view he or she holds of his or her contribution to the ministry. "What does the pastor or the staff member do?" This question is not necessary when the role and duties are communicated clearly.

Staff members expect the senior pastor to initiate staff meetings and work to maintain open relationships and adequate communication.[2] The senior pastor should do all that is possible to help the staff member be successful in his or her work. This may require enough funds in the church budget to develop and/or maintain a ministry or it may mean that additional specialized training is provided at the expense of the church.

The principle of administration at work here is that the success of the pastor is measured directly by the success of those working under his or her supervision. It is at least good common sense to encourage and provide staff members with the resources necessary to do their ministry. By doing so, the senior pastor also is seen as being successful.

The senior pastor has obligations as the leader of the staff team to support them, to provide guidance, and to offer overall pastoral wisdom to assist the staff team to be successful in ministry. The staff members, in their turn, have obligations to the senior pastor of loyalty, support, submission, and Christian love.[3]

Team Ministry

Ministry, to be biblical and to have any chance to be successful, must be a whole ministry to the entire church. All who serve, staff or lay, employed or volunteer, are concerned with this total ministry. All who minister share in this common purpose and joint responsibility. If harmonious and satisfying staff relationships are to be realized, each member of the staff must sincerely want each other member to have the fullest possible success with his or her assignments. Good staff relations are not created only by a proper set of job descriptions or a definite assignment of ministerial duties. They come when there is acceptance, understanding, and a steadfast allegiance to a common overall purpose.[4] This underscores the importance of the mission statement which is to be developed and agreed upon through congregational deliberation, prayer, and allegiance.

Churches expect staff people to work together and be supportive of each other in ministry. Teamwork, cooperation, and collegiality are essential. Those who do their ministries alone and are critical of other staff, destroy the team principle.

Beginning with our belief that God wants the entire congregation to work together in harmony as it fulfills its mission statement, then it is logical to assume that the church staff as a whole would model this type of harmony and teamwork as well. This is not the place to implement the "Do as I say and not what I do." Building a team means that the leader does not force others into submission, but leads them to active participation by empowering them to be involved in decision-making as a group or team.[5]

The church's stated *purpose* and *mission statement* are vital to the teamwork concept expressed here. Friendly and collegial relationships can be strengthened when the purpose and mission statement are part of the commitment of the entire staff. Staff members will want to be a part of the team. They experience this when they are welcome at deacon's meetings and at other leadership and planning sessions. It is true that most do not want to spend all of their time with committees, but when staff members are kept from these crucial decision-making meetings, they question the sense of teamwork and togetherness in ministry.

Healthy teamwork accomplishes more than merely getting people to work together. It enables people to produce extraordinary accomplishments through mutuality and cooperation. More can be accomplished when a church staff works together as a team than when the work is done by a collection of individuals. The health of the team is measured by the way the team is able to set goals and strategies, make and implement decisions, resolve conflicts, change, maintain accountability, and satisfy team members.[6] Healthy teams have satisfied members who rely on one another for a sense of uniqueness, belongingness, fellowship, and accomplishment.[7]

Also healthy teams are open to new people coming in to share in the ministry. Each new person adds a different dynamic. When several new people are added, the complexity of staff relationships are multiplied significantly. Care should be taken to assist the new members to become integrated into the already assembled staff.

Years ago while attending a church growth seminar, a pastor made the statement, "I don't feel God wants every church to grow." The group was stunned. The pastor explained that in recent months new people had moved into their community and some had joined the church. Many of these people had gifts superior to those who were already in the church, and they began to assume some of the leadership positions. "The church just wasn't like it was and it had lost something." Some of us said, "Praise the Lord," but the shock was that this pastor was expressing his insecurity openly. The changes caused by bright new leadership challenged everyone to face change in the faces of new people. However much a church wishes to grow and change, they are usually not prepared for the discomfort of giving up leadership to strangers who will "only change things to their own way."

This is an example of a fear to use gifted people because it will make things different. Is it possible that "different" might mean "better," or at least more of what God wants the congregation to be and do?

Unfortunately some proud leaders nearly kill a church, or at least starve the church infrastructure by withholding leadership positions to those who are best prepared to lead. The church suffers because the old leaders, including the staff, won't tap other willing and available leaders to help the team. This includes both the "paid" professional staff as well as the volunteers.

When change is openly feared and when people are not willing to study new ideas and new thoughts, the potential for an effective team ministry is greatly reduced. The truth is that to move forward in ministry today, change must be at the forefront. This is not change for the sake of change, but change to help us reach the mission statement of the church in a more effective way.

Church staff members, who are team members, must be willing to question and challenge each other in a Christian environment, with give and take, developing a rationale for implementing change. This usually results in the staff working together and providing a greater ministry.

Other elements relating to a team ministry that facilitate good staff relationships include: accountability, valuing each other and the church, loyalty, mutual respect, a supportive understanding of all of the church's ministries, a common theology, and a servant leadership style.

Accountability in ministry, especially for church staff members, is a continual concern. One person said that the ministry is one job where you can be lazy and no one will find out. That person was wrong. We are all accountable to our Lord. We are also accountable to the individual supervising us. In churches, this accountability also reaches to the members of the congregation. It is important that each staff member have just one person as supervisor to whom he or she is responsible. This is true even if the individual works in different areas of ministry. It is difficult, if not impossible, to work directly for a supervisor, a committee, and a congregation at the same time. In fact, it could amount to major stress if and when two or more supervisors have conflicting expectations of a person for whom they provide partial supervision.

Good relationships between staff members are essential for a church. This requires an openness to "give-and-take" with understanding, forgiveness, and respect for each other. Church ministries are hindered when the staff members cannot get along or work only within their own sphere of ministry without regard for the entire church ministry as a whole.

Relationships are hindered when staff members do not see the value and importance of other aspects of the church's ministry. Here are some examples:

• The youth minister only works with young people and ignores their parents and the other ministries of the church. This results in a youth ministry that is separate from the whole church.

• The children's ministry is only called upon to supply child care and baby-sitting for "adult" functions without the consideration of integrating all ages together in some of the church ministries. Children's workers feel "used" when this happens. Yes, they do provide this service for the church, but they will feel more a part of the ministry if they can also be included in ministries that involve them.

• Music ministries set meetings, rehearsals, and performances without consideration of the total church calendar. This portrays an attitude that only *their* ministry is important, and everyone else must bow to their demands.

Other illustrations could be provided, but the ones given portray the fact that working together does require a great deal of give-and-take with a willingness to adjust so that the total ministry of the church can progress. Basic consideration and respect demands that staff leaders work together as a single unit and not perform in a competitive, isolated ministry.

Loyalty is a quality that must be fostered and developed in church staff relations. This does not mean that all staff members must agree on everything. However, it does mean that if disagreements emerge more often than agreements, serious problems are likely to develop. It is possible to disagree agreeably and still have good relationships and loyalty. If staff members, including the pastor, cannot be loyal to each other, good staff relations are virtually impossible. In Christian grace, every way possible to develop this loyalty must be sought.

Respect is a term like loyalty. It should be part of every staff member's appraisal of his or her colleagues. Each member is to be valued and respected for his or her contribution to the staff team and the church's overall ministry. This respect must be both on the personal and professional level and includes a high regard for the competency and ability of each staff member.

This respect carries over to the role and responsibility of the pastor. Members of the staff need the inspiration, nurture, and care provided by the pastor. This role should also be reciprocal, and staff members are to be alert to the need for them to minister to the pastor as well. Either way, respect for each staff person facilitates positive staff relations. The pastor and staff must learn to work together as a team.

A good understanding of all of the church's ministries is unquestioningly important for each staff member, especially the pastor. The pastor needs to be very familiar with the educational program as well as all other ministries for which staff have been employed to serve. This includes the purpose statements, expected outcomes (goals/objectives), and the ways in which each group carries out its ministry. The pastor builds positive relationships by indicating publicly appreciation for the various ministries along with the staff members who lead and the host of volunteers who serve. A sincere "thank you" costs so little, but it goes so far and accomplishes so much. We are all grateful when the person who supervises us also appreciates us and shows this publicly.

Obviously this understanding is not just for the pastor. All staff members should have a good understanding of each other's ministries so they can pray more intelligently, help to recruit prospective workers with more confidence, and have a sense of what's happening in all parts of the church.

A successful restaurant chain requires all new workers to begin by washing dishes. Then they can move on to setting up the salad bar. Eventually, when they have worked in all the various jobs, they can become waiters or waitresses. Everyone on the restaurant staff is trained to do any job. What a concept! This gives them an appreciation as well as a knowledge of how important each job is. I'm not suggesting that each church staff member work in all areas of ministry, but it would be good to have some experience helping one another to lead in his or her respective area of ministry. This will provide mutuality, collegial support, and will assist staff members to gain a more accurate overview of the various ministries.

Obviously a basic prerequisite for good staff relations and teamwork is a *compatibility in theology*. Agreement on the essentials with the freedom to disagree on issues where the basic truths are not denied is an acceptable principle. Certainly if staff members differ over the significant issues of the faith, then it follows as night follows the day that conflict, disagreement, and disharmony will result.

An important feature of the church is *leadership*, and especially the biblical style of *servant leadership*. Actually, one of the important keys to productive staff relationships is the practice of mutual servanthood.[8] Finzel talks about the top down style of leadership which leads to abusive authority, deplorable delegation, lack of listening, dictatorship in decision-making, lack of letting go, and an obviously egocentric manner.[9] The pastor and other staff are leaders, and they must work more toward the servant leadership style rather than that of "top down." This does not negate the existence of authority and the necessity of supervision within the church's or religious agency's staff, but it does strongly suggest that attitudes and relationships exchanged by staff members working together are best based on the servant leadership model.

CONCLUSION

We have focused mostly on paid, professional staff in this discussion, but the suggestions and principles given can be applied to support staff as well as to volunteers.

The concept of the church staff is biblical. The need of the church for specialization in ministry to train and equip its people justifies their existence. Church staff members can work in harmony when there is a high level of understanding of expectations. Also, the elements of teamwork, reviewed above, accountability, good relationships, loyalty, respect, understanding of the church's ministries, compatible theology, and servant leadership must be implemented.

N O T E S

1. Harold Westing, *Multiple Church-Staff Handbook* (Grand Rapids: Kregel, 1985), 43.

2. Ibid., 29.

3. Michael S. Lawson and Robert J. Choun, Jr., *Directing Christian Education* (Chicago: Moody, 1992), 79–80.

4. Herman J. Sweet, *The Multiple Staff in the Local Church* (Philadelphia: Westminster, 1963), 42–44.

5. James E. Means, *Leadership in Christian Ministry* (Grand Rapids: Baker, 1989), 64.

6. Philip M. Van Auken, *The Well-Managed Ministry* (Wheaton, Ill.: Victor, 1989), 157–58.

7. Ibid., 158.

8. Lawson and Choun, *Directing Christian Education*, 69.

9. Hans Finzel, *The Top Ten Mistakes Leaders Make* (Wheaton, Ill.: Victor, 1994), 23.

F O R   F U R T H E R   R E A D I N G

Finzel, Hans. *The Top Ten Mistakes Leaders Make.* Wheaton, Ill.: Victor, 1994.

Gangel, Kenneth O., and Samuel L. Canine. *Communication and Conflict Management in Churches and Christian Organizations*. Nashville: Broadman, 1992.

Judy, Marvin T. *The Multiple Staff Ministry*. Nashville: Abingdon, 1969.

Lawson, Michael S., and Robert J. Choun, Jr. *Directing Christian Education*. Chicago: Moody, 1992.

Means, James E. *Leadership in Christian Ministry*. Grand Rapids: Baker, 1989.

Sanders, J. Oswald. *Spiritual Leadership*. Chicago: Moody, 1967.

Schaller, Lyle E. *The Multiple Staff and the Larger Church*. Nashville: Abingdon, 1980.

Stubblefield, Jerry M. *The Effective Minister of Education*. Nashville: Broadman & Holman, 1993.

Sweet, Herman J. *The Multiple Staff in the Local Church*. Philadelphia: Westminster, 1963.

Van Auken, Philip M. *The Well-Managed Ministry*. Wheaton, Ill.: Victor, 1989.

Westing, Harold J. *Multiple Church-Staff Handbook*. Grand Rapids: Kregel, 1985.

Williams, Dennis E., and Kenneth O. Gangel. *Volunteers for Today's Church*. Grand Rapids: Baker, 1993.

18

AUTHORITY IN MINISTRY[1]

WALTER C. JACKSON

And when Jesus finished these sayings,
the crowds were astonished at his teaching,
for he taught them as one who had authority,
and not as their scribes.
MATTHEW 7:28-29
And Jesus came and said unto them,
"All authority in heaven and on earth has been given to me."
MATTHEW 28:18

A DEFINITION OF AUTHORITY

Authority is a combination of the ability and the right to exercise power. As we humans understand authority, it has both an internal dimension related to personality and abilities and an external dimension related to authorized use of power, which is seen as an authenticated privilege to act.

Internal Authority
When viewed internally, authority is *ability* in the sense that it (1) grows out of natural talents, traits, or gifts you possess from a loving creator God, which you develop or achieve as you mature; it is (2) rooted in the skills and competencies you selectively develop in the dedicated exercise of those traits, talents, and gifts; it is (3) the result of the affirmations you have received from others along the way that you have converted into sustaining self-awareness; and it is (4) the result of those teachings you have

Walter C. Jackson is the former Lawrence and Charlotte Hoover Professor of Ministry at the Southern Baptist Theological Seminary, Louisville, Kentucky.

accepted into yourself as "true" which you silently use to praise yourself when you do the "truth." As you grow older, others may also give words of praise, but the abiding strength for affirmation then shifts to your own internal discernment. In this way, you have developed your capacity for self-affirmation.

All of this produces in you a personality which has a degree of personal strength, whether great or small, that is often recognizable by yourself or others. While you may shield or reveal the full extent of your own achieved authority, your own life is lived in the light of this internal confidence (*con* meaning *with* and *fide* meaning *faith*) you have developed. The power of your internal confidence, however, is unmistakable when observed by others who discern your abilities. Part of your power at any given time is derived from the substance of your inner "being," the inner seat of your authority.

External Authority

Authority also has an external side. This is the part of authority that is given to you from outside yourself, from some external force concerning the status or office you as an authority are to fulfill. In a democracy, you may be elected to an office. That election grants you the power of office with its attendant authority. In a monarchy, the leader assumes high office because one's genetic heritage places him or her in power with all of its attendant authority. In a time of chaos, a leader may emerge triumphant and rise to a position of authority. This provides a wide opportunity to develop new protocols and traditions. In times of crisis, heroes emerge to carry the rod of authority until the crisis subsides. Sometimes, the mantle of authority is withdrawn after the crisis; at other times, the situational bearer of authority remains in office to become the recognized one with authority.

External authority carries a level of insecurity for the officeholder who receives it, but that sense of authority may become secure when it is subsequently legitimated in some way. The first and most powerful way to legitimize externally received authority is to demonstrate that your own gifts, skills, competencies, and accomplishments give positive testimony to your worthiness to hold office. A second way is to demonstrate that you, while exercising authority, are fulfilling the tradition(s) for which the office was established or improving them by your creative exercise of those traditions. Traditional validation is a powerful force to be possessed by anyone in authority even in the face of widespread discomfort with that same tradition. Flexibility to change the tradition in ways acceptable both to traditionalists and to revisionists is a masterful method of exercising authority. When such negotiated change is not possible for you as an authority to achieve, you must make a choice of where to stand: with the tradition, with the revised tradition, or with the revision.

A third way to legitimate authority is to demonstrate rationally that the office you hold is necessary, productive, and well organized. The job is getting done. Any freedoms surrendered by the populace or membership to give you the authority are compensated by your accomplishments using your power to provide what they need and cannot do by themselves. When the authority granted in any office you hold is judged to accomplish what was intended, the placement of external authority is again validated.

By whatever external circumstance you gain office, and by whatever manner you have legitimated your right to remain in office, you usually have the continuous right to legitimate others to places of authority. To assist you in your work, you may choose to appoint certain persons with authority to accomplish specified things. It is well in democratic organizations to seek consultation on appointees, to seek additional specific confirmation of the "persons" you have chosen, but remember that those in appointed offices are primarily "legitimated" in office both by their internal authority and by your own delegated authority.

CHRISTIANITY AND AUTHORITY

Ever since the Apostle Peter lifted his sword to defend Jesus and was rebuked by his Lord, Christians have had ambivalent feelings about expressing power and authority. Jesus urged his disciples to be kind, gentle, caring, and peacemaking persons. He also pressed them to be initiative-taking, strong, and aggressive in the causes of righteousness.

Throughout the period of the Roman Empire, many Christians were passivists and would not serve in the military. In the Middle

Ages Christians controlled feudal armies. They led their troops in battle against their enemies, but against each other too.

Many of today's Christians still have ambivalent feelings about power and authority. Some continue to practice lifestyles of pacifism. Others appear gleefully militant in the use of authority and power. They exercise political power, exert themselves forcefully in legal and social issues, compete tirelessly in sharp and ruthless business practices, engage in abrasive interpersonal encounters, and practice party spirit within the churches and its various institutions. Still others verbally reject the use of power and authority. They speak courteously, even to their enemies, and follow a strict code of kindness in public and in private. But some make use of nonviolent methods such as public marches, sit-in demonstrations, and other passively resistant activities. These latter methods are no less militant in confrontational value than the hostile ones, however. Both methods are clearly ways to exert power and authority.

Is the exercise of authority necessary? The answer to that question is certainly, yes! Ancient history as well as the history of the Christian church teaches an unavoidable lesson. Some form of authority and power is necessary in personal, family, church, organizational, and societal life if there is to be any corporate peace. Some recognized authority must be in place to avoid anarchical chaos; and some reliable persons must be in places of power to enforce the recognized order. The experience of all known civilizations testifies to this truth. But even where there is legitimated power behind the acknowledged authority, there is no scarcity of competitive volunteer authorities in our contemporary world.

The main difficulty among Christians today is sorting through the claims of multiple would-be authorities to discover authentic authority. The primary issues at debate for Christians relate to the actual center of power and authority in every generation. Who are the person or persons (office or offices) authorized to possess such authority and power? What are the appropriate causes in which power and authority may legitimately be exerted? What is the appropriate degree of absoluteness persons wielding power and authority may exert? And finally, what are the best methods available to evaluate and/or provide appropriate checks and balances in response to those who exercise power and authority? The focus of this chapter is to stimulate an introductory discussion about the place of power and authority in Christian ministry.

THE DEVELOPMENT OF MINISTRY AUTHORITY

For Christians, there is no question about the source of power. God is the supreme authority, and that authority is expressed primarily through Jesus Christ, the "captain of our souls" who makes God's authority known. Concerning the church, Jesus Christ is its eternal leader. Matthew 28:19-20 clearly describes the locus of power and authority for Christian ministry. Jesus declared himself to be the possessor of God's power in spiritual and eternal matters, and Jesus gave his blessing and authority to the church. It was to the church, the gathered group of believers present on the mount of ascension, to which Jesus gave his great commission. It was to the church that Jesus promised the gift of the Holy Spirit to empower its members in ministry (Acts 1:6-8). It was to the church gathered in prayer to which the gift of the Holy Spirit came (Acts 2:1-4). The biblical witness clearly identifies the church as the focus of Christian authority.

The Authority of the Minister
While ministry is the responsibility of the church, ministry is the activity of ministers of the church. The church is the external validator of the testimony and observed competencies of men and women who function in the name of the church as ministers. Ministers are people like you who possess self-affirmed and externally discerned internal authority for ministry. We usually know them only when they have achieved adulthood and have been elected to a place of office or authority in ministry. What is usually unavailable to see is the long period of infant, childhood, and adolescent development of a minister. Of course, you can never know all of that about another person who is a minister, but you do know that about yourself.

You are the product of your own heritage, background, and development. You have been molded by your own lifelong experiences. Your ministry has developed from God's gifts to you personally and from your lifelong experiences since birth. To these experiences you can continually add the teachings of the Bible and the church about ministry, especially in your seminary days. You can also add additional clarifications of meaning granted through the leadership of the Holy Spirit, your own personal devotional life, and from the testimonies of other Christians. Primary, of course, are your experiences of worship, study, and service in and through the church and its agencies.

As you grow, remember power and authority are intentional gifts of God—good gifts—and are to be used with gratitude, although also with extreme sensitivity and caution in the exercise of Christian ministry. Therefore, Christian ministers are enjoined to offer whatever parts of their personalities are available for the task.

The major task after accepting the challenge to develop power and authority in ministry as gifts relates to the choice of intensity, style, and integrity. Can you develop the ability to be transparently strong and openly exercise power and authority as a good gift of God or will you live in a more passive style? Many Christians choose to live quietly, to give the "soft answer (that) turneth away wrath," "to agree with (an) adversary quickly," and to exert power and strength only in clear cases of self-defense. Other Christians seeking to affirm power and authority and to exert themselves in dynamically forceful ways have ample biblical support. In Ephesians 4, Paul instructs believers to be "speaking the truth in love" (v. 15). Christians are to "put off falsehood" (v. 25) and are to "be angry but not to sin." These passages direct believers to engage in open and direct face-to-face relationships which are honest and truthful. The powerful energies of anger and rage are declared here to be appropriate, just so long as they are used within ethical bounds. However, no one is to use the potentially explosive power of hostility in sinful ways. Most specifically, believers are not to allow anger to accumulate over long periods of time, but are to release it "before the sun goes down."

The Scriptures treat many other expressions of power and authority, but in no instance is power and authority more clearly established as a legitimate part of a Christian lifestyle than in the exercise of ministry. Jesus' commission to minister was proceeded by a declaration that "all authority" had been given to him. His tremendously inspiring commission extended that authority and power in the direction of his disciples for them to be the witnesses, representatives, and teachers of his life and thought. Ministers of Jesus Christ are not to represent themselves, exploit their positions of ministry for personal gain, or misuse their authority to convert the house of God into a den of thieves. To exercise power in self-effacing ways requires a Christian committed to a life of integrity. Generations of ministers continue to ask, "Where does one discover such power?" "When one finds it, how does one live with such integrity?" Attention will now be given to some of the formative ingredients in the development of authority for ministry.

Personal Authority

An awareness and growing understanding of authority is part of your intimate heritage. You were born with little actual power or authority. You were dependent upon your parents or parent substitutes for your first and lasting impressions of human power and strength. As you grew toward maturity, your accumulated experiences with all persons in positions of power and authority each had their influence on your basic understanding. In our society, power and authority characteristics are clearly focused and promoted through media projections as well as in interpersonal experiences. It is of interest, however, to note that the characteristics of power and authority in the developmental process are somewhat polarized in relationship to male and female gender characteristics, preferences, and behavior.

A review of the major themes discoverable in human child-rearing and the process of human maturation is instructive in the search for a personal development dimension of power and authority. Infants easily become aware of the trustworthiness of their original environments—or of the untrustworthiness of those environments.

Initial tendencies toward faith or unfaith are experienced similarly by children of both genders and are consciously or unconsciously remembered by each child based on actual events. Then, as each child grows and develops, themes from the strong female and male cultural models begin their influential activity. *Male nurturing* trends reward and positively reinforce independence and autonomy. Male identity is developed by achieving a "well-differentiated" personal uniqueness which is designed to be productive, initiative-prone, and even aggressive. Intellectual prowess with an emphasis upon formal and abstract thought is honored as a good male characteristic. Competitive strivings are introduced early and are encouraged. Winning, being dominant, and avoiding the subordinate position is forwarded as the method most likely to lead to success.

Studies of *female nurturing trends* are equally instructive. Interdependence is the major goal of increased competence in the use of authority and power in female developmental patterns. Intimacy, sensitivity, and deeper levels of relationship between persons from early intimacy are far to be desired in the female approach to life than the isolated and autonomous developmental style of males. One's attachments are highly valued. Your family of origin and of faith are to be nurtured, encouraged, and cared for by you, rather than to become venues of competition and competitive strivings. Your own personal development of gifts is encouraged, but your attainments are to be seen as valuable for family or group enrichment rather than exclusively possessed as trophies of your own individual achievement. Equality is the accepted norm of relationships. While this equality is temporarily out of balance in cases of child-rearing or education, the goals of each are similar. Parents give birth to children who are to grow through the child-rearing process to become "friends" of their parents, free and equal partners as adults in the celebration of the God-given and God-sustained created order. Teachers (especially Christian ones) are to teach with authority and then to nurture students to the level of colleagues and friends. While there will likely always be a "junior/senior" dimension in the relationship, both teacher and student will grow into a relationship which is free and equal before God and each other. From this perspective, child-rearing and education are processes of temporary inequality related to the need for growth and development. They have equality and friendship as their common goals. They are not designs for permanent inequality where the plan is to "get ahead," to "stay ahead," and to "lord it over" others in a system of stratified hierarchy or permanent socialized oppression.

Most parents and teachers have adopted an individualized

blend of the above characteristics. Some few adhere rigidly to the purely male or purely female characteristics, but most children report they have grown to value selected characteristics from both lists. In the process of their own development, persons called to ministry have frequently developed a firm and healthy sense of authority for ministry by utilizing the best individual traits of both their father and mother.

Whatever their early predispositions to authority and power, it is true that developing ministers may consciously choose to alter, expand, or curtail the characteristics of behavior affecting the authority patterns they routinely practice. A person who has developed a firm and healthy sense of authority for ministry or who would review and continue such a development will certainly give attention to the following areas:

Personal Authority

First, *your personal identity* is a major source of authority. Many ingredients are part of personal identity, but some of the more important ones are: (1) supportive parental love, affirmation, nurture, and blessing or, in the absence of these items, a sustaining experience of God's love attesting to the truth that "if [your] father and mother forsake [you], then the Lord will take [you] up" (Ps. 27:10, NRSVB); (2) the joy of faith in God; (3) a history of pleasure in work, study, and creative activity; (4) the ability to discover and accept the valuable aspects of your past and conversely to make peace with those unhappy or traumatic aspects of your past; and (5) an awareness of yourself as a unique person before God with all the rights, privileges, and responsibilities of selfhood. These items conspire to nurture a firm personal identity.

Additionally, personal authority grows out of *one's experience with tragedy.* When you comprehend that all of life is dotted with "less than expected outcomes" and that pain is an ever present part of human experience, you become prepared to deal with life in a more realistic way. God created life with the counterpoint melodies of celebration and agony as an expected part of human experience. The sooner you become able to expect the warming presence of God in the valley of shadows as well as in the picnic of celebration, your foundation for personal authority in the face of life's complete offerings is broadened.

Interpersonal Authority

Second, personal authority is established when an individual develops *comfort with interpersonal intimacy*. The ability to give and receive love from other persons, to be known by others as nearly as you know yourself, and to know others as they share themselves in friendship are the major tasks of interpersonal intimacy. Others are: to be able to be the target of anger and to work through to an experience of reconciliation in such a relationship and to be able to express anger without subsequent destruction of relationship. To have shared and experienced a wide range of interpersonal relationships and have achieved a degree of comfort and confidence is to have a firm basis for interpersonal authority.

The Authority of Self-Acceptance

Third, personal authority grows out of a realistic experience of *personal self-acceptance*. Most other people are usually more forgiving of your own mistakes than you are. Individuals routinely continue in some self-accusatory vein far beyond the time when persons injured by your blunders or mistakes have forgiven you and forgotten. For most persons, failures of the past accumulate a residue from which a negative self-image is easily constructed. When you become able to deal with your mistakes, defeats, and failures merely as sad events, you have grown in grace. But when those same mistakes, defeats, and failures become foundations upon which to build deeper relationships and new competencies, then you have cleared a row of high hurdles in the path of acquiring self-acceptance. Such an accomplishment broadens the foundation of your potential for authentic personal authority.

Authority of One's Call to Become a Christian

The most basic authority-producing factor in your or any person's life is to become a Christian; to accept God's love through the redeeming work of Jesus Christ and to commit yourself to Christ as Savior and Lord. To know in your inner self that God has called you to Christian discipleship in spite of your arrogance, hatred, selfishness, greed, and destructive competitiveness is to have the most freeing and power-infusing experience in life. For those for whom previous life has produced a negative self-image, the call to become a Christian presents the liberating experience of a second chance. For those with a positive personal identity, the gift of Christian faith is a blessing beyond all possible previous gifts. For both, having joined the ranks of the children of God establishes a unique and authoritative selfhood.

Some persons come to the moment of conscious faith commitment in Christ in a sudden way. For others, the process is longitudinal. Some have known of the availability of saving faith in Christ previously, but have resisted it, only to "turn around" suddenly to faith at the time of conversion. Others have seized upon faith in Christ as a new discovery in a radical conversion and change to a new way of life. Still others have been reared in Christian families and, while their own faith in Christ is unique and personal, have embraced faith as becoming a full child of God after having lived a lifetime in his presence.

By the time faith in Christ has grown within a person to embrace a positive response to a call to vocational ministry, faith has begun to grow and develop beyond the "sincere milk" stage to the more weighty matters of the Christian way. Again, some careful research information is available to assist in identifying characteristics and patterns frequently followed by believers as they develop.

Most vocational ministers, especially those who were Christians in their pre-teenaged years, can identify a period in life when matters of faith were simply and clearly understood. Belonging to God and to the family of faith was comforting. Learning the beautiful stories of the Bible and the "mysteries" of the faith were central. Sensing the joy and pride of belonging to Jesus Christ and to his church were fulfilling. As time passed for you, the challenges of justice, fairness, and equal treatment prescribed in the Bible seemed always to be good ideas, but became much harder to carry out. Always the seemingly simple ideals were challenged and required some sorting out. A deeper, more personal walk with Christ became an appealing and desirable way to grow in faith.

In the careful study by James Fowler and his associates about the development of faith as a pilgrimage, the move from the more simple, narrative faith to a more relational one is described as the transition from a more dependent faith to a more individually responsible one.[2] In this stage, hunger for a God who provides companionship during the task of sorting out sometimes conflicting "externally authoritative" messages from home, church, school, media, peers, work environments, and society in general is the driving engine of faith. One exerts much energy in the task of the identity struggle or rejoices in a faith stage which celebrates the personal, intimate, relational side of life. Values are assembled and defined to explain the tumultuous events of adolescent and young adult life challenges. The struggle to discover one's own God directed if not God's escorted "way" in the midst of conflicting authorities and conflicting identities is paramount. A primary part of the battle is to avoid or to overcome the paralysis which comes when you are unable to decide between conflicting possibilities.

A major form of temptation at this point of development is for you to succumb to the numbness and shock of it all by withdrawing your mental self and repressing your emotional self. A more spiritually healthy response is to forge ahead into the next stage of development. This stage is one in which you still appreciate the group, but give more focused attention to yourself as an independent self before God. In this stage, you learn to love yourself for God's sake and the sake of the Christian community. This is a very high spiritual stage of humility, as Bernard of Clairveaux has suggested. Beliefs, lifestyle, outlook, vocation, and all one's commitments are forged into an authentic and congruent identity which is at the same time autonomous/individual and committed/collegial. The ambiguities of the previous stage may not all have been resolved completely, but they are set aside as temporarily expendable to pursue the immediate task of finding a deeper personal and relational selfhood in God.

The processes of being with God and participating with him in the ongoing tasks of the work of the kingdom of God are given more importance than settling the great theological issues of the ages. Content of the faith, as always, is important, but its precise definition in every contemporary cultural and classical idiom is balanced by the development of the life in the spirit.

When you have forged this kind of deep personal spirituality or relationship with God and made peace with the ever present and seductive temptation to formulate the perfect theological clarification for your own time, the source of authority and power for ministry has moved within you from one bound by time and space (human language) to an eternal one (personal relationship).

Actually, the issues discussed by Fowler in stages III and IV are of vital importance to ministers in training during their seminary days, as well as at later times, both for one's self and for those to whom clergy are called to minister.

Authority of One's Call to Become a Minister

In addition to participating in the general call for all persons to become Christians, the minister derives a clear sense of authority from a personal call to ministry. Whether the call comes at a precise and documentable time, or whether it arises developmentally from a deep inner conviction over a long period of time that God has invited you to become a minister, your call to ministry is a deep reservoir of strength and power undergirding your ministerial authority. From the moment your call is acknowledged and accepted, all initiative and activities in the direction of fulfilling that call become a part of a "ministry covenant" you have forged with God. This strengthens your authority to be a minister. As you discover and refine your gifts and talents useful in ministry, you are already being faithful to the call. As you improve as a person and give yourself to the task of Bible study, spiritual development, the study of Christian history and theology, and the practical gifts and skills of performing ministry, you increase in power to follow the calling of Jesus Christ to vocational ministry.

Authority of One's Election to a Specific Ministry

When a specific group of Christians elect you as a minister to serve them, you will receive a new burst of power and authority. The authority of your office or stated position has a place in the authorized thought of many people. In the case of the minister, the Christian group electing you stands with you to undergird and support you as necessary. In every case, the authority of the office to which you have been elected both increases your ministry power and gives specific focus for the exercise of your responsible authority.

The Authority of Servanthood

Whatever your ministry, your role identification as Christian minister is always the same. You, the minister, are to be a servant! You will serve the Christians who have called you to their ministry location and lead them to care for and to serve each other and all humankind. The role of the servant-minister and the servant-church is clearly presented in the Scriptures and in the life and teachings of Jesus Christ. One of your major tasks of ministry is to be a servant in increasingly more imaginative, creative, and Spirit-led ways. Confidence that you are living and functioning as a servant nurtures your authority for ministry.

Authority of One's Spiritual Life

To imagine a person attempting to be a Christian minister without an active and growing spiritual life is impossible. The absence of a dynamic spiritual life would doom you to live with an ever diminishing reservoir of nourishment to sustain your power for ministry. Practicing ministers testify that energy and authority in ministry are fostered most powerfully by a consistent inner relationship with God. The great biblical characters relied heavily on spiritual disciplines. Jesus Christ was constantly withdrawing to engage in prayer to maintain private intimacy with God. The church is filled with examples of leaders who declare the greatest source of power and authority to be just such an intimate, prayerful relationship with God. A sustained and disciplined inner spirituality is an essential resource for authority in ministry.

Authority of Personal Competence

Whatever else ministry is, it includes the actual performance of tasks to be accomplished: worshiping and leading in worship, witnessing, discipling, educating, supporting, challenging and inspiring, reconciling, and leading believers in a variety of ways. Securing appropriate Christian understanding of the nature of these tasks and accumulating the proven ability to perform them with competence and strength is the ongoing task of developing competence in ministry.

Every Christian possesses skills useful for ministry. To identify those skills, to add others, and to practice each as an expression of daily worship to God is the manner in which ministry competence is built. That is to say, first, it is in the actual service of others for Christ's sake that ministry competence is developed. Second, ministry competence is developed through face-to-face consultation, and in the activity of responsible dialogue between yourself and other Christians, both laypersons and ministers, where you are enabled to see more clearly your strengths, faults, and growing edges in ministry. Having accepted the wisdom of the congregation, the third method of developing competence may occur. It is in the consistent and prayerful self-reflection before God that you develop an awareness of personal growth in ministry. Out of such increasing competence in ministry, personal authority in ministry develops.

Authority of the Christian Message

There is enormous energy in the Christian message in and of itself. First, power and authority in ministry is directly related to the sense of urgency you generate to proclaim the gospel. When a minister believes forcefully that the Christian message is essential for all humankind, massive reservoirs of power are made available for ministry. The more clearly one sees the desperate nature of human life apart from a relationship with God, the more eager one will be to witness and do the other tasks of ministry.

Second, when one is able to look at human life through the eyes of the gospel, he or she is enabled to see clearly the inhumane and unjust treatment people receive from their contemporaries and the many ways in which humans have permitted their lives and activities to become continuous expressions of the demonic. The more precisely one is able to see the sources and the results of such evil activity, the more convinced the minister will become of the urgency to present the gospel of Jesus Christ as an antidote for that evil. Such promise of victory encourages the use of authority and power to achieve justice and mercy as well as salvation for all the earth.

DEVELOPMENT OF AUTHORITY IN THE CHURCH

Jesus gave his blessing and authority to the church. It was to the church, the gathered group of believers present on the mount of ascension, to which Jesus gave his great commission. It was to the church that Jesus promised the gift of the Holy Spirit to empower its members in ministry. It was to the church gathered in prayer to which the gift of the Holy Spirit came. The biblical witness clearly identifies the church as the focus of Christian authority.

Models of Church Government

Throughout its history, the church has used several models of government. Three main ecclesiastical types survive today. The *episcopal* form is illustrated by the Roman Catholic, Orthodox, Anglican, and Methodist churches. Although practiced with some differences by each of these groups, in this model power and authority is conceived to proceed from the higher orders of clergy (pope, archbishop, bishop, etc.) whose task it is to govern the lesser clergy, laypersons, and the local churches. In each denomination listed, power is believed to descend through a hierarchical order with the most powerful positions being on top of the pyramid. In most cases, the rights of Christians to follow their individual consciences in the matters of personal morality is mentioned, but the official doctrine and the ethical pronouncements of the higher clergy are considered binding on clergy and laypersons alike.

A second prominent type of church organization is the *presbyterian* form. Continued in present-day Lutheran, Presbyterian, and Reformed denominations, the presbyterial form of church government rules the church through a hierarchy of courts. The lowest court, the session, is the court of the individual congregation and consists of the ordained ministers (teaching elders) and elected (ruling) elders from a single congregation. The second court, the presbytery, consists of all ministers and certain elected elders from a group of churches in geographical proximity. The third court, the synod, consists of elected ministers and elected elders from several presbyteries. In some instances, the synods are the highest courts of the church. A general assembly, a jurisdiction to which a synod may elect to belong, consists of representatives of two or more synods. Decisions of the general assemblies are advisory. In the presbyterial system, power is exchanged. It is generated from the called and elected leaders of the local churches and is delegated to the higher courts. The decisions of the presbyteries and synods are binding upon the churches.

The third type of church government is the *congregational* form. Present-day Baptist and many independent evangelical churches along with other so-called "free churches" practice this form of church government. Customarily, constitution and by-laws designed specifically for an individual church set forth policies and practices. Many small churches, however, do not possess such documents. Whether with or without documents, however, these churches cling to the individual autonomy of the local church. Among congregationally governed churches, each local church may choose to join with other churches in the formation of associations and conventions, groups of churches created for the purposes of missions, evangelism, education, and benevolence ministries. Unlike churches and courts, these larger organizations are not arranged in hierarchical fashion. Their annual meetings are held for fellowship, the receiving of reports, inspiration, and to allocate cooperative funds. Non-binding resolutions are frequently made to express the wishes of messengers present and voting in the regular meetings of the associations and conventions. These resolutions as well as the associations and conventions themselves have no authority to dictate policy to the churches, but act in an advisory relationship to them.

CONCLUSION

The power and authority for Christian ministry is derived from several sources. In general, these sources may be cataloged as internalized and personal on the one hand and external and covenantal on the other hand. First, ministerial power is derived from a deeply sensed inner and personal call to faith in Christ and a companion call to use your life and its gifts in vocational ministry service. Second, power and authority for ministry is derived from the act of exercising one's self and gifts in ministry as a servant of all in the name of Jesus Christ. In the actual service of others for Christ's sake, power for ministry grows and matures. Third, authority for ministry is derived from one's deep and ongoing spiritual encounter with Jesus Christ, in ongoing study of the Bible and the historical and theological traditions of the church, and deepened in the continual proclamation of his message with power. The very gospel of Christ contains the greatest foundational bedrock source of power for ministry. Authority for ministry is concentrated in the church, the called body of believers commissioned to do his will on earth. Fourth, authority for ministry is derived from the specific call of a minister to serve a congregation or a single group of Christians on mission for Christ. It is in the togetherness of ministry with other Christians that ministry is best conducted today and into the foreseeable future. Finally, as ministers discipline themselves in a living relationship to a congregation of believers and with them reach out to minister to the world in the name of Christ, authority for ministry is confirmed in daily practice.

N O T E S

1. Gratitude is here expressed to the *Review and Expositor* for permission to include much of my chapter, "Authority in Ministry" previously published in the first (1981) and subsequent editions of the book *Formation for Christian Ministry*, edited by Anne Davis and Wade Rowatt, Jr.

2. James W. Fowler, *Stages of Faith* (San Francisco: Harper & Row, 1981), 151–83.

F O R   F U R T H E R   R E A D I N G

Erikson, Erik. *Childhood and Society*. Second Edition. New York: W.W. Norton, 1963.

———. *Identity: Youth and Crisis*. New York: W.W. Norton, 1968.

Fowler, James W. *Stages of Faith*. Harper and Row, 1981.

Gilligan, Carol. *In a Different Voice*. Cambridge, Mass.: Harvard Univ. Press, 1982.

Maring, Norman H., and Winthrop Hudson. *A Baptist Manual of Polity and Practice*. Valley Forge, Pa.: Judson, 1963.

Miller, Jean Baker. *Toward a New Psychology of Women*. Boston: Beacon, 1976.

Sullivan, James L. *Baptist Polity As I See It*. Nashville: Broadman, 1983.

GLOBAL FORMATION AND CONTEMPORARY ISSUES IN MINISTRY

19

CHRISTIAN MINISTRY IN GLOBAL CONTEXT

DAVID F. D'AMICO

The purpose of this chapter is to sensitize the reader to the realities of Christian ministry in our multiethnic society and world. It will survey the multiethnic nature of our nation and of the evangelical community in the United States. In addition, it will briefly describe some aspects in prejudice in light of New Testament principles about the nature of humanity and the realities of ethnic diversity in the world. To assist engagement with the realities of the student population of evangelical colleges and seminaries, it will also discuss mission in a global sense (the process of globalization) affecting the lives of those communities and the ministry of leaders in training who will serve in cosmopolitan or multiethnic settings during the twenty-first century.

Those who enroll in evangelical colleges and seminaries arrive with diverse spiritual, family, church, geographical, and denominational backgrounds. They may have experienced some

David F. D'Amico is the former Billy Graham Professor of Evangelism at the Southern Baptist Theological Seminary and currently serves as Representative to the Diplomatic Community at the United Nations for the Cooperative Baptist Fellowship.

ethnic diversity interacting with "international" students. If they come from a short-term mission experience they may have been exposed to ethnic diversity. If they had a first career in the military, law, engineering, or business they have encountered some type of ethnic diversity.

Sometimes, however, in church and denominational life a superficial dichotomy has been proposed and practiced. Many tend almost exclusively to classify those different from us as "foreign" and those "who are like us" as "homegrown" persons.

An American student of Korean extraction who is studying at the University of Chicago will almost invariably be asked: "Where are you from?" The expected answer will be that she is from some Asian country because the student has Asian features. When the student answers: "I am from Chicago," the questioner will pursue the dialogue with "Where is your *original* home?" When the respondent replies, "I am from Chicago," the questioner will continue the conversation until he or she asks about the student's parents or grandparents, finding satisfaction only in discovering the identity of the "foreignness" of the person, finally concluding that the student is not really from Chicago, but is from Korea via her parents or grandparents.

If the person approached were of Caucasian features, the questioning would not be as insistent, unless she spoke with a Slavic, German, or Spanish accent. The same type of questioning goes on in the corridors and classrooms of colleges and seminaries, when faculty, staff, and students encounter persons who "are different from us," in color of skin, speech patterns, or some other distinctive feature of "foreignness," different as defined by Caucasian standards.

The world in which we live is, in fact, multiethnic, whether we have experienced some features of it or not. The challenge presented to a college or seminary student, therefore, is whether she has the ability to perceive the differences not through ethnocentric lenses, but instead in light of the realities that are there to be observed if we make an effort.

Some years ago there was on the Southern Baptist Theological Seminary campus a family that demonstrated some aspects of multiethnicity. The student was born in Korea and reared in Illinois. He graduated from college, worked in a business, and went as a missionary to Asunción, Paraguay. He ministered there for a year, and then went to Bolivia, ministering with Korean congregations, learning some Spanish, and ultimately marrying a young woman from the city of La Paz. They have three multicultural children. They came to study at the seminary. While students, he served as a church planter, starting a Korean congregation in Indiana, and his wife worked in the library. At present he is pursuing a Doctor of Ministry degree. Any attempt from us to place this family into an ethnic stereotype will fail. Their Seoul-Chicago-Asunción-La Paz-Louisville pilgrimage may become a type of what will be normative in the ministry setting of the twenty-first century. It provides a modern missiological parable that helps enhance our vision.

HUMAN PREJUDICE:
NEW TESTAMENT PRINCIPLES AND
ANTHROPOLOGICAL INSIGHTS

Prejudice is a sign that we are not fully under the grace and lordship of the Lord Jesus Christ. The New Testament church wrestled with an inherited prejudice against Samaritans and Gentiles. Several narratives in Acts and some teachings from Paul's epistles clearly indicate that the gospel message had to struggle to overcome cultural prejudice (see John 4; Acts 10; 15; Gal. 3).

Peter's discovery of "other than his" cultural and religious heritage became a hallmark in his self-understanding and in the mission of the church toward the Gentiles. The key to the narrative is Acts 10:34: "I perceive that God has no favorites" (MOF). If you are searching for a biblical attitude of equality, if you seek a wide and open stance toward persons different from you, if you wish to be a "world Christian," you may consider making Acts 10:34 your platform for self-understanding and ministry.

Many of us face the potential limitations of our experiences. If while on our educational pilgrimage we recognize the fact that our training may have been "culturally conditioned," we are on the way to discovering new insights about ourselves. To continue our development it is important to avail ourselves of principles suggested by Christian anthropologists and missionaries who have a commitment to a universal gospel and a thirst for understanding peoples different from themselves. Their writings offer Christian attitudes and principles helpful to us as we confront our prejudices, ethnocentrism, and defense mechanisms. They provide useful insights into the nature of human beings, the barriers that are erected in our attempts to adapt to "other-than-me" persons, and the Christian responsibility to deal openly with the potential walls that hinder the spread of the gospel of Jesus Christ.

Cross-cultural citizens of the kingdom interested in learning about others should seek dialogue with persons different from themselves, learning from them about their culture, language, and religious perspectives. The theological and anthropological perplexities we face relate to our view of culture and how it ought to be changed by the principles of the gospel. H. Richard Niebuhr developed a classic treatment of Christ "against," "in," and "above" culture in his book, *Christ and Culture*.[1] Charles Kraft has amplified this discussion and provided illuminating insights into the transmission of Christianity, including the principle of "dynamic-equivalence translation." This principle is applicable to Scripture translations, which are the first means for cross-cultural evangelization. Dynamic-equivalence translations express the message of the source documents in the language of the receptor so that the hearers/readers can, by employing their own interpretational reflexes, derive their proper meaning. Such translations seek equivalence of response rather than equivalence of form. Three examples of this type of Bible translation are the versions by J.B. Phillips, *The New English Bible*, and the *Today's English Version* (commonly called "Good News for Modern Man"). Kraft declared: "If an equivalent meaning is to be conveyed, the forms employed must be as appropriate for expressing those meanings in the receptor culture as the source forms are in the source culture."[2]

Ministry to persons of other cultures always includes the realm of caring and counseling, especially as displaced and refugee persons move to our cities and become desperate. Without proper guidance, sincere but inadequately trained future ministers can limit missionary opportunities.[3]

Marvin K. Mayers discusses a significant number of anthropological principles that are pertinent to understanding cultural enclaves. He argues that in cross-cultural evangelization persons will face culture shock, the emotional disturbance that results from adjustment to a new cultural environment. Others will be victims of ethnocentrism, the notion that "my culture is superior to other cultures." Most ministers will have to deal with biblical absolutism amid cultural relativism and will seek cultural adaptability to communicate the gospel across cultural barriers.[4]

FACING THE REALITIES OF A CHANGING WORLD

It is important for seminarians to have a clear sense of the world in which they will soon be ministering. Let's consider some population trends. In the next two decades the world's population will increase far more rapidly, proportionally speaking, in developing nations than in developed nations. The impact of Christianity in the world compared with that of other world religions may diminish unless some changes take place.[5]

Meanwhile, many persons will seek to immigrate to the United States. The U.S. will continue, with some restraints, to make room for these immigrants. The decade of the 1990s has seen an increase of Asian and Latin American immigrants in proportion to Europeans, a trend, no doubt, which will continue.

The following statistics are presented to show the impact that foreign born peoples who are residing in the United States will have on the culture. As "the world comes to us," these peoples constitute a significant mission field for any person considering holistic ministry during the twenty-first century.

AMERICAN ETHNICITY[6]

Ethnic Group	1990	2000 (Projected)
Asian	4,063,894	4,663,167
Caribbean	805,709	924,522
European*	51,112,484	58,649,696
Hispanic	23,254,836	28,761,893
North African & Middle Eastern	1,301,550	1,493,481
Native American	2,848,087	3,268,076
Pacific Islander	304,305	349,179
Sub-Saharan African	386,151	443,094
Totals	84,077,016	98,553,108

U.S.	253,024,479	271,493,439
% of U.S. Population		
Ethnic/Language Culture	33.2%	36.3%

*Excludes English, Welsh, Scottish, Irish, and multiple ancestry.

These projected statistics correlate with population changes in this country that occurred during the 1980s. The white percentage of the U.S. population fell from 83 percent in 1980 to about 80 percent in 1990. The black population increased 13 percent during the 1980s to a total of 29.9 million. There are estimates that 6 million legal and 2 million undocumented immigrants came to the U.S. during the 1980s.

The Asian-American population in the United States increased nearly 108 percent during the decade. The five largest Asian groups living in the U.S. are: Chinese, 1.6 million or 23 percent; Filipino, 1.4 million or 19 percent; Japanese, 847,000 or 11 percent; Korean, 798,000 or 11 percent; and Indian, 815,000 or 11 percent.[7] Many choose to reside in urban centers. An analysis of the 1990 census shows that 46 percent of Asian-Americans live in central cities, 47.8 percent in suburbs, and 6.2 percent in rural areas. During the 1980s the traditional bastions of Asian-American population—Los Angeles, San Francisco, and New York—experienced increases of 138 percent, 104 percent, and 136 percent respectively, while Washington, D.C. and Houston experienced 144 percent and 149 percent increases. The largest Asian-American population in the U.S. is found in Los Angeles with 2.5 million.[8]

According to the U.S. Census Bureau, the Hispanic population in the United States is divided as follows: 52 percent, or approximately 13.5 million, are of Mexican descent; 24 percent, or approximately 6.2 million, are of Puerto Rican descent (both on the island and the mainland); 20 percent, or approximately 5 million, are "other Hispanics"; and 4 percent, or approximately 1 million, are of Cuban descent. During the 1980s the Hispanic population grew 53 percent to a total of 22.3 million. This population has spread to all fifty states. Only seven states experienced decreases in Hispanic population, while forty-three states experienced considerable growth, including the states where Hispanic population is greatest (California, 69 percent; Texas, 45 percent; Florida, 83 percent; and New York, 33 percent). Two-thirds of the Hispanic population in the United States live in three states: California (7.6 million), Texas (4.3 million), and New York (2.2 million).

A sampling of some major cities reveals the following increases in "traditionally" Hispanic centers, all of them with growth above 70 percent: Dallas-Fort Worth: 109 percent; San Diego: 86 percent; Los Angeles: 73 percent; Houston: 72 percent; and Miami: 71 percent.[9] The Hispanic population has surpassed the black population in twenty-six U.S. cities, including four large cities in the Southwest—Los Angeles, Houston, Phoenix, and San Antonio. The Hispanic population was already a majority in Miami, El Paso, and Santa Ana, California. The political implications are significant. Projections suggest that the Hispanic population will surpass the African American population in New York in the future.[10]

GLOBALIZATION CURRENTS IN CHRISTIAN MISSION

Let me begin a consideration of globalization in contemporary Christian mission by presenting a brief overview of Southern Baptist data concerning cross-cultural evangelization in the U.S., which is representative of major evangelical denominations. Due to limited space, I will highlight only the largest ethnic groups. A conservative estimate based on current data indicates that Southern Baptists have at least 4,000 units or congregations scattered among 101 ethnic groups and 97 American Indian tribes. These units utilize ninety-eight different languages. The largest ethnic groups, by congregations, are: Hispanic (1,578), American Indian (478), Deaf (477), Korean (400), Chinese (159), French (150), Vietnamese (89), Filipino (58), and Haitian (48).[11] During 1991, 466 new units were established. During the decade from 1980 to 1990 all the ethnic congregations, in cooperation with the SBC, experienced a growth rate of 147 percent.

The fact that Christians in the Third World outnumber Christians in the First World is one of missiology's best kept secrets. The research and writing of David Barrett have awakened many to these realities. Asia, Africa, and Latin America will have domination of world population by the year 2000. The majority of the world population of Christians resides in the Third World. This majority is committed to the radical claims of the gospel, increasingly urban, and mostly poor. The task of world evangelization is immense. The First World church, especially in the U.S., has been very slow to recognize the impact of "ethnic" evangelical groups who are doing creative evangelism in the United States. Few are aware of the Third World mission agencies which are evangelizing effectively in many countries of the world.

A popular hymn, "You Shall Be My Witnesses," is sung by many choirs in evangelical churches. Its refrain paraphrases the words of the Great Commission: "Jerusalem, Judea, Samaria, and to the ends of the world." In contemporary global mission circles some adaptation of the hymn would reflect the fact that evangelicals are fulfilling in a limited way the implications of the Great Commission. Such a refrain could be rephrased: "Rio de Janeiro-Quito-Jamaica, N.Y.—to the ends of the world." Consider Levi Penido, a Brazilian who pastored a large church in Rio de Janeiro. He was sent as a foreign missionary by the Brazilian Baptist Foreign Mission Board to Quito, Ecuador, where he served for five years. He was called to pastor the Brazilian Baptist Church in Jamaica, Queens, New York City, where he served for more than five years. This church has started two new congregations in the metro New York area and is fast becoming a sending church.

GLOBALIZATION IN THEOLOGICAL EDUCATION

Many evangelical colleges and seminaries have been mission-sensitive institutions with commitment to their graduates going to serve overseas and in the United States and to students coming from other parts of the world. They have recognized the trends toward globalization, leading them to reflect about the needed adaptations that are required of their faculty and staff.[12] An example of how "the world has come to us" is the increasing foreign student population one finds in colleges and seminaries. For example, at the Southern Baptist Theological Seminary in the 1995-96 academic year, 126 international students were enrolled, representing thirty countries as follows: Africa: 21; Asia: 81; Europe: 11; Latin America and the Caribbean: 9; North America:

4. Of these the largest representations were from Korea (54), followed by Nigeria (12), Taiwan (6), and Japan (6).[13]

Those preparing themselves for ministry for the twenty-first century should become aware that serving in God's kingdom will require diverse preparation. Some will minister as pastors, others may be called to be pastoral counselors, many will serve the multitude of international students as campus ministers; and many will become social workers assisting refugees, teaching English as a second language, or guiding those immigrating to the United States in cultural, economic, and religious adaptation. For those involved in ministry to foreign-born persons, it is possible to project several trends. There will be a continuing flow of immigrants from developing nations. Many recently arrived immigrants will settle in urban areas, especially those of lower socioeconomic levels. There will be a lack of trained ministers for these populations. Many new evangelical congregations will start ministering to these and other persons of lower socioeconomic status.

Leaders of Asian descent seeking higher educational attainments likely will wish to minister to the middle and upper classes, people of their own kind. Ethnic churches will tend to reduplicate, among Asians, the patterns of church life they have observed in white churches. Economic concerns will motivate pastors and congregations and the result will be many middle- and upper-class churches that are culture-captive and not prophetic. The lower class immigrants, then, may well be drawn to churches such as the charismatic and Pentecostal, as has occurred in certain countries of Latin America. These churches offer more affective, emotional, and elementary religious experiences.

In the life of evangelical denominations a concern for the breaking of racial barriers will increase. The distinctions between "foreign" and "home" missions will slowly decrease and many will attempt to engage in "global mission." As persons become better informed about the reality of mission in the twenty-first century, they will seek to avoid paternalism and instead move to embrace egalitarianism.

In the area of *world mission* the following issues are highlighted for the consideration of college and seminary students interested in a holistic Christian worldview. An understanding of the strengths of Christianity in different areas of the world will become a priority. First World Christians will seek to face the challenges of population increase, dislocations, political turmoil, and poverty. Many evangelicals will seek a creative connection between direct evangelism, mission, and ministry (care). Denominational mission agencies will recognize the limitations of traditional means of delivery of mission and ministry.

In the area of *evangelism* the following issues will become crucial. Varied patterns of evangelization contextualized to the needs of "people groups" will be used for a better harvest. Some First World methods may continue to be effective, but "contextualized" evangelism will highlight the differences between the United States and other areas of the world. College and seminary graduates will be better attuned to cross-cultural concerns. A few will see the immensity of the urban mission challenges and will seek to become "world-class ministers." Some local churches will continue in the survival mode (chaplaincy model) while many will be inspired to greater outreach (apostolic model).

In the area of *pastoral care*, envisioning with love how to minister to foreign-born populations living in the United States will require consideration of the following issues. Methods of contextualized counseling recognizing cultural differences in understanding human personality will develop. One example relevant to counseling the large population of Asians in the United States will be to understand the Asian view of guilt. In addition, pastoral counselors will have to consider becoming multilingual to assist foreign-born populations. Those coming from other countries will force pastoral counselors to consider crucial issues other cultures bring with their worldview, such as the role of the extended family, medical practices, the role of the minister as an authority figure, and male and female roles that differ from the American culture.

To minister in a changing world during the twenty-first century will be challenging, exciting, and rewarding. Ministry students will have to rely on the power and guidance of the Holy Spirit and the training they will receive for a lifetime of ministry.

N O T E S

1. H. Richard Niebuhr, *Christ and Culture* (New York: Harper, 1951).

2. Charles H. Kraft, *Christianity and Culture* (Maryknoll, N.Y.: Orbis, 1979), 273. See pp. 276–312 for his discussion of dynamic-equivalence transculturation and theologizing of the message.

3. See David W. Augsburger, *Pastoral Counseling Across Cultures* (Philadelphia: Westminster, 1986); and Craig W. Ellison and Edward S. Maynard, *Healing for the City: Counseling in the Urban Setting* (Grand Rapids: Zondervan, 1992).

4. Marvin K. Mayers, *Christianity Confronts Culture: A Strategy for Cross Cultural Evangelism*, revised and enlarged ed. (Grand Rapids: Zondervan, 1987), 192, 249. Mayers, Dean of the School of Intercultural Studies and World Mission at Biola University, provides significant case studies dealing with the anthropological principles listed. See also David F. D'Amico, "Urban Ministries in a Multiracial Nation," in *Proceedings of the Christian Life Commission Conference: Southern Baptists and Race* (Nashville: Christian Life Commission, SBC, 1989), 27–32.

5. David B. Barrett, "Annual Statistical Table on Global Mission: 1993," *International Bulletin of Missionary Research* 17, no. 1 (January 1993), 22–23.

6. U.S. Census population reports, as cited in Oscar Romo, *American Mosaic: Church Planting in Ethnic America* (Nashville: Broadman, 1993), 43.

7. *Commerce News*, U.S. Census Bureau (5 July 1991), 14.

8. "Asian American Demographics," *The American Enterprise* (Nov.-Dec. 1991): 87.

9. *Commerce News*, U.S. Census Bureau (5 July 1991), 15.

10. Sam Roberts, "Census Reveals a Surge in Hispanic Population," *The New York Times* (9 October 1994), 15.

11. Language Church Extension Division, HMB, SBC, *Co-Laborers: Achievements, Projections* (Atlanta: Home Mission Board, SBC, 1992), 5, 14. For a typology of several ethnic enclaves in evangelical circles in the United States, see David F. D'Amico, "Evangelization Across Cultures in the United States: What to Do with the World Come to Us?" *Review and Expositor*, 90 (Winter 1993), 83–99. For different aspects of methodology of ethnic church planting in selected urban areas of the United States, see David F. D'Amico, "Ethnic Ministry in the Urban Setting," *Review and Expositor* 92 (Winter 1995), 39–56. For a developing missiology related to evangelical ethnic congregations in the United States, see David F. D'Amico, "A Pilgrim Missiology for the Stranger in Your Midst," *Review and Expositor* 92 (Fall 1995), 491–503.

12. See Alice Evans, Robert Evans, and David Roozen, eds., *The Globalization of Theological Education.* Maryknoll, N.Y.: Orbis, 1993.

13. The Southern Baptist Theological Seminary, "International Student Directory, 1995–1996," 16.

For Further Reading

Augsburger, David W. *Pastoral Counseling Across Cultures*. Philadelphia: Westminster, 1986.

D'Amico, David F. "Ethnic Ministry in the Urban Setting." *Review and Expositor* 92 (Winter 1995): 39–56.

———. "Evangelization Across Cultures in the United States: What to Do with the World Come to Us?" *Review and Expositor* 90 (Winter 1993): 83–99.

———. "A Pilgrim Missiology for the Stranger in Your Midst." *Review and Expositor* 92 (Fall 1995): 491–503.

———. "Urban Ministries in a Multiracial Nation." In *Proceedings of the Christian Life Commission Conference: Southern Baptists and Race*. Nashville: Christian Life Commission, SBC, 1989, 27–32.

Ellison, Craig W., and Edward S. Maynard, *Healing for the City: Counseling in the Urban Setting*. Grand Rapids: Zondervan, 1992.

Evans, Alice, Robert Evans, and David Roozen, eds. *The Globalization of Theological Education*. Maryknoll, N.Y.: Orbis, 1993.

Kraft, Charles H. *Christianity and Culture*. Maryknoll, N.Y.: Orbis, 1979.

Mayers, Marvin K. *Christianity Confronts Culture: A Strategy for Cross Cultural Evangelism*. Revised and enlarged edition. Grand Rapids: Zondervan, 1987.

Niebuhr, H. Richard. *Christ and Culture*. New York: Harper, 1951.

Romo, Oscar. *American Mosaic: Church Planting in Ethnic America*. Nashville: Broadman, 1993.

20

CHRISTIAN MINISTRY IN LOCAL CONTEXTS

ROBERT DON HUGHES

In Okelerin Baptist Church in Ogbomoso, Nigeria, the organist is accompanied by a drummer as everyone dances by the altar table, depositing their offerings as they pass. At a large church in Louisville, Kentucky, the black-robed minister leads the liturgy in a highly formal worship service, reading the Scripture at a stately, dignified pace. Not far away another church bounces to the rhythms of contemporary Christian rock as a drama team prepares to "play" the gospel before the crowd. Fifteen miles from that church a rural congregation worships God through a service almost identical to services held in that same church building fifty years before. Besides the lordship of Jesus Christ, what do these churches share in common?

One thing they share is their contextual nature—that is, they each "fit" with their location and their people. While each church may worship in a different manner, all these churches worship in a manner appropriate to their context.

Robert Don Hughes is Professor of Missions and Communication and Director of Continuing Education and Extension Studies at the Southern Baptist Theological Seminary, Louisville, Kentucky.

WHAT'S A CONTEXT?

A context is anything—a room, a town, a lifestyle, a language, a culture, a telephone link, a tradition—that people share in common and which binds them together. We might talk of "the American context," by which we would probably mean things common to and well-understood by people in the United States. We could speak of "the Baptist context," by which we might mean the common understandings and traditions of a particular denomination of Christians. We might use the term "a seminary student context" and mean all things that seminary students everywhere share in common. We might, on the other hand, be meaning what students at a particular seminary share in common—a context which is part of the worldwide seminary-student context, but which is more particular, more exclusive. It would include only *these* students at *this* seminary. When we speak of the "local church context" we might be meaning characteristics common to all local churches, or we might be speaking of a particular local church. However we use the language of context, it is obvious that we all belong to many different contexts, and that these contexts can be quite different from one another.

WHY IS THE CONCEPT OF *CONTEXT* IMPORTANT TO A MINISTER?

If you were to grow up in a particular church—a particular context—learn the Scriptures as taught by that church, yourself become a teacher in that church, and ultimately become a leader of that same particular congregation, then the question of context might never be of importance to you. Oh, you might learn that other churches did things differently from your own church, and you might shake your head in confusion. Why would those churches want to do things differently from the way your church has always done things? Yet even in such a closed context you would still be touched periodically by church *differences*—when a new member joined your church from some other context, perhaps—or when a visiting missionary shared slides revealing Christian practices in other lands.

The truth is, the more we learn about Christians who think,

worship, or practice differently than we, the more we are confronted by the reality of differing contexts. The more we visit other congregations, have fellowship with other Christians, or even study the history of those first-century churches so powerfully depicted in the Book of Acts, the more clearly we see that differences in *context* make for a wide diversity of Christian experience.

Some Christians may be threatened by such diversity, asking "Isn't there one right, true, *correct* way for churches to operate and for Christians to behave?" Such believers might feel motivated to do all in their power to make other Christians conform to their own practices. Other Christians may become so enamored of diversity that they begin to view *all* Christian thought and practice as "contextual," and slide toward a relativism that essentially says, "It doesn't matter what you believe, so long as you believe something." Such a view is not far from actually saying, "We believe nothing." Clearly, the impact of context upon Christianity raises difficult questions, ones that strike at the very heart of what a church should be. Ministers who will be called upon to lead churches in a wide variety of local contexts need to face the issue of content vs. context head-on.

BIBLICAL MODELS
OF CONTEXTUALIZATION

The early church, as seen in the Book of Acts, quickly encountered exactly these problems. The Jerusalem church was a Jewish church, filled with Jewish believers who understood Christ and his commands in a very Jewish way—a Jewish context. But by Acts 6 we see that the cultural questions raised by differing languages had already begun to divide the fellowship. Greek-speaking Jews within the church began to perceive that their widows were being overlooked in the daily distribution of food. The twelve apostles met with the congregation and defined this as an administrative problem, offering a solution which apparently worked. The church was called upon to select seven men of high reputation who were filled with the Holy Spirit and with faith. Once selected, they were placed in charge of this task. Not incidentally, the names of the seven that were selected are all Greek names, indicating that the church was seeking to incorporate more than just the original Hebrew (Aramaic-speaking) context into what they all understood to be the *ekklesia*.

Philip, one of these seven, helped enlarge the context of the faith even further, first by preaching among the hated Samaritans—with wonderfully fruitful results (Acts 8:4-25)—and then by responding to the leadership of the Holy Spirit to share the gospel with an Ethiopian eunuch (Acts 8:26-40). The "context" problem became even more acute when the Lord asked Peter to swallow his Jewish prejudices and share the truth of the gospel with that righteous Gentile, Cornelius (Acts 10–11). Peter sounded almost apologetic when he later had to explain this happening to his Jewish brethren. Then when Paul and Barnabas began their ministry *directly* to the Gentiles, establishing church after church through Asia Minor without requiring these new believers to undergo the circumcision required of proselytes by the Jews, the intense conflict that ensued is a matter of biblical record (Acts 15). Some Jewish Christians definitely did not want to see the church contextualized. Why? Because they feared that something basic, an essential principle, a fundamental of the faith, would be compromised thereby. The resultant split necessitated a conclave of the early church leaders to seek some resolution of this heated issue—the meeting often referred to as the Jerusalem Conference.[1]

We can easily understand the feelings of these apostles and elders as they met together to pray and debate. Each person present certainly believed with great sincerity that his own position was the correct one. And yet—they differed. The question they faced was thorny then, just as it is for us today: What parts of our "faith and order" are the essential, nonnegotiable truths of the gospel, and what parts are our contextual traditions—the cultural trappings that we have allowed to become attached to those truths because they make us feel more comfortable?

For the sake of the gospel, Paul was willing to sacrifice much of what was, for himself, culturally comfortable. After all, this is the missionary who wrote, "I become all things to all people, that I might by all means save some" (1 Cor. 9:22, NRSVB). Did he mean by that that he was willing to compromise the gospel itself? Certainly not! But it is clear from his running battle with the Judaizers that he was willing to compromise far more of his

Jewish religious *tradition* than were they. How Jewish listeners would have cringed to hear Paul stand in the Areopagus in Athens and relate the God of Abraham, Isaac, and Jacob to some dirty foreign altar labeled TO AN UNKNOWN GOD! (Acts 17:16-34) Yet all Paul was attempting to do was to help the Athenians understand the God of the Jews in their own context. As we seek to communicate the gospel with a multicultural world, should we be following the example of Paul, or the example of the Judaizers?

A MAJOR ISSUE FOR MISSIONS

The problem of separating the con*tent* of the gospel from the con*text* of the culture has continued to plague missionaries to this day. Is it our responsibility to make *American* disciples of all nations—to turn Zambians into American Christians, or Taiwanese into American Christians, or Brazilians into American Christians? Of course not. But American missionaries are American Christians, and it is out of that context that our faith has grown. What can we share except what we know?

The cultural circle can be drawn much smaller than the differences between nations. I was born in Southern California to parents who had moved to that state from the South to grow a newly planted Southern Baptist church. In the early days of my denomination in that state, it was primarily transplanted "Southerners" who joined Southern Baptist churches. But there's a vast cultural difference between L.A. (Los Angeles) and L.A. (Lower Alabama). Ministry in California had to be *contextualized* to meet the needs of Californians—and it was. A large component of today's Southern Baptist Convention of California is "ethnic" in makeup. There are many Latino churches, African American churches, Korean and Chinese churches, Cambodian churches, Lithuanian churches—in short, the world has moved to America, and Christians of all contexts have responded with the gospel. Even the "Anglo" member of a California church is likely to be different from his or her counterpart in the South. Glance at the picture of laid-back "Saddleback Sam," the target of Saddleback Valley Community Church in Laguna Hills, California,[2] and you see a very different churchgoer than Mr. Southern Charm in a sport coat and penny loafers, or

Mr. Serious Christian in a vested, pin-striped blue suit and Brooks Brothers tie.

Does this mean their values are different? Some of them are, probably. But what about *Christian* values? Aren't Christian values universal? Are Christian values compromised in the contextualization of the gospel? Is it our task to *judge?* Are we not left with the same basic problem as were James and the rest of the Jerusalem church when faced with expressions of Christianity that differ from our own? The Jerusalem church prayed, swallowed hard, wrote a letter spelling out what it thought were some *essentials* that the Gentile churches needed to adhere to, and embraced their new brothers and sisters in Christ (Acts 15:23-29). What was their alternative? To attempt to control the context of new believers?

THE MISSIONARY STEREOTYPE

Consider the popular culture's view of "the missionary"—stern, rigid, unsympathetic, unreasonable, demanding, dour, dictatorial, paternalistic—in other words, the character played by Max von Sydow in the movie version of James Michener's *Hawaii.* This missionary stereotype may have been amplified recently by such films as "At Play in the Fields of the Lord" and "Black Robe," but the image was already clearly fixed in the popular imagination. Why? Any basis in truth?

In fact, many missionaries of what Kenneth Scott Latourette called "The Great Century"[3] did act in a way that enabled such a stereotype.

> Some of them were bungling and did unnecessary damage to those whom they had come to help. Some were shocked by the costume, or lack of costume, of the natives and sought to induce them to wear the white man's clothes. Unwashed and unadapted to the local conditions, the clothing often bred disease. Customs were uprooted which seemed to the missionary unchristian, but which in some instances were either morally neutral or could not be destroyed without working more harm than good.[4]

These were surely very well-intentioned people, but they ran aground on the same problem that troubled the Jerusalem church in the first century: "If they don't talk as we do, act as we do, dress as we do, and worship as we do, how can we be certain they *believe* as we do?" The answer of the Judaizers was clear: "The safest course is to make them as much like us as we can." Paul's answer seemed to focus instead on what missionary strategists call the principle of indigenity or the indigenous principle.

WHAT IS THE INDIGENOUS PRINCIPLE?

Just as the culturally bound thinking of the Judaizers hampered the expansion of the church in the first century, it has sometimes hampered the growth of churches in other contexts—on "foreign mission fields." In the 1800s mission boards tended to pay native pastors to lead churches that were carbon copies of those back in England or America. Missionaries often maintained tight controls on the churches through this financial authority. The churches only grew when native populations agreed to the directions of the missionaries. Roland Allen, a missionary of that "Great Century" to China, was sharply critical of such methods in his books *Missionary Methods: Saint Paul's or Ours?* and *The Spontaneous Expansion of the Church.* Why is it, he wondered, that Paul could establish multiple churches over a period of just a few years, while modern missionaries sometimes struggle to keep one limping congregation alive? "We naturally expect our converts to adopt from us not only essentials but accidentals. We desire to impart not only the gospel, but the law and the customs. With that spirit, St. Paul's methods do not agree, because they were the natural outcome of quite another spirit, the spirit which preferred persuasion to authority."[5]

Henry Venn, Rufus Anderson, John Nevius, and other missionary strategists also tried to help the church to return to a less authoritarian, more contextual approach to sharing the gospel. The result is that the indigenous principle has become foundational for modern missions. This principle has classically been explained by the "three-self" model—that the local church ought to be encouraged from the beginning to become self-*supporting*, self-*governing*, and self-*propagating*. In other words, every local church should pay its own way, call its own shots, and actively seek to plant new churches, just as it was itself planted. The result of this strategic approach to missions has been vigorous national churches in many contexts around the world. This was, in fact, the approach of the Apostle Paul.

BUT WHERE ARE THE LINES?

Does this mean Paul was willing to allow *any* cultural practice to remain within the fellowship of the churches he helped to establish? If that had been the case, the New Testament would have been a much shorter book! In fact, Paul's letters are full of teaching, scolding, encouraging, arguing, counseling, forbidding, suggesting, and (in sum) *revealing* by inspiration of the Holy Spirit the direction of God. Ministers today are called upon to do the same tasks, based upon that same revelation. Would that the lines between essential Christianity and cultural religion were sharply drawn!

They are not. Christians still differ on many issues that revolve around this same critical question: Is this practice/ view/attitude/method/approach/program/system a Christian essential, or a contextual option? Because we differ in our responses to that question, the result is likely to be more conferences like that first one in Jerusalem, more debates, more struggles and splits and controversies. We each must be true to ourselves and to our own understanding of God's leadership. But it is helpful to realize that many of our issues *do* have a contextual element embedded in them which *may* provide us room for flexibility. Sometimes—as happened in Acts 15—it is possible to find a solution to the problem that does not involve a break in fellowship. We need to be careful to let God draw the lines, rather than allowing our own culture or tradition to draw them for us.

HOW CAN I APPLY ANY OF THIS
TO MY LOCAL CHURCH?

Up to this point it may seem that this chapter has been rather theoretical. Is there any way that this "contextualization" idea can be practically applied in the life of a local church? Many ways. Here are some ideas as you embark on your ministry.

Every Context Is Local

First, it's important to remember that every church is a local church *somewhere*. Until there is a "First Church of Cyberspace," all contexts are "local" to someone, even that megachurch whose services you occasionally watch on television. And if every context is local, and you do not originate *from* that locality, it will be helpful to your ministry to learn that local context as quickly as possible. It's helpful to begin by listening to the people who belong to that context. Often ministers called to a new situation assume that they've been called because they have something to *say*. While that's true, they have much to *hear* as well, if they expect to be able to illustrate their messages effectively to their "listeners."

Along with the idea of listening goes the idea of observing. Remember that Paul began his Areopagus sermon by relating what he had *observed* (Acts 17:22-23). This was a good foundation for beginning to reach the Athenians "where they lived," as we sometimes say. It certainly wouldn't hurt to write down some of your early observations of a particular context. Missionaries comment frequently on the fact that they take few pictures late in their term because the context is too *familiar* for them to be able to see it clearly. Writing down your first impressions of a new ministry situation can be a very effective tool for planning how to get in touch with these people in the future.

As you listen and observe, ask questions. Most people are happy to share their own interpretations of a place or of a church. If every context is local, you must come to understand the local context effectively to share your message effectively. All of this might seem obvious, but there have been times when ministers have failed to learn their new context—and have failed to minister, as well. They perhaps forgot that each context differs.

Every Context Is Different

I have a friend who had led a church to very effective growth. After that church was well-established (and his own reputation as a dynamic pastor was established as well) he changed pastorates, confident that he could do the same thing in the new situation. Several years later I heard he had again changed pastorates, leaving behind a church less vigorous than the one he'd come to. We talked later about his inability to help that church grow, and he shrugged and confessed, "It's really my fault. I assumed I knew these new people without ever taking time to get acquainted with them." It wasn't only the people he'd failed to get in touch with—it was the whole changed context. What had worked in one place did not necessarily work in another.

Missionaries *do* gossip—or at least, they compare notes about other missionaries, in part to learn what to do and what not to do. It is sometimes said of missionaries that "they never unpacked their bags." This is said of pastors as well, those who never appear to make the effort to become "at home" in a situation. While we may sing "This world is not my home, I'm just a-passing through," in fact, people want us to build foundations with them, to put down roots, to make plans to stay beside them if we intend to minister among them. If this requires you to do things differently, is that too great a sacrifice for the gospel?

Every Context Is Changing

Remember too the incredible changes going on in the world today. Consider this: Our generation has witnessed more technological changes *in a single life span* than witnessed by all the previous generations of humanity on this earth *put together*. Nor does the pace of change appear to be slowing. Rather, the inertia of our exploding technology is likely to carry us into contexts visualized by no one except science fiction writers. Have you ever thought about the impact the copy machine has made on church life— much less the computer?

Whatever situation God calls you to minister in *will* be experiencing "future shock" at some level or another. The pace of technological change will doubtless exert pressure upon the gospel to change as well: It is, after all, a new culture that is emerging, and the values and practices of every new culture have confronted the gospel with their own agenda. And, as it has in every other age of history and each new cultural situation, the gospel will need to be *contextualized* for that future-to-be which we all face. How can the minister help people who are assaulted by changes that appear to threaten the very fabric of their lives?

Ministers can welcome change—or at any rate, greet it cheerfully. If the people to whom we minister are going to be forced to suffer through it, they might appreciate our giving them some informed guidance as to how to weather the storm. Ministers can *plan* for change, recognizing that it *is* going to come and that the church will need to be there—wherever "there" is—to minister effectively to new needs. Don't we sometimes describe ourselves as "change agents?" Ministers can also remind their people that the gospel *can* and *will* be preserved in the face of oceans of change. After all, we believe we understand the gospel clearly and can share it effectively—and hasn't our world undergone enormous change since the Lord gave the early church the Great Commission?

CONCLUSION

The contextualization of the gospel is a critical element in effectively communicating that good news to people in need. It is a difficult proposition, however, for Christians sometimes disagree about what constitutes an essential of the message and what is instead culturally conditioned. It is critical for the minister to be aware of the need to be up to speed with his or her context. To do this effectively, it might be helpful to remember that each context is local, each is different, and each is changing.

It is equally critical for the minister to recognize the tension between effective communication and fidelity to the Word of God. Most of us are familiar with the so-called Serenity Prayer— "God grant me the strength to change those things I can change, the patience to endure the things I cannot change, and the wisdom to know the difference." Perhaps we need to consider praying a "Contextualization Prayer": "Lord, give us the stability to maintain all the essential values of the Christian faith, the flexibility to adapt our presentation of the gospel so that all might come to understand it, and the wisdom to know the difference."

N O T E S

1. For an excellent treatment of these passages, see John Polhill, *Acts*, vol. 26 of The New American Commentary (Nashville: Broadman, 1992).
2. See Norman Shawchuck, et al., *Marketing for Congregations* (Nashville: Abingdon, 1992), 200.

3. See Kenneth Scott Latourette's seven-volume *A History of the Expansion of Christianity* (New York: Harper, 1937–1945).

4. Latourette, *The Great Century: The Americas, Australia, and Africa,* vol. 5 of *A History of the Expansion of Christianity,* 199.

5. Roland Allen, "Introductory," in *Missionary Methods: St. Paul's or Ours?* (Chicago: Moody, 1959).

FOR FURTHER READING

Engle, James F. *Contemporary Christian Communication.* Nashville: Thomas Nelson, 1975.

Hesselgrave, David. *Communicating Christ Cross-Culturally.* Grand Rapids: Zondervan, 1978.

Hughes, Robert Don. *Talking to the World in the Days to Come.* Nashville: Broadman, 1991.

Kraft, Charles. *Christianity in Culture.* Maryknoll, N.Y.: Orbis, 1979.

Mayers, Marvin. *Christianity Confronts Culture.* Grand Rapids: Zondervan, 1989.

21

CHRISTIAN MINISTRY IN THE AFRICAN AMERICAN CHURCH:
A CHALLENGE FOR SEMINARIANS AND SEMINARIES

T. VAUGHN WALKER
AND
ROBERT SMITH, JR.

Dr. Gayraud Wilmore, the renowned African American church historian, often speaks of the irrepressible, indomitable spirit of the black religious experience in America in terms of three themes: *survival, elevation*, and *liberation*. From 1619, when twenty slaves were brought to these shores and began to work the fields of the Virginia colony, to January 1, 1863, when the Emancipation Proclamation took effect, African Americans *survived* 244 years of slavery without benefit of a payday or a paycheck. It was a time in which "hope unborn had died," a time of "I shall not be moved" determination.

During the brief Reconstruction era, African Americans aspired to live an *elevated* life. They experienced a semblance of their dream during the years between 1867–1877, a time referred to by W.E.B. DuBois as "those mystic years." These were the years of "climbing Jacob's ladder" and the recognition of a present reality where "every round goes higher, higher."

T. Vaughn Walker is Professor of Black Church Studies, and **Robert Smith, Jr.** is the Carl G. Bates Associate Professor of Christian Preaching, both at the Southern Baptist Theological Seminary, Louisville, Kentucky.

Yet Reconstruction makes its last move in 1877. Rutherford Hayes moves into the presidency. Checkmate! The wheels are wrenched off the short-lived Reconstruction period. The newly elected President orders the withdrawal of federal troops from the Southern states, thus denying African Americans protection from Southern whites. African Americans would experience lynchings, beatings, and other inhumane treatment in the aftermath of Hayes' decision. Now the flame of *liberation* is lit in the African American experience. Refusing to allow the clock of justice to be rolled back in silence, black people begin to sing: "Oh, Freedom, Oh, Freedom, Oh, Freedom over me. And before I'll be a slave, I'll be buried in my grave, And go home to my Lawd and be free."

African Americans have experienced uprooting from their ancestral home in Africa, nearly four centuries of *survival* against all odds, a quest for *elevation*, and a continuous pursuit after *liberation*. There is an undeniable thread running between this distinctive African American heritage and the contribution blacks have made to this nation. American Christianity is no small part of their investment. For example, as African American congregations continue to unite with the Southern Baptist Convention, and as many ethnic churches start as dually aligned congregations, increasing numbers of African American churches and Christians seek to be a viable and vital part of the life of the Southern Baptist Convention. Inevitably, this means that more African American students will find their way to SBC seminaries. Their presence poses a number of great challenges, both to the seminaries and to the seminarians themselves. These challenges are the topic of this chapter.

THE BLACK STUDENT ON THE WHITE CAMPUS

At the turn of the twentieth century, W.E.B. DuBois eloquently articulated the challenge facing the African living in America.

> One ever feels his two-ness, an American, a Negro; two souls, two thoughts, two unreconciled strivings; two warring ideals in one dark body, whose dogged strength alone keeps it from being torn asunder.[1]

Is this the dilemma of first-semester African American students who enroll in predominantly white Southern Baptist (and evangelical) seminaries? Can African American students attending such seminaries experience collegial, intellectual, and spiritual inclusivity without being inculturated, losing their distinct cultural identity? This is the internal struggle facing incoming students of African American descent who desire, in the words of James Weldon Johnson's *Lift Ev'ry Voice*, to be "true to our God, true to our native land."

In an address delivered at the Christian Theological Seminary in 1990, Dr. James Earl Massey, Dean of the Anderson University School of Theology, declared:

> Whether one wants to admit it, and however one assesses it, the American churches and society are changing along racial lines. As the Hispanic presence continues to burgeon, as Southeast Asian immigrants make their impact, and as Black Americans continue to affirm their impact in the collective process, new challenges to ministry steadily increase. Some of those challenges are rooted in racial and ethnic factors, which must be understood and rightly treated in the theological seminary if they are to be appreciated and regarded within the churches.[2]

Massey admonishes theological seminaries to pay attention to the changing racial complexion of the U.S. population. He challenges seminaries to respond to this phenomenon by coloring their curriculum, faculty, administration, and resource offerings and to be sensitive to the needs of their entire student constituency. His is a call for a thorough "retooling" and "refocusing" of theological education. Massey asserts that "seminaries must be about the business of making all of our seminarians 'insiders.'"[3] Of course, all of the responsibility for adaptation and adjustment does not lie upon the seminary; some of it must be borne by the African American student.

The overarching purpose of Southern Baptist seminaries is to serve churches in the Southern Baptist Convention by training and equipping students to serve those churches upon graduation. With the increase of "black presence" in the form of black churches in the Southern Baptist Convention, Southern Baptist seminaries need to be sensitized to the black religious experience in America. They need greater knowledge of the black presence in Scripture and in twenty centuries of church history. This comprehensive reorientation will increase the seminaries' ability to train African American students effectively to serve black churches both within and outside the Southern Baptist Convention.

To understand the black church, Southern Baptist seminaries must look through the lens of the black community which the black church serves. Conversely, the black community cannot be understood if the black church is neglected. Both Southern Baptist and other white evangelical seminaries must offer theological education that is genuinely useful to black students, enabling students to move from being "outsiders" to "insiders." This is a particularly critical issue for predominately white seminaries which have a significant African American student population. African American theologian J. Deotis Roberts offers this penetrating critique of white seminaries' training of black students: "Black graduates are more qualified to minister to white suburban congregations than to their own people. Seminaries are generally 'miseducating' black seminarians for ministry in black churches."[4]

What shall we say then to these things, to this two-ness of being a black student on a predominantly white theological campus? Is it possible for the African American to acquire a functional theological education through the process of *adaptation* (retaining African identity and culture) instead of *adoption* (surrendering African identity and culture to white/American theological worldview)? In what follows we offer a proposal to African American students to help them bridge the gap between the mind-set of the white theological institution and the mind-set of the black religious experience; between the African past and the American existential reality; between the "rock" of African identity and the "hard place" of American relevance. If this proposal is to be actualized within the theological educational experience of African Americans attending SBC and evangelical seminaries, it will require some bridge building on the part of black students as they matriculate through these institutions. The ultimate goal is for African American students, who study in the white arena of theological education and worship in the fellowship of the black religious experience, to stand between these two worlds, holding them in tension and extracting the best from both. This posture is critical because African American students not only serve black congregations, but are sometimes called to minister in all-white, bicultural, and multicultural contexts. Additionally, African American churches are exhibiting a greater openness to globalization and are sometimes calling non-African Americans to serve, especially in non-pastoral roles. Seminarians—both black and white—are challenged with the charge to prepare themselves to serve Christ in a much more pluralistic society.

PREPARE FOR THE INTELLECTUAL CHALLENGE

African American students will not only experience culture shock at Southern Baptist and white evangelical seminaries (especially those who have attended black colleges or colleges where blacks are a significant population group), they will also experience *syllabus* shock. High intellectual demands are made upon the entire student body. Black students must seek to integrate their theological education into their cultural heritage. Given the burgeoning field of Black Church Studies and the proliferation of black scholarly writings in all theological disciplines, black seminarians must integrate European/American theological thought with African American perspectives. Class bibliographies should be examined for black visibility and inclusivity. Students should encourage professors to include and increase books written by black scholars and urge them to require all students to do some work in black (or other ethnic) scholarship, in order to acquaint the entire student population with black scholars and to insure a more complete theological education for everyone.

FORM HEALTHY RELATIONSHIPS

The extended family is a vital relational structure within black culture. Black students must transmit the reality of this concept from their community to the campus of the seminary. However, the "new extended family" must not be "for blacks only." The underlying meaning of the Negro Spiritual, *"Were You There When They Crucified My Lord?"* is the slaves' ability to identify with the ignominious suffering of Jesus the condemned Jew, because like him they too had been to Calvary. African Americans are not the only group of people who have suffered grave injustice. They need to bond with persons who "sit where they have sat" and share existential commonalities. Some of them will come from Africa; others from the Caribbean and Asia; still others will come from South America and Appalachia. This bonding must evolve into *koinonia*, as black students attempt to "live peacefully with all" (Rom. 12:18, NRSVB). In Christ, Paul reminds us, the walls of partition are torn down. In Christ, there is neither Jew nor Gentile, bond nor free, male nor female, for we are all one in Christ Jesus (Gal. 3:28). It is indispensable that students nurture healthy relationships, not neglecting such relationships because of the demands of academics. Friendships provide cushioning during times of emotional upheaval, financial reverses, and spiritual ambiguity.

CULTIVATE SPIRITUALITY

Admittedly, oftentimes it requires greater effort to sing the Lord's song on predominantly white seminary campuses. Such places represent a "strange land" to many incoming African American students. Consequently, they join with the sixth-century Hebrews in their response to the Babylonian request: "How can we sing the Lord's song in a foreign land?" (Ps. 137:4, NASB) African American students must not refuse to sing. White America did not bestow religion upon the African slaves; they brought their religion to America with them. They artfully synthesized African tribal religion and American Christianity, formulating an intensely personal religion that was both Christian and distinctively African. African American students must bring their religion with them and cultivate their spirituality, so that they can "have church" on a predominantly white seminary campus, practicing the spiritual discipline of "singing the Lord's song in a strange land." The alternative yields disastrous consequences. If you "stop singing," it is not only possible but likely that you will experience shipwreck on the rocks of spiritual catastrophe, a wide chasm in your relationship to God, and a loss of faith. Take precautions to prevent the encroachment of these hindrances; take measures to cultivate your spirituality.

PRACTICE THE ART OF BLACK BIBLICAL INTERPRETATION

The black biblical interpretive tradition has relevance not only for blacks but for all, especially for persons who experience depersonalization and oppression. There are a variety of responses to religious experience because there are a variety of needs. Black students must read the scriptural text in such a manner that they experience the truth of Phillips Brooks' directive to find the place where the truth of the text touches down upon life. Black students must wear "shoes that fit their feet" as they traverse the terrain of the verities of God's Word. They must let the Bible use them, instead of using the Bible. This type of textual reading will enable black students to interpret biblical passages by looking through cultural lenses and discerning how God is specifically speaking to their particular reality.

BE OPEN TO OPPORTUNITIES FOR CHRISTIAN SERVICE

Seminarian Issac Durosinjesu of Nigeria has expressed surprise at the present state of American Christianity. One of his greatest frustrations was the lack of ministry opportunities offered to him as a visiting African preacher. He correctly observed, "When American ministers visit us in Africa, we allow them full-time ministry opportunities—preaching, baptizing—no restrictions, but here that is not the case. I wonder if they feel we cannot minister."[5] It is imperative that African American students attending Southern Baptist and white evangelical seminaries be involved in a local church ministry. Like other students, they need opportunities to balance theory with practice. Ministry does not begin after graduation; ministry begins while one is in seminary.

WHAT SEMINARIES CAN STILL DO

We want to say a word particularly relevant to Southern Baptist seminaries. Such seminaries must make a concerted, sincere, and history-making commitment to diversify their faculty, curriculum, and administration with a significant African American presence in all areas. Most likely this will require creative and flexible policies which are more germane to specific cultural realities. For example, the seminaries should allow African American faculty to serve simultaneously in long-term local church ministry positions (including senior pastorates). They should permit such faculty to remain affiliated with black Baptist denominations (faculty could align dually if they choose to do so). Such affiliation patterns would enable black faculty to maintain credibility with the larger African American Christian community. Many may never choose to be Southern Baptist, but perhaps could be persuaded to continue as well as increase cooperative ministry opportunities with Southern Baptists.

Southern Baptist seminaries can also make concerted efforts to attract sabbaticant and retired African American scholars for short-term teaching commitments. It would be altogether feasible that some cooperative programs with non-Southern Baptist institutions could be explored to offer experiences that cannot be provided under present circumstances.

Every effort must be made to provide students with wholesome and meaningful supervised ministry and practicum experiences which focus on the most probable or likely ministry type and setting for all students. These experiences become acutely critical when preparing students to serve in distinct cultural settings such as the African American community. The black church is not the white church in blackface. Such ministry settings may prove most beneficial for all students who feel a call to serve in transitional, urban, or other specific or unique cultural settings.

ADDRESSING PLURALISM

Ministry training for the twenty-first century clearly will have to be more inclusive. Ministers of all ethnicities will encounter cultural, racial, and ethnic diversity as in no prior period. In North America, where specific ethnic groups have dominated, undoubtedly there will be a major shift. As society continues to open, and educational and social integration advance, the church—previously branded as the most segregated institution in the land—will invariably become more diverse and multiracial as well as multicultural.

Ministers for a new era must move beyond "sensitivity" to

other races and cultures toward a greater level of appreciation and affirmation of the diversity of God's creation. The seminary experience can serve as a marvelous beginning point for this greater affirmation of diversity. Seminaries will be challenged constantly, however, to be inclusive in all curriculum areas, not simply be content to establish special black church or African American programs. Church history cannot be taught adequately without the inclusion of the contribution of the African American church—nor can Christian theology, Christian ethics, or Christian preaching. All must include the enormous contributions of African Americans and scholars of other ethnic groups.

CONCLUSION

The African American church, along with *other* ethnic expressions of the people of God, also must be challenged to produce provocative and scholarly contributions to the academy. African Americans have a critical contribution to make in the years ahead. It is the seminary that will produce tomorrow's scholars. It is the seminary that will inspire, encourage, and train such gifted researchers and writers for leadership in the academy. It is the seminary that will provide mentors and role models who will be the catalysts for the scholars of the future.

N O T E S

1. W.E.B. DuBois, *The Souls of Black Folk* (Chicago: A.C. McClurg, 1907), 3.

2. James Earl Massey, "The Coloring of the Theological Curriculum," Public Lecture, Christian Theological Seminary, Indianapolis, Indiana, 8 November 1990.

3. Ibid, 4.

4. This condition exists even in black seminaries where the desire to please accrediting agencies, whose standards are set by white leaders, is stronger than the desire to provide black seminarians with an immersion in ministry leadership in the "black experience." J. Deotis Roberts, *The Prophethood of Black Believers: An African American Political Theology for Ministry.* (Louisville: Westminster/John Knox, 1994), 143.

5. Quoted in *Towers*, Southern Baptist Theological Seminary, 11 September 1995, 1.

FOR FURTHER READING

Bailey, Randall C., and Jacquelyn Grant, eds. *The Recovery of Black Presence: An Interdisciplinary Exploration*. Nashville: Abingdon, 1996.

Cone, James, and Gayraud Wilmore, *Black Theology, A Documentary History: 1966-1990*. Maryknoll, N.Y.: Orbis, 1990.

DuBois, W.E.B. *The Souls of Black Folk*. Chicago: A.C. McClurg, 1907.

Felder, Cain Hope. *Stony the Road We Trod*. Minneapolis: Fortress, 1991.

————. *Troubling Biblical Waters: Race, Class and Family*. Maryknoll, N.Y.: Orbis, 1989.

Fischer, Miles Mark. *Negro Slave Songs in the United States*. New York: Citadel, 1963.

Higginbotham, Evelyn Brooks. *Righteous Discontent*. Cambridge: Harvard Univ. Press, 1993.

Lincoln, C. Eric. *The Black Experience in Religion*. Garden City, N.Y.: Doubleday/Anchor, 1974.

Lincoln, C. Eric, and Lawrence H. Mamiya. *The Black Church in the African American Experience*. Durham, N.C.: Duke Univ. Press, 1990.

Lovell, John, Jr. *Black Song: The Forge and the Flame*. New York: Collier-Macmillan, 1972.

McCall, Emmanuel. *Black Church Lifestyles*. Nashville: Broadman, 1986.

Meyers, William H. *God's Yes Was Louder Than My No: Rethinking the African American Call to Ministry*. Grand Rapids: Eerdmans, 1994.

Parrillo, Vincent N. *Diversity in America*. Thousand Oaks, Calif.: Pine Forge, 1996.

Roberts, J. Deotis. *The Prophethood of Black Believers: An African American Political Theology for Ministry*. Louisville: Westminster/John Knox, 1994.

Stewart III, Carlyle Fielding. *African American Church Growth*. Nashville: Abingdon, 1994.

Washington, James Melvin. *Frustrated Fellowship: The Black Baptist Quest for Social Power*. Macon, Ga.: Mercer Univ. Press, 1986.

West, Cornel. *Race Matters*. Boston: Beacon, 1993.

Wilmore, Gayraud. *Black Religion and Black Radicalism*. New York: Doubleday, 1972.

Woodson, Carter G. *The History of the Negro Church*. Washington, D.C.: Associated Publishers, [1921] 1945.

22

MORAL ISSUES FACING THE CONTEMPORARY CHURCH

DAVID P. GUSHEE

It is not possible to be a fully effective minister in the late 1990s without serious attention to the moral issues that confront us in our time. Sometimes these concerns scream out at us from the daily newspaper—racism, homosexuality, family breakdown, abortion, the environment. Other times we are confronted directly with moral issues through those in need of crisis counseling: a teenager is pregnant; parents find out that their child is a homosexual; children of a terminally ill parent face decisions concerning medical treatment; a business executive contemplates ordering a layoff that will cost hundreds of jobs.

Many times a congregation or Christian agency must make moral decisions as a body. Consider these contemporary issues which a church might face. A qualified African American applies to serve as a predominantly white church's minister of education. A family in which the father and daughter have AIDS seeks to join a congregation. The numerous homeless and hungry people in a community request the church's help in meeting their needs.

David P. Gushee is Associate Professor of Christian Studies at Union University, Jackson, Tennessee.

A church budget must be passed, and arguments over ministry priorities raise significant moral issues. A political party seeks to distribute its election flyers at a church's Sunday morning service. A divorced and remarried individual is nominated as a deacon.

The Southern Baptist Convention (SBC), my community of faith, addresses new moral concerns at its annual meeting. A significant portion of each year's resolutions involve moral issues— race, abortion, assisted suicide, genetic engineering, church/state issues, and so on. The SBC Christian Life Commission (soon to be renamed the Ethics and Religious Liberty Commission) repeatedly finds itself in the national press, from the *New York Times* to "Nightline." State and local ethics-related commissions and bodies proliferate. The Southern Baptist Convention by now is fully engaged in addressing contemporary moral issues, and its witness is taken seriously by cultural and political leaders. The same is true today of other leading evangelical bodies and parachurch organizations.

And let us not forget the personal moral life of the called-of-God minister. Every Christian faces daily moral challenges. Christian discipleship is about meeting those challenges in a way that is pleasing to our Lord Jesus Christ, through the power of the Holy Spirit. A minister's character and conduct has profound consequences, either for good or for ill (see chap. 10).

This chapter will focus on several moral issues of particular importance today: abortion, the role of women, racism, sexual ethics, and war. Of course, these are just a few of the dozens of moral issues that confront Christians today. Others that could be discussed include religious liberty, capital punishment, marriage and divorce, the family and Christian parenting, new reproductive technologies, euthanasia, genetic engineering, economic ethics, world hunger, children's rights, and stewardship of creation (environmental ethics). You can probably think of other important moral issues. Because there is no area of life unaffected by sin, and because the Bible does not allow us to be complacent about sin anywhere it is found, moral issues arise across the length and breadth of human existence. I hope that this chapter will at least help get you started in thinking about the moral challenges that you will face in ministry.

ABORTION

In two 1973 decisions, the United States Supreme Court interpreted the U.S. Constitution in such a way as to create a "right" of a woman to pay a physician to "terminate her pregnancy" if she so chooses. She need meet no burden of proof for this decision. The only criteria for the deliberate extinguishing of the human life developing within her body is her desire to terminate that life. This state of affairs is rightly called abortion-on-demand. It is the single most contested moral, legal, social, and political issue in the United States. Well over 30 million abortions have been performed in our land since 1973, an average of 4,400 per day.

Although the Bible doesn't speak of abortion specifically, it does address the issue through the theological/moral norm of the sacredness (or "sanctity") of human life, a critical concept for Christian ethics. The Bible testifies that human beings are made in the image of God (Gen. 1:27), and that God is intimately involved in the conception, development, and birth of every human being (Ps. 139:13-16). The repeated prohibition of murder (Ex. 20:13) also bears eloquent witness to the value God places on our lives. Further, God's love for each of us has been demonstrated supremely by the incarnation and the atoning death of his Son, Jesus Christ. By these signs and others God has declared each human life to be of immeasurable value. We human beings are obligated to adjust our perception of, and actions toward, other people so that these correspond to God's perception and action. This is especially true for Christians, those of us who are called to follow the way of Jesus in the living of our lives.

The tragic record of human history is that we continually fail to protect and nurture human life in the way that God requires of us. While there is no biblical evidence that the sacredness of human life somehow does not apply to conceived-but-not-yet-born human life, many contemporary societies *draw* this distinction, permitting the "termination" of "fetal" life while prohibiting the killing of those who have had the opportunity to see the light of day. Many—Christians as well as non-Christians—believe that this is a false distinction. They believe that human biological life begins at conception (if not then, when?) and that life in the womb is fully human life in its earliest stages, not some kind of prehuman, pre-sacred, potential form of life. The biblical witness speaks strongly to God's intimate overseeing of the process of conception, pre-birth development, and birth, particularly in the narrative accounts of the life of Jesus—which begin, naturally enough, with his (miraculous) conception, not with the barn in Bethlehem (Matt. 1:18; Luke 1:26-38). To kill a developing human child in the womb is to take a human life. Whether or not the child is wanted by the biological parents does not affect this moral reality in the least.

In its concern for the sanctity of human life, the Bible establishes, at the very least, a strict burden of proof concerning killing. Abortion, as the deliberate taking of a developing human life, must meet the same burden of proof as any other such act. That burden of proof involves demonstrating a direct mortal threat to self or to others. An unborn child poses such a threat to his or her mother only in cases in which continued pregnancy endangers the mother's physical life. This is not to discount the mental and emotional anguish caused by an unwanted pregnancy. But only a mortal threat clearly meets the burden of proof for the taking of a human life. We lighten that burden of proof at our peril, for that barrier stands between civilization and the deluge. If no other way can be found, abortion is morally permissible in the case of a mortal threat to the physical life of the mother and ought to be legally available for such circumstances.

Statistics show that a very small percentage of those seeking abortions are the victims of incest or sexual assault. The continuation of pregnancies under such circumstances can be extremely traumatic. Through the grace of God and the provision of the support needed, often by Christians, many women today can attest from experience that they have endured such trauma and grown to love their babies as gifts from God. Those children conceived and preserved under such horrendous circumstances walk the earth as a living testimony to the love of their mothers and of those who supported them during pregnancy. While abortion in the cases of rape or incest does not meet the mortal threat criteria, many morally sensitive Christian people believe that abortion in such cases should be legally permitted, even if it is *morally* questionable.

Evangelical Christians sometimes engage in bitter argumentation over this issue, failing to realize that the point is moot in the current U.S. context. We remain in the wilderness of abortion-for-any-reason-whatsover as the law of the land. Frankly, a "three-exception" law has far more chance of passing in our lifetime than does a one-exception or no-exception statute and if enacted would prohibit all but a tiny minority of the abortions currently performed. Can evangelicals agree to work for a three-exception abortion law in this country and then reexamine the situation after the glorious day when such a law is enacted?

A woman seeks an abortion because an unintended pregnancy creates a crisis in her life, and in response she chooses to obtain an abortion. However, as Frederica Mathewes-Green argues in her wonderful book on abortion, this "choice" often is no choice at all, as parents, husband, boyfriend, or one-night-stand-man pressure the confused and distraught young woman into an action that she will likely regret and grieve for the rest of her life.[1] Christians are responsible for protecting and cherishing the lives of both the pregnant woman and her baby.

We must respond with compassion and with concrete forms of help so that a woman can "love her baby to life," in the words of Matthewes-Green. Often she needs a place to stay, medical care, parenting instruction and adoption counseling, food, education and/or employment opportunities, help in planning a future, child care help, spiritual and emotional counsel, therapy, and so on. Until the day that the laws are changed—indeed, especially if the laws are changed—if unwanted pregnancies continue at current rates, such help is urgently required. Every community needs to have a crisis pregnancy ministry based on a model that has proven successful, such as St. Elizabeth's Regional Maternity Center, a ministry I was a part of in Louisville, Kentucky.[2] Your church can be the one that leads the way if such a ministry does not currently exist in your community. Pro-life preaching and political activism, though necessary, are not a sufficient response to the abortion crisis.

This reminds us that abortion happens in a particular context. In terms of the individuals involved, abortion is usually sought because a pregnancy has resulted from a consensual sexual act outside of marriage. The father of the child most often wants no part in raising that person whom he has conceived, and his unloving and unjust act is not prevented. The mother of the child judges that the harm to her life plans, circumstances, and relationships outweighs the value of her unborn child's life, especially when the father will not provide any kind of support.

In terms of the broader culture, the leadership of the national feminist movement argues that abortion-on-demand is fundamental to the well-being of women. Politicians fear a backlash at the polls if they vote pro-life. Meanwhile, government representatives cut funds used to aid pregnant women and single mothers. Most churches remain complacent and uninvolved in crisis pregnancy ministry. Thus, widespread male and female sexual irresponsibility and profoundly misshapen priorities, disregard for the sacredness of life, distorted forms of feminism, political cowardice, government hard-heartedness, and churchly noninvolvement, all create and reflect a cultural climate in which abortion-on-demand remains deeply entrenched. It is most unlikely that the law of the land will change until this climate changes. In turn, it is most unlikely that this climate will change unless pro-life Christians lead the way.

THE ROLE OF WOMEN IN THE CHURCH

This discussion of abortion brings into view a broader set of issues related to the life circumstances and role of women in our society and in the church. Our focus here will be issues related to church life.

Over the last thirty years or so, cultural changes in gender roles, and responses to those changes, have created considerable turmoil, confusion, and unresolved conflict. Southern Baptists are among those Christian bodies which in recent years have found themselves wrestling with this issue. It has taken various forms. During the 1980s, the discussion focused on the role of women in ministry—in particular, the ordination and pastoral service of women. It was not long before this conversation became deeply enmeshed with the overall controversy that wracked the Convention. If the issue can be said to be "resolved" by now, which is arguable, this resolution has occurred only through an excruciating process of ecclesiastical civil war, culminating finally in the cold and sullen quasi-peace that now exists among and between estranged brothers and sisters in Christ. Readers from other divided evangelical bodies probably find this a familiar scenario. It may not be possible to write anything about this subject that does not contribute to further division. Yet it seems critical to offer Southern Baptist and evangelical seminarians a perspective on an issue that *will* surface in one form or another in your ministry, and that requires your most faithful and biblical reflection.

Let us begin with some basic biblical truths. The Bible teaches that men and women are both created in the image of God, and share equally in the immeasurable worth, dignity, and sacredness that God has bestowed upon every human being (Gen. 1:26-27). Women and men are thus of equal worth before God as persons. It is God's will that men and women together exercise loving stewardship over the created order (Gen. 1:28-29). Both men and women stand in need of redemption from their sin, and the blessings of salvation in Jesus Christ—who died for all—are available to men and women without distinction. It is important to emphasize the full baptismal equality among Christians (Gal. 3:26-28), an equality in which distinctions of class, race, and gender are transcended. Further, all Christians, male and female, are commanded first to seek God's kingdom and righteousness (Matt. 6:33). Christian men and women are required to take the gospel to all nations (Matt. 28:19-20), to build up the body of Christ (1 Cor. 10:23), to care for the needy (Matt. 25:31-46), to bear witness to the salvation we have experienced in Jesus Christ (John 4:39; 20:17-18; Acts 1:8), to be ambassadors of reconciliation (2 Cor. 5:16-21), to stand boldly for the will of God for human life, and so on—in short, to live faithful Christian lives in a world desperately in need of our mission and witness. The gifts of the Holy Spirit (Rom. 12:1-8; 1 Cor. 12:1-11; Eph. 4:7-13) are made available both to Christian men and women to enable the church to fulfill its commission.

The domination, exploitation, and marginalization of women by men—both historic and contemporary—constitute offenses against their sacredness before God and a barrier to the work of the church. Pope John Paul II named and repudiated some of these offenses in his rich and thoughtful 1995 "Letter to Women."[3] Men frequently use their superior physical strength to inflict violence and physical harm upon women, even within the marital relationship. Men assault women sexually and force other forms of sexual exploitation upon them. Men often use their social and cultural power to marginalize and subjugate women; in some times and places women have functioned as little more than slaves. Far from treating women with an appropriate dignity, some men consider women to be constitutionally inferior in intellect, worth, or psychological and spiritual capacity. Men have denied women educational opportunities, thus preventing the full exercise of their God-given gifts. Likewise, where men have permitted women to enter the workplace, women frequently are denied equal pay for equal work and fail to receive fair treatment related to promotion and career advancement. Only in this century have women in the Western countries, after arduous efforts on their part, won political rights such as the right to vote and hold office. Such rights belong to all persons as fundamental human rights. Historically, Christians have participated in all of the wrongs just named, many of which continue today. Signs of outrage, repentance, and active engagement on behalf of women are few. Where is the love of Christ in our silence and complicity?

New Testament evidence concerning the treatment and role of women bears witness to a remarkable spiritual and social revolution, a revolution inaugurated by our Lord Jesus. In the context of a rigorously patriarchal society, Jesus treated women with uncommon and obvious dignity and respect. He associated and conversed freely with women from all stations in life. Women were among those who sat at his feet as his students (Luke 10:39) and traveled with him on his journeys (Luke 8:1-3). Women were last at the cross and first at the empty tomb, and were the first to proclaim the good news of his resurrection (Luke 24:1-12).

David Dockery has claimed that "women had widespread influence in the early church."[4] Female disciples helped to elect Matthias as a replacement for Judas (Acts 1:15-26). They were among the first believers (Acts 5:14), as well as among those who early on received the power and gifts of the Holy Spirit (Acts 2). Along with her husband Aquila, Priscilla was a teacher of Apollos (Acts 18), and Philip's four daughters were described as having "the gift of prophecy" (Acts 21:8-9, NRSVB). Phoebe (Rom. 16:1) is described in a word "best translated deacon," according to Dockery.[5] Paul asks the Roman Christians to welcome Phoebe when she visits in a manner that is "fitting," and to "help her in whatever she may require from you" (Rom. 16:2, NRSVB). First

Timothy 3:11 offers a set of qualifications for either women deacons or wives of male deacons, while Titus 2:3-5 describes a ministry of older women to younger women within the body of
Christ. Eight of the twenty-six church leaders Paul singles out for
special greeting in Romans 16 are women.

Certain New Testament texts, however, reflect and/or assert
gender-based distinctions in role and in behavior between
Christian men and women, both in family life (Eph. 5:21-33; Col.
3:18) and in the church. In 1 Corinthians 11:2-16 Paul argues that
when a woman "prays or prophesies" (11:5), unlike a man, she
ought to have her head covered, or veiled. While most evangelical scholars recognize the veiling command as contextual, the
passage is significant in offering a creation-based argument for
the distinctness and diversity of the sexes, for female modesty in
public dress, and for voluntary female submission. It is, though,
important to observe that in this passage women are described,
without criticism, as praying and prophesying in public worship.
In 1 Corinthians 14:33-36, Paul commands that "women should
be silent in the churches" (NRSVB). Dockery argues, along with
many evangelical biblical scholars, that here Paul is addressing a
particular problem: verbal interruptions of worship services by
women.[6] Rather than disrupt the orderly and dignified worship
that ought to occur, women who have questions should hold
them until worship is over. A blanket prohibition of female participation in worship cannot be meant, given what Paul says in 1
Corinthians 11:5.

Another critical passage related to this matter is 1 Timothy
2:11-15, especially verse 12, "I permit no woman to teach
[didaskein] or to have authority [authentein] over a man; she is to
keep silent" (NRSVB). Again, some interpreters point to a particular
contextual issue. In this case, certain scholars have suggested that
the church in Ephesus was plagued by "heretical or uninstructed
women teachers [who] were seeking to expound their beliefs."[7]
Given other New Testament evidence, including in the pastoral
epistles themselves, the passage cannot mean that women are permitted no speaking role in worship and no place whatsoever in
the church's teaching ministry (Titus 2:3-5). Exactly what the text
does mean, and what it ought to mean for the church today, continues to be hotly debated. One interpretation pulls together the

apparent prohibition on a woman teaching and the other apparent prohibition on a woman having authority over a man into a synthesis in which Paul is understood to bar women only from any church *office* in which they would have "final teaching authority" over a congregation. The "final teaching authority" position in traditional Southern Baptist polity is normally viewed as that of pastor, or senior pastor in a multi-staff church. This interpretation would understand Paul as leaving most or all other church offices and functions open to women without distinction. This interpretation of 1 Timothy 2:12 is plausible, though it must be seen as an *interpretation* of a difficult passage and not an obvious reading of a simple text. No New Testament text states explicitly and directly that women are barred from service as pastors/senior pastors. First Timothy 2:12 is one text among several that can plausibly be synthesized so as to lead to that conclusion (cf. 1 Tim. 3:2). The practice of a clear majority of Southern Baptist churches, as well as many other evangelical bodies, reflects this interpretation of the biblical evidence.

On the other hand, it is also plausible to suggest that limits on the service of women in the life of the church simply do not cohere with the sacredness and equal worth of female life, with the foundational biblical moral norm of justice, with the liberating, inclusive, boundary crossing nature of the ministry of Jesus our Lord, and with the evidence of female leadership in the early church and the church's transcending of social and cultural boundaries of all types. A significant number of evangelical scholars and institutions have come to this alternative conclusion in recent years.

This divergence of opinion reflects the fact that these two strands in the biblical witness are most difficult to reconcile. The issue can and ought to be the subject of continuing fruitful conversation and exploration. Unfortunately, when Christians encounter a hermeneutical dilemma of this type we frequently resolve it by conflict and schism. We choose up sides. These sides tend to dismiss or at least suppress the biblical materials that do not advance their point of view. As the conflict deepens it is frequently politicized. A difficult yet fascinating hermeneutical, ecclesiological, and discipleship question becomes enmeshed in the dispiriting factionalism, self-interestedness, and lovelessness that the New Testament clearly and repeatedly condemns. This is what has happened among Southern Baptists on this issue.

As a Baptist, I am glad that both ordination and appointment to church office are decided by each local congregation. Each such body is responsible to seek God's will diligently through Bible study, prayer, and intensive conversation together. I believe that the Spirit is not through speaking to local congregations about these matters. I am encouraged by the respectful and responsible nature of the conversation about this issue that many evangelical scholars are having and the help that this conversation is offering the local evangelical churches that must decide this issue. I fervently hope and pray that Southern Baptist scholars and ministers will be able to serve our people as well. May we who are called to equip the saints and to facilitate the church's ministry make our minds and hearts open to the Spirit's direction on this issue, as on every issue.

RACISM AND RACIAL RECONCILIATION

Few offenses against the biblical norms of love, justice, and the sacredness of life rival racism. As an ideology, racism is the mistaken belief that "race" is the primary source of human characteristics and abilities and that racial differences produce the intrinsic superiority of a particular race and the inferiority of others. As a behavior, racism is the perpetration of this belief through both individual and institutional activities. Both as ideology and behavior, racism flatly contradicts the Word of God. As an ideology, racism marks an explicit rejection of the biblical doctrine of creation (Gen. 1–2) and its moral corollary, the sacredness of *every* human life. While there are indeed distinct human groups who inhabit the face of the earth, it is God who made each individual and group. Every human being is equally *precious* in the sight of the Creator. God "shows no partiality, but in every nation whoever fears him and works righteousness is accepted by him" (Acts 10:34-35, NRSVB). "From one ancestor he made all nations to inhabit the whole earth" (Acts 17:26, NRSVB). It is persistent, stubborn, human sinfulness that turns God-given human differences into an occasion for hatred and contempt.

As a behavior, racism is a particularly insidious and pervasive sin, penetrating into the structures of the individual soul and the most intimate relationships, affecting the life of the church, even distorting political and social structures such as the economy, the criminal justice system, even international relations. At its worst, racism kills. In our own century we have watched Nazi racism against the Jews and other groups destroy millions of people. More recently, the racism manifested in Serbian "ethnic cleansing" operations in the former Yugoslavia has meant displacement for millions and death for tens of thousands. There are few regions of the world in which racism does not wreak its havoc in one form or another.

Southern Baptists have recently faced squarely their own history of racism. I am thrilled to have played a small part in the drafting of the "Resolution on Racial Reconciliation" that passed overwhelmingly at the 1995 SBC meeting in Atlanta. That resolution acknowledges for the first time in denominational history "the role that slavery played in the formation of the Southern Baptist Convention." It admits that many of our SBC forebears "defended the 'right' to own slaves" and later, after slavery had been abolished, sometimes opposed "legitimate initiatives to secure the civil rights of African-Americans." The resolution confesses the sometimes intentional and sometimes unintentional segregation of our churches, the painful racial divisions that have been inflicted on the body of Christ, and the distorted understanding of the gospel and of Christian morality that racism both caused and reflected.[8] As Martin Luther King, Jr. so frequently argued, racism damages the racist and not only his or her victim. "Hate is just as injurious to the person who hates. Like an unchecked cancer, hate corrodes the personality and eats away its vital unity."[9] Thankfully, Southern Baptists as a people have decided corporately and publicly to repent of the corrosive evil of racism. We will benefit from this "moral cleansing" more than we can imagine. The same is true for other evangelical bodies that have renounced or will renounce the racism in their own histories.

Having decided to renounce racism, Southern Baptists must now take the concrete steps necessary to root it out of our corporate life and to move toward full racial reconciliation. We must also look to the social and political arenas, seeking ways to incarnate our commitment to racial harmony and justice. In the life of the local church, we must hear clear teaching and preaching on the equality and sacredness of every human being and human group. Churches must be open—genuinely and fully—to prospects, members, visitors, and staff members from different races. Likewise, a wide range of racial reconciliation activities are possible, from pulpit or choir exchanges to occasional joint worship services and shared mission projects. Simply making friends across racial boundary lines is as critical as anything else that can be done. Meanwhile, at the denominational level, the growing ethnic diversity of the SBC, as well as our commitment to full racial reconciliation and an end to corporate racism, demands more adequate ethnic representation in the makeup of agency staffs and trustee boards as well as in the elected leadership of the Convention as a whole.

At the social and political level, Southern Baptists and other evangelical Christians must be vigilant about working for progress toward justice for historically mistreated racial groups as well as for racial reconciliation. Racial injustice remains pronounced in such areas as education, housing, employment, and criminal justice. Tensions between racial groups continue unabated, as was demonstrated by the racially polarized response to the recent O.J. Simpson verdict and by continued acrimony over affirmative action. We must reject racial injustice and racial hatred and work toward a peacefully integrated nation with civic justice, economic opportunity, and social equality for all. The extent to which this is a priority for us will be reflected in the intensity of our activity. By this shall the meaningfulness of our repudiation of racism be judged.

SEXUAL ETHICS AND HOMOSEXUALITY

Sexual intimacy is intended by God to be shared by one man and one woman within the lifetime covenant of a loving marriage. This is the classic Christian sexual ethic, rooted in Scripture (Gen. 2:24-25; Matt. 19:4-6; 1 Cor. 7:2-3; 1 Thes. 4:3-8), affirmed across confessional boundaries in the historic Christian moral tradition, and attested to by the experiences (both positive and negative) of millions of persons. This is the only sexual ethic that does full justice to God's purposes for human sexuality—partnership (Gen. 2:18-25), procreation (Gen. 1:28), and pleasure (Prov. 5:18-19)—

and to our human nature as male and female embodied sexual persons.[10] It is also the only sexual ethic that takes full account of the immense destructive power of misused sexuality.

Yet, especially since the 1960s, this sexual ethic has been challenged by two major competitors. In ministry, you will sometimes hear people articulate these competing approaches to human sexuality. One competitor is what we might call the "mutual consent ethic." Those holding this view believe that adult men and women should feel free to have sexual relations with whomever they want, provided that there is mutual consent. One does not have to "channel-surf" very long on cable television, or flip through the radio dial, before finding some kind of expression of this approach. While orthodox Christian tradition rejects this stand, its impact in the culture is obvious. One place this ethic can be noticed is in law. Today, state laws related to sexual behavior in our society generally reflect this minimalist approach, normally prohibiting only nonconsensual sex (rape, incest), and sex between an adult and a minor (statutory rape, incest). All other forms of nonnormative sexual behaviors are legal in most states.

The "loving relationship ethic" is in some ways the more insidious competing sexual ethic in our culture. Here the belief is that sexual relations are morally acceptable within any "committed" or "loving" relationship. Such a view is insidious because it contains a slice of the truth. It is indeed the case that a context of mutual commitment and loving partnership is God's intention for sexual expression. However, heterosexual, monogamous marriage is the *particular* context of mutual love and commitment that the Scriptures have in mind. The loving relationship ethic leaves open premarital sex (among unmarried people, including fifteen-year-olds, who "love" each other), homosexual sex (among committed, monogamous partners), even adulterous relationships (when the unfaithful spouse really "loves" his or her partner in adultery rather than the marriage partner). Human beings have an endless ability to rationalize behaviors that the Bible calls sin. While the mutual consent ethic ("if it feels good, do it") gives little comfort to persons of moral sensitivity, the loving relationship ethic ("how can it be wrong when we love each other so much?") is more alluring to those who want to feel they are operating according to some moral code. Both fall short of scriptural truth, and the moral, emotional, and relational carnage caused by sex outside of a loving heterosexual marriage bears clear witness to the inadequacy of anything other than the biblical ethic.

Before closing this section, the issue of homosexuality requires extra attention. The church has been forced to respond in recent decades to the claim that it ought to reconsider its historic view of homosexual behavior; pressure has come both from within her walls and from without. The cultural impact of the organized gay-rights movement has been considerable. Struggles over this issue have divided the mainline denominations, where conflict over the matter sometimes has been extremely intense. The SBC and other evangelical Christian bodies have been more united (though not unanimous) in rejecting any reconsideration, and thus the issue has been less divisive in our own context.

The Bible does not frequently address homosexual conduct. However, the several scriptural references that directly consider the matter are uniformly negative. In Old Testament law, consensual sexual contact between two men is condemned as an "abomination" to be punished with the death penalty (Lev. 18:22; 20:13, NRSVB). On two other occasions, the Scripture offers narratives of attempted homosexual rape (Gen. 19:4-9; Jud. 19:16-30). Some scholars focus on the rape aspect of these stories, but it seems clear that both the attempted homosexual conduct and the rape are seen as deeply sinful. In the New Testament, Jesus does not address homosexuality directly. However, he does affirm the Genesis teachings related to the creation of human beings as male and female for a divinely ordained marital/sexual partnership (Mark 10:2-12). The Apostle Paul addresses both female and male homosexual conduct in Romans 1:18-32 in the context of a theological account of human sinfulness, particularly on the part of Gentiles. He lifts up homosexual practices in that account for particular attention, while also naming many other characteristic forms of moral confusion and error (envy, murder, strife, deceit, etc.) that demonstrate the Gentiles' willful rejection of the knowledge of God and of his will. Two other New Testament references to homosexual conduct (1 Cor. 6:9; 1 Tim. 1:10) are offered in a similar manner, as part of long lists of behaviors that place persons outside of the will of God.

One reason some morally sensitive Christians have drifted

(or rushed headlong) toward the moral legitimation of homosexual conduct is their revulsion at the hatred, contempt, injustice, and sometimes even violence with which certain other believers treat homosexual persons. People who struggle with homosexual inclinations need the compassion, love, and ministry of the church, just like those who struggle with other issues. We are just as obligated to act in a loving and fair manner toward homosexuals as toward anyone else. We are just as obligated to act on behalf of the basic civil rights of homosexuals as we are of any other group. The life of the homosexual is just as sacred before God as anyone else's life. It is possible, and necessary, for individual Christians, local congregations, and other Christian bodies to be both uncompromisingly biblical about Christian sexual ethics and uncompromisingly biblical in obeying Jesus' command to love our neighbor as ourselves.

WAR, PEACE, AND PEACEMAKING

"Now the earth was corrupt in God's sight and was filled with violence" (Gen. 6:11). And so God decided to send a flood that would destroy all but a small remnant of the earth's inhabitants. Human beings have been killing each other since Cain slew Abel (Gen. 4:2-16). This violence is an affront to God, whose will is harmony between human beings and the reconciliation of broken relationships at every level. Yet one of the consequences of sin is violence, including that violence on a mass scale that we call war.

The biblical witness on the issue of war is complex. As with other issues, the moral norm of the sacredness of human life is of central importance. Those human beings who die in war are all "fearfully and wonderfully made" in the image of God. God loves each more than we can imagine. Surely the God who knit together each of us in our mother's womb (Ps. 139:13-16) did not intend the extinguishing of our lives on a battlefield or underneath an artillery shell or nuclear bomb. On the other hand, a not inconsiderable portion of the Old Testament is devoted to descriptions of wars, some of which are fought with the blessing of God. There are narratives of conquest and "holy war" in Joshua, numerous defensive skirmishes during the Judges period, many battles, wars, and threats of war during the kingship era, and finally decisive military disasters for Israel (at the hands of Assyria) and for Judah (at the hands of Babylon). The devastation and carnage of war are depicted in all of their terror and horror (cf. Lam.).

In sending his Son, Jesus Christ, God has acted to make peace with sinful humanity and both requires (Matt. 5:9) and enables us to make peace with each other. Christ himself is our peace (Eph. 2:14). Jesus, and Paul after him, instructed Christians in the methods and mechanics of peacemaking (Matt. 5:21-48; 18:15-18; Rom. 12; 15:1-13). The eschatological vision of the Scriptures is a vision of peace (Isa. 2:1-4; Rev. 21:1-4). In that time when the will of God is perfected we will no longer lift up weapons against one another. There shall be no more tears of mourning over war's many victims. As Christians, then, the question of war arises within the particular moral/theological horizon established by the biblical narrative. We are the called-out, set-apart people of God, seeking to be faithful to a God whose intention is peace, to a Savior who taught peacemaking and whose death achieved peace, living in the midst of a world that will be susceptible to the ravages of war until that Savior comes again in glory. Given these realities, how shall we deal with war?

A look at our Christian tradition is instructive. At its best, the Christian moral tradition abhors war. The two major historic moral options for Christians have been *pacifism* and the *just war* tradition. Christian pacifism is the refusal to participate in war under any circumstances, as a commitment to follow the way of Jesus and to bear witness to his lordship. Christian just war theory is the view that peace is indeed God's will, but in a tragic and sinful world some wars are justifiable and Christians are called to participate in such wars (and *only* such wars). A strict set of criteria has been developed to test whether or not a war is justifiable or whether, once entered, it is being fought in a just manner. In theory, the difference between these views is whether the obligation not to participate in war is seen as an essential and nonnegotiable part of the way of Jesus or as a moral principle open to occasional exceptions. The just war theory has become the "establishment position," both in the church and in government, while the pacifist view has remained the consistent witness of particular strands of the Christian community.

The witness of human history, and especially of this bloody century, is that war is not easily restrained. It is difficult to unleash the demons of mass killing and then keep them civilized. Technological innovations have heightened this ancient problem. It is easier to kill hundreds of thousands of people with chemical, biological, and nuclear weapons than with swords and spears. The just war theory has proven itself to be easily abused, manipulated, and overwhelmed. In terms of entering wars, every government claims its war is just, and most Christians tend to go along unquestioningly. In terms of fighting wars, few if any of this century's many wars have been fought in adherence to the ancient, noble just war criteria. In particular, the principle of noncombatant immunity has been ignored if not openly rejected (the Holocaust, Hiroshima, Bosnia).

While pacifism is not a fully adequate response to the challenge of war, I am persuaded that we need to reclaim the deep resistance to war that pacifism has always incarnated. As well, we need a politically realistic and usable set of criteria and steps to help us to actually participate in the prevention of war and the making of peace. Glen Stassen has helped to lead the way toward a new Christian approach to war, called (as the title of his book on the subject indicates) "just peacemaking."[11] Picking up on Jesus' words, "Blessed are the peacemakers" (Matt. 5:9), this view sees the essential Christian obligation as the active making of peace, rather than merely not participating in war or trying to figure out if a war is justifiable. He offers seven essential steps of peacemaking, based on Jesus' teaching in the Sermon on the Mount and Paul's in Romans 12 and 15. Besides being consonant with the teaching of Jesus, such an approach is practical and profoundly applicable to our own time. Our weaponry is so advanced now that we can no longer fight with all of our might and survive. We either learn how to make peace or we commit collective suicide. Christians must lead the way in making peace, as we are commanded to do.

CONCLUSION

The moral issues facing the church are challenging and daunting. Yet we cannot be excused from intense moral effort to understand

and to incarnate God's will. The faithful Christian minister has an enormous responsibility in leading the people of God in this dimension of their existence. May God find us—his ministers—ready and willing to meet this responsibility, until Jesus Christ comes in glory.

N O T E S

1. Frederica Mathewes-Green, *Real Choices* (Sisters, Ore.: Multnomah, 1994), 18.

2. For information about the ministry of St. Elizabeth's, write them at 621 E. Market St., New Albany, Indiana 47150, (812) 949-7305.

3. John Paul II, "Letter to Women," *Origins* 25:9 (27 July 1995): 138–43.

4. David S. Dockery, "The Role of Women in Worship and Ministry: Some Hermeneutical Questions," *Criswell Theological Review* 1:2 (1987): 374.

5. Ibid.

6. Ibid., 370.

7. Ibid., 371.

8. For the full text of the resolution, see *Light* (September–October 1995), 3.

9. Martin Luther King, Jr., *Strength to Love* (Philadelphia: Fortress, 1981), 51.

10. See Stanley Grenz, *Sexual Ethics* (Dallas: Word, 1993).

11. Glen Stassen, *Just Peacemaking* (Louisville: Westminster/John Knox, 1992).

F O R   F U R T H E R   R E A D I N G

Bendroth, Margaret Lamberts. *Fundamentalism and Gender*. New Haven, Conn.: Yale Univ. Press, 1993.

Bernardin, Joseph Cardinal. *Consistent Ethic of Life*. Kansas City, Mo.: Sheed & Ward, 1988.

Bonhoeffer, Dietrich. *Ethics*. London: SCM, 1955.

Davis, John Jefferson. *Evangelical Ethics*, 2d ed. Philipsburg, N.J.: Presbyterian & Reformed, 1993.

Dockery, David S. "The Role of Women in Worship and Ministry: Some Hermeneutical Questions." *Criswell Theological Review* 1:2 (1987): 363–86.

Feinberg, John S., and Paul D. Feinberg. *Ethics for a Brave New World*. Wheaton, Ill.: Crossway, 1993.

Grenz, Stanley. *Sexual Ethics*. Dallas: Word, 1993.

Grenz, Stanley J., with Denise Muir Kjesbo. *Women in the Church: A Biblical Theology of Women in Ministry*. Downers Grove, Ill.: InterVarsity, 1995.

Gushee, David P. *The Righteous Gentiles of the Holocaust*. Minneapolis: Fortress, 1994.

John Paul II. "Letter to Women." *Origins* 25:9 (27 July 1995): 138–43.

King, Martin Luther, Jr. *Strength to Love*. Philadelphia: Fortress, 1981.

Lovelace, Richard F. *Homosexuality and the Church*. Old Tappan, N.J.: Revell, 1978.

Mathewes-Green, Frederica. *Real Choices*. Sisters, Ore.: Multnomah, 1994.

Smedes, Lewis B. *Mere Morality*. Grand Rapids: Eerdmans, 1983.

Stassen, Glen. *Just Peacemaking*. Louisville: Westminster/John Knox, 1992.